THE AESTHETICS OF CULTURAL STUDIES

ABOUT THE COVER

The cover features a detail from Liza Lou's monumental work *Kitchen*, a room-size sculpture measuring 8 × 11 × 14 feet and covered with an estimated 10 million beads. *Kitchen* took Lou five years (1991–5) to create, and it made its public debut in 1996 at the New Museum of Contemporary Art in New York as part of the "Labor of Love" show curated by Marcia Tucker. *Kitchen* has since traveled to museums around the world.

In 2002, Liza Lou was awarded a MacArthur Foundation Fellowship for her work.

Many thanks to Marcia Tucker for introducing me to Liza Lou's work, and to Liza herself for her kind permission to reproduce this detail from *Kitchen* as an emblem of the dazzling and ingenious aesthetics of cultural studies.

Thanks also to Janet Lyon for pulling Marcia Tucker's *Labor of Love* off the shelf, opening it to the photo of *Kitchen*, and saying, "this would make a *great* cover."

THE AESTHETICS OF CULTURAL STUDIES

Blackwell
Publishing

Edited
by Michael Bérubé

BLACKWELL PUBLISHING
350 Main Street, Malden, MA 02148-5020, USA
108 Cowley Road, Oxford OX4 1JF, UK
550 Swanston Street, Carlton, Victoria 3053, Australia

First published 2005 by Blackwell Publishing Ltd

Library of Congress Cataloging-in-Publication Data

Bérubé, Michael, 1961–
    The aesthetics of cultural studies / edited by Michael Bérubé.
       p. cm.
    Includes bibliographical references and index.
    ISBN 0-631-22305-3 (hardcover : alk. paper) — ISBN 0-631-22306-1 (pbk. : alk. paper) 1. Aesthetics. 2. Culture. I. Title.
    BH301.C92B47 2004
    111'.85—dc22

                                                                    2004010913

A catalogue record for this title is available from the British Library.

Set in 10/12.5pt Minion
by Kolam Information Services Pvt. Ltd, Pondicherry, India
Printed and bound in the United Kingdom
by MPG Books Ltd, Bodmin, Cornwall

The publisher's policy is to use permanent paper from mills that operate a sustainable forestry policy, and which has been manufactured from pulp processed using acid-free and elementary chlorine-free practices. Furthermore, the publisher ensures that the text paper and cover board used have met acceptable environmental accreditation standards.

For further information on
Blackwell Publishing, visit our website:
www.blackwellpublishing.com

Contents

CONTENTS

Notes on Contributors

Michael Bérubé is the Paterno Family Professor in Literature at Pennsylvania State University.

Barry Faulk is Assistant Professor of Victorian Literature and Cultural Studies at Florida State University. He is the author of *Music Hall and Modernity: The Late Victorian Discovery of Popular Culture* (2004).

Rita Felski is Professor of English at the University of Virginia. Her most recent book is *Literature after Feminism* (2003).

John Frow is Professor of English at the University of Melbourne, and the author of *Marxism and Literary History* (1986), *Cultural Studies and Cultural Value* (1995), *Time and Commodity Culture* (1997) and – with Tony Bennett and Mike Emmison – *Accounting for Tastes: Australian Everyday Cultures* (1999). A book on Genre is forthcoming in the Critical Idiom series in 2004/5, and a Handbook of Cultural Analysis, co-edited with Tony Bennett, in 2006/7.

Jane Juffer is an assistant professor of English and Women's Studies at Pennsylvania State University, where she specializes in Latina/o and feminist cultural studies. She is the author of *At Home with Pornography: Women, Sex, and Everyday Life* (1998) and other work on pornography and domesticity. She has also published on lingerie, single mothering, Sammy Sosa, Latina/o studies at the corporate university, and various aspects of the US–Mexican border.

Irene Kacandes is Associate Professor of German Studies and Comparative Literature at Dartmouth College. She is author of *Talk Fiction: Literature and the Talk Explosion* (2001) and co-editor of *A User's Guide to German Cultural*

Studies (1997) and *Teaching the Representation of the Holocaust* (forthcoming in the MLA Options for Teaching Series). Author of articles on German and Italian cultural studies, narrative theory, feminist linguistic theory, trauma studies and Holocaust studies, her current research focuses on violence in the Weimar Republic.

Laura Kipnis is the author of *Against Love: A Polemic* (2003); her previous book was *Bound and Gagged: Pornography and the Politics of Fantasy in America* (1996). She is a professor of media and cultural studies at Northwestern. Her next book will be about scandal in the 1990s.

Steven Rubio has taught literature, film, American studies, mass communications, and humanities at several institutions in the San Francisco Bay Area, and is currently teaching English at American River College. He believes "adjunct faculty" is just a fancy way to say "temp." During his most recent trip to Spain, he saw a graffiti version of Guernica that covered an entire brick wall.

David Sanjek has a Ph.D. in American Literature from Washington University and has been the Director of the BMI Archives since 1991. He is co-author with his late father, Russell, of *Pennies From Heaven: The American Popular Music Business in the 20th Century* (1996), and is completing *Always On My Mind: Music, Memory and Money*. He is at work on a project, *Keeping It Real: The Persistence of Authenticity in American Popular Music*.

David Shumway is Professor of English and Literary and Cultural Studies, Carnegie Mellon University, and Acting Director of its Humanities Center. He is also director of the Film and Media Studies Minor, and he teaches courses in film, American culture, and cultural theory. He is co-editor of *Knowledges: Critical and Historical Studies in Disciplinarity* (1993), *Making and Selling Culture* (1996), and *Disciplining English* (2002), and the author of *Michel Foucault* (1989), *Creating American Civilization: A Genealogy of American Literature as an Academic Discipline* (1994), and *Modern Love: Romance, Intimacy, and the Marriage Crisis* (2003). He is at work on *Classic Rockers: the Cultural Significance of the Stars* and on a book about film director John Sayles.

Jonathan Sterne teaches in the Department of Art History and Communication Studies at McGill University. He is author of *The Audible Past: Cultural Origins of Sound Reproduction* (2003) and numerous articles on media, technologies, and the politics of culture. He is also an editor of *Bad Subjects: Political Education for Everyday Life*, the longest-running publication on the internet.

Introduction:
Engaging the Aesthetic

MICHAEL BÉRUBÉ

In 1991, in an essay entitled "Always Already Cultural Studies," Cary Nelson, my former colleague at the University of Illinois at Urbana-Champaign and one of the three organizers (with Lawrence Grossberg and Paula Treichler) of the 1990 conference "Cultural Studies Now and in the Future," surveyed the prospects for American cultural studies in the wake of the Illinois conference and made the following prediction:

> of all the intellectual movements that have swept the humanities in America over the last twenty years, none will be taken up so shallowly, so opportunistic-ally, so unreflectively, and so ahistorically as cultural studies. . . . A concept with a long history of struggle over its definition, a concept born in class conscious-ness and in critique of the academy, a concept with a skeptical relationship with its own theoretical advances, is often for English in America little more than a way of repackaging what we were already doing. (1991: 54)

This is a monitory passage, filled with bitterness and cynicism. And yet, as I write these words in the late fall of 2003, I wonder: who among us, in 1991, could have known that Nelson would prove to be so spectacularly wrong?

I hope this question sounds strange – since, of course, over the past decade, cultural studies has indeed been "taken up" shallowly, opportunistically, unre-flectively, and ahistorically. Allow me to explain. By 1991, the Illinois conference had come under attack for many reasons: it was too academic and jargon-ridden; it was too Anglocentric (one prominent American leftist called it "a festival for Stuart Hall" – as if that in itself would be a bad thing); it did not include the voices of all the attendees; it was organized with an eye to its eventual publication;

it was organized so as to lay claim to being the "definitive" word on cultural studies; and in the words of one of the attendees who had been "silenced" and whose remarks are reproduced in the conference volume, it "duplicate[d] the traditional structures of power which practitioners of cultural studies almost uniformly claim to be committed to subverting" (Grossberg et al. 1992: 293). Nelson's response to these criticisms was, perhaps understandably, brittle and defensive; badly stung, he lashed back by contrasting his own conference with the University of Oklahoma's fall 1990 conference, "Crossing the Disciplines: Cultural Studies in the 1990s," and, in the course of breaking that particular butterfly on the wheel, laid out a series of propositions about what cultural studies should and should not be – while duly expressing the usual caveats about how cultural studies should not be defined by a series of propositions about what cultural studies should and should not be.

All well and good: for those of you who were keeping score at home in 1990, the Illinois conference was much better than the Oklahoma conference, and the citizens of the free world rejoiced. But that's not what makes Nelson's essay look so mistaken in retrospect. Quite apart from Nelson's conflation of American cultural studies with American English departments, it's his insistence that cultural studies will be *incorporated*, that it will become just another name for what "English in America" (and I believe we are supposed to hear the echo of Richard Ohmann's ground-breaking work here) is "already doing." In 1991, in other words, it looked to some English professors as if other English professors would try to glom onto cultural studies as the Next Big Thing, even if these other English professors had never heard of cultural studies until sometime around 1990. What Nelson did not anticipate – and what no one, myself included, managed to anticipate – was that cultural studies would be positioned *even more opportunistically than this*. By the end of the 1990s, cultural studies had not only become a name for what some English professors insisted they were always already doing; it had also become a name for what some other English professors were already *no longer* doing. When the real backlash in English departments came, it did not present itself as a return to an uncomplicated past, before the critical twilight, when all was sunny and clear. On the contrary, it presented itself as the next Next Big Thing, and the next Next Big Thing was the aesthetic: finally, it seemed, scholars in English departments were going to be allowed to talk about the pleasant and the beautiful, all the sensual textual details overlooked or actively derided by the teeming hordes of cultural studies mavens.

For the most part, the Return to Beauty was little more than a publicity moment, consisting of a curious essay in the December 4, 1998, issue of the *Chronicle of Higher Education*, in which Marjorie Perloff opined that "people are really tired of the old cultural studies," and Emory Elliott declared that aesthetics was "the forbidden subject" (p. A15). Perloff's remark is all the more remarkable when one realizes that very few US scholars had been doing work that was recognizably in the cultural studies tradition in the 1970s and 1980s, and that she was speaking only eight years after the Illinois conference; for comparison's sake, you would have to imagine E. D. Hirsch in 1974, eight years after the Johns Hopkins conference ("The Languages of Criticism and the Sciences of Man") that introduced figures like Derrida and Lacan to American literary critics, claiming that "people are really tired of the old poststructuralism." Elaine Scarry's *On Beauty and Being Just* was cited as the bellwether of the critical shift, as if Scarry had been toiling away in Birmingham's dark satanic mills of cultural studies these many years and had just emerged to find that the sky was a radiant blue, after all, and the flora of the Earth were really quite exquisite when you stopped to look. Soon thereafter, the University of California Press published a pleasant little *festschrift* for Murray Krieger, ably edited by Michael Clark, under the preposterous title *Revenge of the Aesthetic,* as if the House of Aesthetics had been wronged by the House of Cultural Studies and was now about to exact its measure of justice by serving Cultural Studies' children to Cultural Studies in the form of a pie. Few of the champions of beauty seemed to know very much about the work of Raymond Williams, or of cultural studies' long history of engagement with what was once called the problem of Marxism and formalism. Accordingly, it was hard for cultural studies theorists – or, for that matter, casual onlookers – to know whether to take any of these invocations of "the aesthetic" seriously, just as it was hard for cultural studies scholars outside English departments to know what to make of what looked like – and was – a parochial, in-house dispute about which English professors at which universities were drawing all the attention and all the graduate students. If you took your cue from Perloff and Elliott, you could be forgiven for thinking that cultural studies had been the sole property of English departments for many years, and that "the aesthetic" was simply synonymous with "the literary."

I will confess that my initial reaction to the Late-1998 Return to Beauty was sheer incredulity – a reaction echoed by Rita Felski's and Irene Kacandes's essays in this volume. As historical irony would have it, I was teaching a graduate seminar titled "Aesthetics and Canons" at the time the *Chronicle* essay came out; I had decided to offer such a course after reading and reviewing George Levine's edited collection, *Aesthetics and Ideology,* which in turn seemed to me to be a response to (among other things) Terry Eagleton's *The Ideology of the Aesthetic.* In my review, I had suggested that Levine and many of his contributors, in their reactions against narrowly politicized forms of criticism that appeared to read right through the sensuous materiality of the text to the layers of ideology lying underneath, were replaying versions of the old debates between Marxism and formalism, and I suggested in so many words that most of the contributors were bumping up against Jan Mukarovsky in the dark without knowing who or what it was they had struck. (I will say more about Mukarovsky – and Raymond

Williams's bump into him in *Marxism and Literature* – below.) But at the same time, I had agreed with Levine that literary theory should, at the very least (or, more accurately, at its very best), inquire into the status of literature as an institution and into the multiplicity of forms of writing of which "literature" – in its myriad historical transformations – can be said to consist. In other words, I had by 1998 read enough of Raymond Williams's work to believe that a "cultural studies" approach to literature entailed, at minimum, an awareness of the process (beginning in the eighteenth century) by which "literature" was gradually distinguished from "literacy" in general and from the field of writing *in toto*, as the social transformations of modernity and the "heightened self-consciousness of the profession of authorship" produced a specialized sense of the literary "which may be understood as well-written books but which is even more clearly understood as well-written books of an *imaginative* or *creative* kind" (Williams 1983b: 185, 186). And because I did not understand the verb "to historicize" as a synonym for the verb "to destroy," I did not see how the study of the historical conditions for definitions of "literature" could possibly be a threat to the institutional study of literature in the late twentieth century.

The first half of my seminar surveyed the canon debates of the 1980s; the second half tried – not always with success or (to be honest) with aesthetic pleasure – to place those debates in the broader context of the emergence of the "aesthetic" (and, or in, theories of the aesthetic) over the past 300 years, starting from the premise that the history of aesthetics is a history of theories of perception. As Williams wrote, in what has since become one of the most famous passages in *Marxism and Literature*, "The replacement of the disciplines of grammar and rhetoric (which speak to the multiplicities of intention and performance) by the discipline of criticism (which speaks of effect, and only through effect to intention and performance) is a central intellectual movement of the bourgeois period" (1977b: 149). A crude restatement of this sentence would insist that the bourgeoisie, centrally concerned as it was with the problem of consumption in industrial capitalism, created a form of attention to art that corresponded to its material interest in its contemporary mode of production: a consumerist discipline for an incipient consumer society. A more subtle paraphrase of the sentence, however, would suggest that the autonomies of the aesthetic and of civil society are somehow mutually interdependent: that the social forces of the eighteenth century, which in the industrializing Western states produced forms of consensual government and plural public spheres (even if the plurality of such spheres proved, for many decades, to be merely latent or deliberately suppressed), also created the conditions for a noninstrumental understanding of art distinguishable from the discourses of church and of state. Kant and Schiller have for 200 years been the central figures in this argument, the former for (among other things) his insistence that the perception of the beautiful and its purposive purposelessness entails the perception of its universal apprehension, the latter for (among other things) his fundamental oscillation over whether the realization of the play-drive (*spieltrieb*) is itself the highest human goal, or whether the play-drive itself serves a still higher purpose, that of promoting peace and human harmony. The second half of my seminar, accordingly, began with Kant and Schiller, wending its twentieth-century way through Jan Mukarovsky, Pierre Bourdieu, Tony Bennett, and John Guillory. By the time the *Chronicle of Higher Education* announced that professors of literature were returning to Beauty, in other words, my students had argued about whether the aesthetic was (as Mukarovsky had strenuously argued) a mere function, or whether it was (as Bourdieu had strenuously implied) a mere fraud. And so I read the *Chronicle* incredulously, wondering how in the world anyone could hope to dismiss three centuries' worth of debate about the constitution of the aesthetic by dismissing four decades' worth of work in cultural studies, some of which had devoted itself to engaging with three centuries' worth of debate about the constitution of the aesthetic.

Even in 1998, I knew the simple answer. As Felski suggests in her chapter below, "cultural studies" had by then become the generic term of opprobrium among disciplinary traditionalists; 10 years earlier, the default position was "postmodernism," and 10 years before that, "deconstruction." Cultural studies was but the latest name for Theory, and Theory, of course, was the cause of all the trouble: these trendy, hotshot theorists and their little cliques and claques, driving down intellectual standards and driving away students – or, even worse, attracting all the students (no doubt by driving down intellectual standards). It was irrelevant that such critics didn't know much about cultural studies, just as they hadn't known all that much about postmodernism or deconstruction. As Felski points out, they just didn't have a clue that Dick Hebdige's epochal *Subculture: The Meaning of Style* was as deeply engaged in the aesthetics of social formations as in the social formations themselves, or that (as Hebdige's subtitle suggested) without an account of the *styles* cultivated by subcultural groups in postwar Britain, one would have no account of the meaning of subcultural groups in postwar Britain. The argument was lost on the partisans of beauty, for whom cultural studies was simply a name for things gone wrong.

But, as it happens, the story of the past decade is more complicated than this, and it is not confined to the disciplinary politics of English departments in the United States. For as many of the contributors to this volume point out, even if one is not utterly ignorant of the work of Raymond Williams and Dick Hebdige, it is possible to critique cultural studies' sense of aesthetics nonetheless, not only with respect to literature but with respect to all forms of artistic practice. Insofar as cultural studies' engagements with the aesthetic have tended to instrumentalize the aesthetic (as Jonathan Sterne suggests in this volume), to see aesthetics as a form of social semiotics that can (and therefore should) be read for its possible use in a war of position, it is plausible to say that cultural studies has been simply missing the point – not just for Kant's definition of aesthetics, but also, say, for Korn's (or any other rock band's). As Simon Frith has argued, it's one thing to map the politics of social semiosis, and quite another to say, as David Sanjek's essay in this volume wryly asks us to do, whether the politics of social semiosis is danceable and has a good tune:

> The teacher now has the authority to explain why Madonna videos or *Aliens 2* matter – not by saying whether they're any good or not, but by assessing their ideological implications, which are, paradoxically (this approach began with the importance of what consumers *do*) all there in the text, for the academic analyst (like any good literary critic) to uncover. The 1990s thus saw a boom in the academic Madonna business – the books! the articles! the conferences! the courses! Scouring compulsively through all this material, I couldn't tell whether Madonna was a good singer (as well as a skilled media operative); whether she was an engaging dancer (as well as a semiotic tease); whether I'd actually want to play her records and videos as well as read about them. (1996: 14)

I think Frith is right to describe the Madonna business in this way, and I can suggest moreover that roughly half of the essays in this volume can be read as extended Frithian meditations on the question of value and evaluation in popular culture. But there are really two questions embedded in this passage, one of which has to do with the formation of an academic Madonna business, and the other of which has to do with whether "Like A Virgin," "Vogue," or "Ray of Light" (to pick three samples from Madonna's early, middle, and late periods) are "any good," apart from their potential importance to the formation of an academic Madonna business. One question asks, why Madonna? The other asks, implicitly, why Madonna instead of Metallica? Why not Radiohead, or Mary J. Blige, or, for that matter, Korn?

In formulating answers to the first question, contemporary cultural studies has characteristically insisted on the importance of popular culture for the formation of (and the analysis of the formation of) social subjectivity. Reading the responses – actual and potential – of mass audiences to popular music and film, it is commonly argued, is critical to any project that seeks to intervene in contemporary politics.[1] Indeed, partly because most citizens of advanced Western democracies tend to be more engaged by and informed about Madonna and blockbuster movies than by the details of tax law or the advantages of proportional representation over against winner-take-all balloting, it has seemed to some cultural studies theorists that popular culture provides a greater range of political possibilities for ordinary people than do contemporary forms of government, and that, accordingly, the prospects for social change appear better with regard to cultural politics than with regard to public policy.[2] According to this line of argument, there are any number of pedagogical purposes to which cultural artifacts like *Die Hard* or *Star Trek* might be put, and therefore any number of justifications for offering courses and writing articles or books about mass-media phenomena and their place in the war of position against All Bad Things, namely, racism, patriarchy, homophobia, imperialism, theocracy, and still last and still not least, late capitalism.

Most of the debates over cultural studies in the past 10 or 15 years have been centered on this line of argument. Curricular conservatives (who do not always map neatly onto the terrain of political conservatism) have complained that popular culture is too ephemeral or trivial to deserve sustained scholarly treatment, and rafts of media-effects theorists on both the left and the right have argued that popular culture is worth our attention only because it is an index of our degraded, fallen era and/or because it makes kids misbehave. To all such critics, cultural studies looks misguided, delusional, or worse. Meanwhile, off campus, many policy-oriented progressives and leftists have wondered querulously why academic progressives and leftists would waste their time on forms of cultural politics that, in their estimation, have no impact whatsoever on matters of distributive justice: and if there's one thing on which left publications as diverse as *The Nation*, *Dissent*, *In These Times*, and *The Baffler* managed to agree in the 1990s, it's that the mode of subcultural analysis pioneered by cultural studies has foolishly overemphasized the liberatory and transformative potential of consumer culture.[3] Interestingly, then, one angle of critique suggests that cultural studies is too topical and too aggressively politicized, and the other angle suggests that cultural studies is too trivial and not politicized *enough*. But both kinds of criticism assume that cultural studies can be fairly described as a place where "Milton has had to share the stage with Madonna for the last two decades" (2003: 14), as writer Curtis White puts it in his extended rant, *The Middle Mind: Why Americans Don't Think for Themselves*.[4] And as long as cultural studies is taken to be identical to Madonna Studies, the critiques of cultural studies follow an altogether predictable path: either because popular culture is not worthy of serious study, or because popular culture does not provide fertile ground for political activism, cultural studies is simply a waste of time.

But what if we returned to the second question – why Madonna instead of Metallica (whom I have chosen not for the sake of euphony but because the band appears on the cover of Frith's *Performing Rites*)? What if cultural studies analyzed popular culture not merely to discover the place of this or that singer or movie in the war of position against late capitalism, but to understand – and to discriminate among – the varieties of evaluative mechanisms by which people actually participate in (or refuse to participate in) popular culture? Cultural studies might then be following the track laid out by Frith toward the end of the first chapter of *Performing Rites*, where he writes,

It is arguable, for example, that there are a number of aesthetic/functional axes around which all cultural judgments work: believability (and its complex relations with both realism and fantasy); coherence (whether in terms of form or morality – and with a great variety of ways in which cause is taken to relate to effect); familiarity (and the constant problem of the new, the novel); usefulness – whether at the most material level (is that painting the right size, shape, and color for this space on this wall in this room?) or at the most spiritual (does this experience *uplift* me, make me a better person?).

What I'm suggesting here is that people bring similar questions to high and low art, that their pleasures and satisfactions are rooted in similar analytic issues, similar ways of relating what they see or hear to how they think and feel. The differences between high and low emerge because these questions are embedded in different historical and material circumstances, and are therefore framed differently, and because the answers are related to different social situations, different patterns of sociability, different social needs. (1996: 19)

Such a program for cultural studies would no doubt build on the work of Barbara Herrnstein Smith's *Contingencies of Value* in stressing the functional and situational character of judgment, and on Pierre Bourdieu's *Distinction: A Social Critique of the Judgment of Taste* in insisting on the place of aesthetic judgment in the system of social differentiation.[5] It would ask, as Janice Radway does in chapter 6 of *Reading the Romance* ("Language and Narrative Discourse"), not only about what various cultural practices do, but also about how they strike the senses – and whose senses, and which senses, and why. It would try, as Simon Frith does in the opening pages of *Performing Rites*, to persuade us that one band (in Frith's example, the Pet Shop Boys) merits our sustained attention, whereas (say) the collected works of Phil Collins (my example, not Frith's) do not. And it would insist, as John Frow does in the closing pages of *Cultural Studies and Cultural Value*, that cultural studies theorists "can act in good faith only as long as we realize that there is no escape from the consequences of possession of cultural capital, just as there is no way of getting outside the game of value judgment and the game of cultural distinction" (1995: 169). It would be a form of cultural studies about which no one would have to write in the conditional or the subjunctive, because – as this very sentence slides subtly into the present indicative – it already exists.

However, although it exists, I have to admit – or complain – that it is not in fact the dominant strain of cultural studies, and it is not the kind of thing most general readers think of when they think of cultural studies. For most people, "cultural studies" is not about evaluating and historicizing complex cultural forms, including literary texts and the idea of the literary; it is all about celebrating the transgressive possibilities afforded by Madonna's video for "Vogue" or the everyday *bricolage* performed by *Star Trek* fans who produce "slash zines" about Kirk and Spock. The problem with the latter does not lie simply with Constance Penley's work on *Star Trek* fandom or on her promotion of the model of the intellectual *as* fan; the problem lies with the way Penley's work has somehow been made emblematic of cultural studies, as if, together with Henry Jenkins's *Textual Poachers*, it had established the *Star Trek* insignia as the international symbol of Cultural Studies®, or as if the aspiring cultural studies theorist could have no higher goal than to find a subculture even cooler than that of the K/S slash fans. In John Michael's discussion of cultural studies in *Anxious Intellects*, for instance, one can find a sustained discussion of Penley, Jenkins, *Star Trek*, and the discourse of the intellectual-as-fan, but one will search in vain for a mention of Frith or Frow. Nor do such figures appear in Tom Frank's broadside against cultural studies in *One Market Under God*, in which he confuses cultural studies with the work of libertarian economist Tyler Cowen and advertising critic James Twitchell.

And in the rest of the bookstore, things are even worse: cultural studies scourge Camille Paglia appears in the "cultural studies" section. Over in the magazine rack, a *New Republic* reviewer is calling Marjorie Garber's book *Dog Love* a work of cultural studies (Faulk's essay calls attention to this strange development as well). In the general literate culture of the US, it would appear, "cultural studies" consists chiefly of stuff about popular culture; popular culture, in turn, contains lots of stuff, like movies and TV shows and bands that matter. Cultural studies must therefore consist of *stuff about stuff*.[6] And the idea that it could have anything perceptive to say about complex cultural artifacts and the means by which people evaluate them, aesthetically and otherwise – this idea is commonly mocked not only by disciplinary traditionalists and partisans of beauty but also by culture-beat writers in the popular and alternative press.

Perhaps, then, it's time to take the Return to Beauty, and the concomitant dismissal of the "old" cultural studies, not as a strange publicity moment but as an opportunity for revivifying questions that cultural studies, old and new, is especially well situated to ask. And if most readers now have little idea that cultural studies has any history of engagement with such questions, so much the better. The questions themselves are not going away anytime soon. Can politically motivated criticism have anything interesting to say about the *form* of cultural forms? What is the role of aesthetic evaluation in such criticism? How should we understand the emergence of the aesthetic as a realm of experience, and its relation to the institutions of modernity? Can an understanding of the aesthetic augment an understanding of social movements, or is one necessarily a distraction from the other? And why should anyone bother with any of the above?

*

In another of the many oft-cited passages from *Marxism and Literature* (cited by Irene Kacandes's essay in this volume as well), Raymond Williams appears to carve out a sensible middle road between the equally "crude" senses of Zhdano-vites and aesthetes:

> If we are asked to believe that all literature is "ideology," in the crude sense that its dominant intention (and then our only response) is the communication or imposition of "social" or "political" meanings and values, we can only, in the end, turn away. If we are asked to believe that all literature is "aesthetic," in the crude sense that its dominant intention (and then our only response) is the beauty of language or form, we may stay a little longer but will still in the end turn away. (1977b: 155)

The passage comes toward the end of Williams's chapter on "Aesthetic and Other Situations," and is embedded in a terse but complex discussion of Jan Mukarovsky's attempt to blend Marxism and formalism in his 1936 mono-graph, *Aesthetic Function, Norm, and Value as Social Facts*. It is a fine (and oft-cited!) passage to be sure, and could be said to sum up the sensibilities of many of the contributors to this volume, or perhaps of many of the literary and cultural critics now working in the world. But as I hope to show in this section, Williams's discussion of the aesthetic is a good deal more complicated than this passage would suggest, and raises the question as to whether cultural studies should properly abandon discussion of "the aesthetic" altogether.

Williams's complaint about aesthetics is of a piece with the project that dominated much of his life as a critic, namely, the Marxist rereading of the key words and cultural forms of the emergence of the mature bourgeois period, from the late eighteenth century to the present. The relation between the key words and the cultural forms is, of course, neither determined nor yet indeterminate; Williams thoroughly repudiated "reflection" theory, refusing to believe that changes in language (or any other element of the superstructure) corresponded to and followed from changes in the means or the organization of production. At the same time, he avoided the poststructuralist evisceration of Marxism, insisting in *Keywords* that "the problem of meaning can never be wholly dissolved into context" (1983b: 22) and preferring instead to argue that "some important social and historical processes occur *within* language, in ways which indicate how integral the problems of meanings and of relationships really are" (ibid.).

We are invited, I think, to speculate just how much pressure the italicized word *within* can bear here. The parallel passage in the 1958 introduction to *Culture and Society* contains a similar hinge: arguing that "in the last decades of the eighteenth century, and in the first half of the nineteenth century, a number of words, which are now of capital importance, came for the first time into common English use, or, where they had already been generally used in the language, acquired new and important meanings," Williams singles out five key words (industry, democracy, class, art, and culture) and writes, "the changes in their use, at this critical period, *bear witness to* a general change in our characteristic ways of thinking about our common life" (1983a: xiii; emphasis added). Historical changes *occur within* language; language *bears witness to* historical change. Which is to say, on one hand, that important social and historical processes are not to be understood as having taken place solely in the dictionary, as if the word "culture" somehow wrestled with its linguistic relation to the world "cultivation" over the course of 200 years, independently of the social transformations of the times. But on the other hand, important social and historical processes are not independent of language; they are to be understood as having involved linguistic change in complex ways that cannot be reduced to the mechanics of base and superstructure. For Williams, then, the elaboration of Western modernity is both recorded and enabled by changes in the meanings of its key words.

Thanks to the wonders of alphabetization, *Keywords* opens with the term *aesthetic*, where its appearance in the nineteenth century is read as "an element in the divided modern consciousness of *art* and *society*" (1983b: 32) and where it is linked to *art, creative, culture, genius, literature, subjective,* and *utilitarian*, which are in turn linked to other terms in the Marxist geology of Romantic and post-Romantic seismic sociolinguistic shifts. Thus, as Williams rejects the idea of the aesthetic as a realm set apart from the social, he recognizes also that the idea of the aesthetic is bound up in what are by now familiar contradictions in Romanticism's response to the rise of industrial capitalism: "it is clear, historically," he writes,

> that the definition of "aesthetic" response is an affirmation, directly comparable with the definition and affirmation of "creative imagination," of certain human meanings and values which a dominant social system reduced and even tried to exclude. Its history is in large part a protest against the forcing of all experience into instrumentality ("utility"), and of all things into commodities. This must be remembered even as we add, necessarily, that the form of this protest, within definite social and historical conditions, led almost inevitably to new kinds of privileged instrumentality and specialized commodity. (1977b: 151)

Williams's sense of the aesthetic as a new niche in the division of labor has been borne out spectacularly by the history of modern art, which has managed to abjure the logic of the commodity so completely as to have become extremely valuable. But where aesthetics went wrong *theoretically* – and Williams is hardly alone in making this claim – was in its attempt to discover either the specific properties of objects or (following Kant) the conditions of possibility for certain modes of apprehension that would allow for a distinct realm of beauty.

In formalist literary theory from Shklovsky through Jakobson and into New Criticism, the attempt was to discover a distinct kind of language that could reliably be designated as literary, or (what amounted to the same thing) the principles of "literariness."[7] The road not taken for most of the first two-thirds of the twentieth century, by contrast, was laid out most comprehensively by Mukarovsky in *Aesthetic Function, Norm, and Value as Social Facts*, where art is defined as a class of objects in which the "aesthetic function" is dominant, but with the crucial proviso (which distinguishes Mukarovsky not only from his formalist precursors but from three succeeding decades of structuralists) that the aesthetic is neither an attribute of objects nor a transcendental realm. "[A]n active capacity for the aesthetic function is not a real property of an object, even if the object has been deliberately composed with the aesthetic function in mind," Mukarovsky writes. "Rather, the aesthetic function manifests itself only under certain conditions, i.e. in a certain social context.... The limits of the province of aesthetics, therefore, are not provided by reality itself, and are exceedingly changeable" (1970: 3). For Mukarovsky, distinctions between the aesthetic and the non- or extra-aesthetic are ultimately referable to the social and historical circumstances in which cultural works are produced and perceived: thus, for instance, Mukarovsky points out that what we now call the aesthetic function is not a transhistorical category (there are "environments in which there is no systematic differentiation of functions, e.g., society in the Middle Ages or in folklore" [1970: 8]), and that even the past two centuries have seen decisive shifts in how the aesthetic function is assigned in various social contexts – as in the case of crafts and decorative art, in which "the atrophied aesthetic function was supposed to replace the lost practical functions of the craft, since those latter were better performed by industrial production" (1970: 14). The aesthetic function is then only one among many functions that can be assigned to objects; it can be assigned to any object whatsoever, even to phenomena such as breathing (1970: 2); and in some contexts it is not even firmly distinguished from other functions. Clearly, Mukarovsky opens the door to a highly specific and variegated analysis of aesthetics, even as he closes the door on the idea of the aesthetic as a realm constitutively opposed to the realm of the social.

Williams's discussion of aesthetics in *Marxism and Literature* must, obviously enough, be read in this light. Williams's response to Mukarovsky is instructive, and not least because Williams is among the very few English-speaking theorists who have given Mukarovsky some of the attention he deserves. Suggesting that Mukarovsky's work is "best seen as the penultimate stage of the critical dissolution of the specializing and controlling categories of bourgeois aesthetic theory," Williams applauds the fact that "almost all the original advantages of this theory have been quite properly, indeed necessarily, abandoned. 'Art' as a categorically separate dimension, or body of objects; 'the aesthetic' as an isolable extra-social phenomenon: each has been broken up by a return to the variability, the relativity, and the multiplicity of actual cultural practice" (1977b: 153). The final words of this passage put a distinctively Williamsian spin on Mukarovsky's method, slipping in a term, "cultural practice," which had played a crucial role in

Williams's seminal 1973 essay, "Base and Superstructure in Marxist Cultural Theory."[8] Here, it sounds as if Mukarovsky reached the conclusions set forth in *Aesthetic Function, Norm, and Value* not by following and extending the debates in Russian Formalism that produced the antiformalist work of Volosinov, Medvedev, and Bakhtin, but by returning to the multiplicity of cultural practices and being reminded, oh yes, there *is* a great deal of variety in the world, isn't there.[9] Be the merits of Williams's argument what they may on this score, the argument about "actual cultural practices" serves as the pivot on which Williams then claims to take the "next step" in the critical dissolution of the specializing and controlling categories of bourgeois aesthetic theory: "What Mukarovsky abstracted as a function has to be seen, rather, as a series of situations" (1977b: 154). On the way from functions to situations, we will acknowledge the full variety of physical and intellectual responses made available to us by the multiplicity of actual cultural practices, but we will not assign a class of such responses, however remote from immediate, practical utility they may be, to a subcategory entitled "the aesthetic." Rather, Williams concludes, we will adopt the language of "situations" in order to jettison the language of aesthetics:

> Thus we have to reject "the aesthetic" both as a separate abstract dimension and as a separate abstract function. We have to reject "Aesthetics" to the large extent that it is posited on these abstractions. At the same time we have to recognize and indeed emphasize the specific variable intentions and the specific variable responses that have been grouped as aesthetic in distinction from other isolated intentions and responses, and in particular from information and suasion, in their simplest senses. . . . Any concentration on language or form, in sustained or temporary priority over other elements and other ways of realizing meaning and value, is specific: at times an intense and irreplaceable experience in which these fundamental elements of human process are directly stimulated, reinforced, or extended; at times, at a different extreme, an evasion of other immediate connections, an evacuation of immediate situation, or a privileged indifference to the human process as a whole. (1977b: 156)

The "specific" concentration on language or form, for Williams, produces both kinds of response: the heightened, "irreplaceable" aesthetic experience which Viktor Shklovsky pinpointed when he suggested that literature makes the stone stony, and the aesthetic "evasion" entailed in the notorious Bollingen Award committee's defense of Ezra Pound's Pisan Cantos in 1948.[10] Fair enough. But if you strip this passage of its most loaded terms – that is, the first sentence's characterization of the aesthetic as a "separate" and "abstract" dimension or function, and the second sentence's insistence on rejecting aesthetics "to the large extent" that it rests on this abstraction – you will, I propose, wind up with a formulation that is more Mukarovskian than Williams cares to admit.

For what Williams does, in taking the "next step" in the critical dissolution of aesthetic theory, is to substitute the term "situations" for Mukarovsky's term "functions," in the belief that Mukarovsky's "functions" still retain some sense of the separation of art from the social world that constitutes the founding gesture of aesthetic theory. As Williams had written earlier in the chapter, that separation is of a piece with the manner in which certain classes of commodities are presented and consumed in capitalist societies: "Art and thinking about art have to separate themselves, by ever more absolute abstraction, from the social processes within which they are still contained. Aesthetic theory is the main instrument of this evasion. In its concentration on receptive states, on psychological responses of an abstractly differentiated kind, it represents the division of labour in consumption corresponding to the abstraction of art as the division of labour in production" (1977b: 154). Williams then immediately follows this claim with the following sentences: "Mukarovsky, from within this tradition, in effect destroyed it. He restored real connections even while retaining the terms of the deliberate dis-connection" (1977b: 154). Perhaps Mukarovsky did retain those terms, but the point remains that by the time we reach the end of Williams's brief chapter, the words *separate* and *abstraction* are almost slurs, and anyone standing within reach of them (or retaining words like them) is tainted by association. For why should we assent to the proposition that "what Mukarovsky abstracted as a function has to be seen, rather, as a series of situations," if not for the sinister suggestion that Mukarovsky has somehow participated in the separation of art and life that bourgeois aesthetic theory enforces (and that, in Peter Bürger's influential reading, the European historical avant-garde sought to undo), by designating as a "function" that process by which different societies and different forces within societies have fixed attention on the formal features of certain cultural practices?[11]

There are, I realize, simpler ways of saying what I'm saying here. One of them is this: Mukarovsky's work is more supple and elusive than Williams lets on. Another is the corollary that Williams's substitution of "situations" for "functions" seems to do more work than it really does. For in claiming that art is "a dialectical negation of actual communication" (1970: 83), Mukarovsky provides a pithy formulation which allows us to weep at Cordelia's death but absolves us from calling the police when Edmund blinds Gloucester; in insisting that the aesthetic function is variably assigned by social collectives in such a way as to affect the reception *and* the production of cultural works, he avoids both the separation of the aesthetic from other functions and the post-Romantic division of labor according to which the discipline of criticism (to return to Williams's formulation) speaks only to the effect of artworks on perceivers. For these reasons, a branch of cultural studies that takes seriously the discourse and the history of aesthetic theory should certainly return to Williams's rereading of Mukarovsky – and to Williams's rereading of the discourse and the history of aesthetic theory since 1750. But more than this, such a branch of cultural studies should return to Williams's rereading of Mukarovsky in part to reread it against the grain of its own assumptions about the kinds of "separations" and "evasions" involved in the aesthetic. Or perhaps, for that matter, we might read through Williams's rereading to a fresh reading of Mukarovsky himself, and of how, for all its limitations of time and space, Mukarovsky's work manages to authorize a complex sociohistorical analysis of how disparate social collectives have constructed and understood the features of cultural practices we commonly – and still usefully, I insist, with a full awareness of the paradox entailed in the invocation of utility – call "aesthetic."

To undertake this reading, however, we will, at the very least, have to turn away from Ian Hunter's polemical proposal that we turn away from cultural studies' history of engagements with the aesthetic. Hunter's understanding of the aesthetic, following Schiller's suggestion that (in Hunter's paraphrase) "an aesthetic judgment can be treated not as a description of the object but as a symptom of the aesthetic condition of the person who judges" (1992: 364), is almost exclusively an understanding of aesthetic *education*, in which aesthetics involves a particularly amorphous and sinister form of self-policing. While it is true that the aesthetic should be understood in an institutional context that gives it form, it is also true that the institutional status of the aesthetic would look rather different (that is, it would look more compatible with the project of human freedom) if we attended to the history of obscenity law rather than the history of schooling. Thus, because Hunter continually elides the aesthetic with the institutions of aesthetic education, he can make (for instance) the otherwise odd claim that "the aesthetic" does not name a function among other functions in a variety of cultural practices, a function that calls attention to the formal features of such practices, but is rather a "technique of person-formation in the educational apparatus" (1988: 115). From this premise, needless to say, the whole enterprise looks like a swindle in which educational authorities get to mess with your mind. "Aesthetic culture," writes Hunter, "is the means by which individuals undertake a special kind of ethical work on the being whose incompleteness they have accepted as their own" (1992: 353). Admittedly, Hunter's reading of Schiller is sound: Schiller takes pains to distinguish "a moral or a material interest" in a work of art from an "aesthetic" interest, and to criticize the viewer who apprehends the work of art by means of the former rather than the latter. But from this approach Hunter draws a strangely "essential" lesson:

What must be observed here is that the work of art is essentially a device in a practice of self-problematization. Its instituted incomprehensibility provides a convenient site for individuals to begin to relate to themselves as subjects of aesthetic experience. This is achieved through the successive counterpointed destruction of one's "ordinary" responses as sentimental or naive, as "too tensed" or "too relaxed," as moralistic or rhapsodic, and so on. (1992: 351)

It is at least conceivable that in Schiller's *On the Aesthetic Education of Man*, the work of art *is essentially X*, such that it makes sense for Hunter, even at this very late hour when few are willing to say such things, to write that in the aesthetic tradition under scrutiny here, the work of art is *essentially* a device in a practice of self-problematization. But if Hunter is only following Schiller's lead, this is, in the end, all the more reason for cultural studies to turn away from Hunter's turn away from Schiller, and to engage with Williams's engagement with Mukarovsky instead. Away from the history and institutions of aesthetic education, away from theories of art's essential nature, and toward the staggering multiplicity of cultural practices and their manifold functions.

*

I do not intend, by means of the preceding sections, to suggest that the contributors to *Aesthetics and Cultural Studies* agree with anything I have to say about cultural studies, Simon Frith, popular culture, *The Baffler*, Raymond Williams, or Jan Mukarovsky. On the contrary, I have grown used to watching people's eyes glaze over when I mention Mukarovsky, usually because they believe there is nothing to be learned from an obscure Central European theorist whose work was already old (indeed, already renounced by its author under the pressure of Soviet totalitarianism) when Raymond Williams was writing the first drafts of *Culture and Society*.[12] Rather, what follows this introduction is a healthy multiplicity of approaches to the question of aesthetics and cultural studies. That multiplicity is probably to be expected. But its specific form, I hope, will be something of a surprise.

As it happens, Rita Felski and I do agree on a great deal: we are suspicious of announcements of a return to beauty, and concerned to reestablish the ways in which cultural studies has made "the case for different forms of aesthetic experience and aesthetic value." Likewise, we are impatient with the populist strain of cultural studies that has dominated discussion for the past decade, not least because, as Felski writes, "romantic visions of the people as 'more real,' as symbols of authenticity, spontaneity, and sexy, sweaty, nonalienated bodies, are eloquent proof of the vivid fantasy life of intellectuals." But even as she defends the legacy of cultural studies against its most recent and most shallow detractors, Felski insists that cultural studies should not be conflated with literary studies – or with any other established disciplinary tradition. Retooling George Levine's complaint (1994: 6–8) that some admirers of Stephen Greenblatt and Eve Sedgwick seem to make a habit of drawing sweeping cultural conclusions from a small body of texts (if not at times from a few anecdotes and subordinate clauses here and there), Felski notes that "it is not uncommon to see textual analysis of two or three films being used as evidence of deep American anxieties (currently a much favored word) about gender or race." Ultimately claiming to side with "both the old fogies and young Turks," Felski's essay not only provides a masterful overview of the past few years of debate but renders a good idea of what the next few years should look like as well.

John Frow opens, by contrast, by insisting that "cultural studies is perhaps not as far removed as it believes from some currents in literary studies and art history." Defining "the project of cultural studies...in shorthand as a concern with the social relations of textuality," Frow draws on his theorization of the "regime" in *Cultural Studies and Cultural Value* in order to argue that the literary regime "shifts attention from an isolated and autonomous 'reader' and 'text' to the institutional frameworks which govern what counts as the literary and the possible and appropriate manners of its use and valuation."[13] For Frow, the concept of the regime includes both spaces (libraries, bookshops, bedrooms) and modes of authority (in all manner of institutions, formal and casual); and the literary regime, far from being isolated from other regimes of cultural practice and cultural value, constantly overlaps and interacts with them – as both Mukarovsky and Bakhtin would heartily agree. Moving from fine close readings to a broad summary of the state of the discipline of literary studies, Frow's essay demonstrates just how cultural studies can both broach and bracket questions of the aesthetic; and closing with a pair of provocations – one, that there is no longer any reason for cultural studies to valorize the study of popular culture at the expense of literary study, which in the early days of cultural studies was "an older and more prestigious discipline which was perceived to be deeply committed to a fetishized object of study"; and two, that cultural studies can lead us to an investigation of the institutionality of literature and the question of "what might count as useful knowledge for a literary propaedeutics" (for undergraduates, no less!) – Frow's essay not only recursively replays its own analysis of the self-reflexivity of the "emergence" of the literary, but manages to delight and instruct along the way.

Jane Juffer's essay proceeds to question the projects of instruction and delight. Juffer provides what is by far this collection's most sympathetic treatment of Ian Hunter's critique of aesthetics, and with good reason. Her reading of Hunter, Tony Bennett, and Lawrence Grossberg makes the best possible use of their claims that the aesthetic designates a realm of self-policing: for what, after all, has been at stake in the vexed distinction between pornography and erotica, but the correct comportment of the reading/viewing subject, and the status of the critic as what Bennett calls a "moral exemplar" qualified to distinguish between worthy and unworthy texts? Hunter's and Bennett's claims may be overdrawn with regard to the history of theories of the aesthetic; it is, for instance, difficult to assent without comment to the Hunter/Bennett proposition (as Juffer rephrases it) that "literary critics rely on moralisms to posit a correct reading that leads to an understanding of subjectivity." And yet, as Juffer points out, this is precisely what goes on when sexually explicit representations are at issue: aesthetics becomes part of the apparatus of governmentality, not only with regard to obscenity trials (obviously enough) but also with regard to the proper behavior of the individual subject. Still, even here the aesthetic turns out to have some relative autonomy from the uses to which it has been put by the state and by the critic-as-moral-exemplar. As Juffer argues, the aesthetic claims made on behalf of erotica have had unintended and even unchartable effects, as myriad forms of sexually explicit representations have begun to circulate at myriad cultural sites, and to myriad cultural ends: "aesthetic claims," it would appear, "open up a realm of possibilities that are not predictably contained by governmentality." Indeed, even when critics of erotica do act as moral exemplars, Juffer points out, "the moralism must be seen for the specific work it does in facilitating erotica's circulation – at which point the moralism disperses and becomes subject to different uses."

Jonathan Sterne then opens what I'm tempted to call a four-essay cluster (containing a Simon Frith subcluster) on the question of value and evaluation in popular culture. Sterne begins by noting that cultural studies theorists tend to duck and weave when it comes to defining cultural politics: one strand of argument claims that "the political dimension of culture is what matters to cultural studies," while the other claims that "culture has to be conceived as something more than an instrument of politics." But at bottom, cultural studies enshrines an instrumentalist idea of culture, an idea Sterne calls "a political dead end" that "carries with it a reactive notion of politics and a deferral of social and political imagination." Sterne then surveys the work of Stuart Hall and John Fiske – refreshingly enough, in the latter case, by pointing out the ubiquity and predictability of Fiske-bashing among cultural studies' detractors. And rather than simply complaining that Fiske-bashing is often conducted in bad faith, Sterne points out that critics of cultural studies populism *themselves* rely on a thoroughly instrumentalist idea of culture, whenever they fault cultural studies for failing to hasten the arrival of the just society: "Some of our biggest inter- and intradisciplinary fur-fights have been around the question of exactly how much and under what conditions cultural practices do contribute to social transformation. But there is a tacit agreement that they should." In what may be an attempt to initiate a whole new genre of fur-fights, Sterne proposes instead that we consider the ways in which culture might *not* be pressed into political service, and proposes also that (to return to a familiar paradox) a noninstrumentalist theory of the aesthetic might be useful for left theorists to have – if, that is, they should ever decide to take a spare moment to entertain the notion that "a better world would include a way of life where all nonsleeping time is *not* work time."

David Shumway predicates his investigation into the problem of value on a rejection of the Kantian distinction between the agreeable and the beautiful; but Shumway then quickly turns that rejection into a critique of the relation between cultural studies and critical judgment – or, more specifically, of cultural studies' curious aversions to and evasions of critical judgment. Shumway argues that cultural studies "must ask culturally specific questions of pleasure and value, and it must make them as central to its project as questions of subversion and affirmation have been." At the same time, Shumway casts a skeptical eye on those oft-rehearsed questions of subversion and affirmation, wondering whether "practitioners of cultural studies find texts that are surreptitiously infected by pernicious ideology more interesting and attractive than those which seem to explicitly endorse or represent the political and moral values on which cultural studies is founded." Where Juffer had largely endorsed Bennett's critique of the moral exemplar, Shumway replies that few cultural studies theorists have merited the critique; on the contrary, "explicitly left-wing artists have seldom been the focus of cultural studies" even as "cultural studies has excluded most of the traditional arts." Perhaps, Shumway suggests, there is more of a challenge in elaborating a counterhegemonic reading of *Die Hard* than of taking seriously the explicitly political works of filmmaker John Sayles or playwright Robert Myers. Shumway accordingly urges scholars in cultural studies "not only to criticize the ideology of the dominant, but also to endorse and explicate works that themselves challenge that ideology."

David Sanjek picks up Shumway's sense of the "inevitability of selection" in mass culture, and runs with it. For Sanjek, the role of evaluation in popular music is crucial not only because music speaks to matters pertinent to identity, solidarity, transcendence, and getting on the good foot, but also because the sheer volume of material produced by the music industry is overwhelming: "in the 1960s," Sanjek writes, "an average of 45 albums appeared each week, whereas the current figure is 710." Tracking recent trends in the music industry, Sanjek, like Felski, is leery of the discourse of trend-tracking – particularly when it comes to making sweeping cultural generalizations on the basis of a tiny assortment of primary texts (in this case, the *oeuvres* of Eminem, J.Lo, or 'N Sync). As he moves from the A&R apparatus of Mercury Records to the work of Thomas Frank in *The Baffler*, Sanjek zeroes in on the role and the image of the music critic: on one hand, the critic as a kind of press flack or "maven" whose job it is to generate "buzz," and on the other hand, the critic as a heroic figure who stands outside the industry and champions the virtues of authenticity and independence. Lester Bangs has long been iconic for rock fans in this latter respect, and Sanjek's analysis of Bangs addresses two texts that amounted almost to a Millennial Lester Bangs Revival: Jim DeRogatis's biography, *Let It Blurt*, and Cameron Crowe's film *Almost Famous*, both of which appeared in 2000. Sanjek juxtaposes his reading of Bangs with a contrasting look at Nick Hornby's *High Fidelity*, thereby making the very necessary but strangely unremarked point that the contemporary culture industry is suffused by, among other things, narratives that foreground the role of criticism, discrimination, affect, and evaluation in the culture industry itself.

Barry Faulk's essay is all about the critic – but for Faulk, criticism as evaluation is only half the story. Construing the backlash against cultural studies as yet another crisis in the ideology of professionalism, Faulk makes a series of telling and counterintuitive points about what he calls the "new populism" of critics such as Richard Rorty, Andrew Delbanco, Thomas Frank, and Ron Rosenbaum. Though, as Faulk notes, the first two of these writers are renowned academics and the latter two are independent journalists, their critiques of cultural studies are fixated on the image of the cultural studies theorist as an academic careerist *par excellence* – smug, knowing, ironic – who parlays his or her pop-culture know-ingness into a self-contradictorily elitist demonstration of expertise. By contrast, the new populists call not so much for the return of Beauty as for the return of Ardor, and thus for a model of criticism in which smugness and irony would be replaced by a priestly combination of humility and passion. Faulk suggests in return that cultural studies theorists did themselves a disservice by failing to speak in more demotic languages. "It would have been far better if cultural studies theorists in America had learned to speak in the language of their 1990s contemporaries, Beavis and Butthead: this is cool, and that sucks," Faulk cheekily writes, insofar as the B&B model would offer "the spectacle of intellectuals relinquishing some cultural capital while at the same time asserting their right to choose and judge objects." Instead, we are now faced with the absurdity of high-culture belletrists claiming to speak for the popular (indeed, enlisting Harold Bloom as a man of the common people) while populists in cultural studies appear as jargon-spouting mandarins. But this latest version of profes-sional antiprofessionalism, Faulk concludes, serves no one at all: "When we think of expertise as an encumbrance, and our identities within the profession as a matter of passion rather than knowledge and know-how, training and credential-ing, the result isn't so much the dissolution of professional structures as the dissemination of the bad faith argument that training isn't necessary in the humanities."

For Irene Kacandes the role of the critic is to attempt and then to disseminate "close readings of specific texts *and* broad knowledge about the societies in which those texts were produced." This, Kacandes writes, is the project that drew her to cultural studies in the first place, and that informs her dissatisfaction with Elaine Scarry and the Return to Beauty. Kacandes's essay consists of three interlocking sections: a piquant discussion of cultural studies' relation to aesthetics (including a look at Williams's "Aesthetic and Other Situations"); a discussion of teaching literature in the age of "secondary orality"; and a close reading of a most curious novel of the Weimar Republic, Gertrud Kolmar's *A Jewish Mother* (written 1930–1, published 1965). While noting that some contemporary critics in and of the humanities are effectively calling for literary scholars to learn more about things that cultural studies has known for many years, Kacandes nonetheless reminds us that cultural studies has to date been heavily Anglophone and Anglocentric. Drawing briefly on historian Celia Applegate's work on Mendels-sohn's revival of Bach's *St. Matthew Passion* and more extensively on her previous work on Kolmar's obscure, melodramatic, and fascinating novel, Kacandes affirms both by example and by precept that there are "aesthetic problems for which the analysis of 'beauty,' and the question of whether it is good or bad art, is completely insufficient." In reading Kolmar's *A Jewish Mother* both for its bathos and for its representation of the marginalization of Jews as "dangerous others," Kacandes demonstrates neatly why Raymond Williams insisted that concentrated attention to the formal features of artworks can be at once "an intense and irreplaceable experience" and "an evasion of other immediate connections."

Steven Rubio picks up another Williamsian thread: culture, in Rubio's essay, is altogether ordinary. Picasso is ordinary, Bugs Bunny is ordinary, Rossini is ordinary, museums are ordinary, Proms in the Park are ordinary, and even American garage doors are ordinary. But what's exceptional about this ordinariness is how complexly articulated it all is, and how difficult it is as a result to disentangle the aesthetic response from the welter of associations it inevitably produces. Rossini's *Barber of Seville* at once reminds American pop-culture aficionados like Rubio of one of Chuck Jones's inspired Bugs Bunny cartoons, *The Rabbit of Seville*, just as few can hear Strauss today (either in waltzing or bombastic mode) without thinking of *2001: A Space Odyssey*. But for Rubio, the point is not that cultural artifacts echo each other in strange and unpredictable ways, nor is the point to find banality in Rossini and brilliance in Bugs; the point is rather that Bugs Bunny somehow led him both to recall his childhood and to resist a British festival's somewhat desperate and ridiculous (re)citations of empire, just as, in a much more rarified (but no less nationalist) setting, *Guernica* recalled to him both the history of antifascist struggle and a curious garage door in the town of Pittsburg, California. Carefully tracing his own complex responses to the sublime and the ridiculous, Rubio struggles to understand all these cultural productions – the Centro de Arte Reina Sofia as well as the 7-minute piece of animation – without succumbing to simple nostalgia or wishful thinking. And in so doing, Rubio reminds us that one of the most extraordinary things about cultural works is that they can afford us intense and irreplaceable experiences precisely in their ordinariness.

Laura Kipnis gets the last word here, not for an analysis of how cultural studies has dealt with the aesthetic but for her analysis of the aesthetic of cultural studies – or, more precisely, of a salient genre of cultural studies writing. Like Faulk, Kipnis discerns an aesthetic at work in cultural studies, in its self-presentation: but this time the self-presentation involves the presentation of the writing self, as evidenced by the profusion of first-person narratives in academic writing. True, the first-person narrative is not an invention of cultural studies; on the contrary, as Kipnis herself acknowledges, the memoir or "autocritography" can be seen as part of the decline or dissipation of cultural studies, as if the American version of cultural studies had taken the field "from Birmingham to Oprah." But it would be a mistake, Kipnis insists, not to see the dynamic at work in first-person cultural studies. "To whatever degree the disciplines have loosened their grip on the profession – 'cultural studies' or 'interdisciplinarity' would be a few of the names this shift goes by – it has meant altered relations to knowledge and writing in the humanities." Most notably, those altered relations have included the demand that scholars in the humanities account for the "situated" nature of their knowledge; and while this demand can be read as a version of the Jameso-nian dictum, *always historicize*, it has perhaps more often been read as a license for a different project: *always personalize*. "It began to seem imperative for researchers to 'locate' or 'position' themselves in relation to their research," writes Kipnis; "those who didn't were subject to charges of universalism, or worse." Kipnis's withering first-person critique of the "cringe factor" induced by the academic first person will, I believe, lead to some altered relations to knowledge and writing in the humanities: some of us will never see the first person in quite the same way again, while others of us will never cringe in quite the same way again. Possibly this will depend on whether readers of Kipnis's essay (including this reader) imagine that her critique includes their own work in, or exempts their own work from, the general cringing.

And though Kipnis gets the last word, I get the first one – with which I want not only to introduce the volume but to thank all its contributors, who graciously endured and accommodated my various requests for rewrites, clarifications, expansions, elaborations, and (finally) patience while I tried to orchestrate their thoughts and (in a much longer process) my own. I have learned much from these essays, and I'm sure that I will not be alone in this respect. Whether they will lead to more work on aesthetics and (or *in*) cultural studies remains, of course, to be seen; for now I will be content if these essays serve to remind readers of some of the incisive and edifying work that has already been done on the aesthetics of cultural practices and the intricacies of social semiosis – and how much work remains yet to be done.

NOTES

1   This "ethnographic" branch of cultural studies is usually traced, in the UK, to David Morley's study *The "Nationwide" Audience* (1980), and in the US to Janice Radway's *Reading the Romance* (1991). For a retrospective account of the simi-larities between the two, see Radway 1991: 1–18, in which she maps out her points of overlap with Morley and others while acknowledging that she was unaware of their work when she was writing *Reading the Romance*.

2   These cultural studies theorists would, in fact, include me. See, e.g., *The Employ-ment of English* (1998: 225–6).

3   This position is now most commonly associated with Thomas Frank, editor of *The Baffler* and author of *One Market Under God*, but versions of it were so

common throughout the 1990s that they could be found even in the work of some of the left's finest journalists (Tomasky, *Left for Dead*) and most distinguished philosophers (Rorty, *Achieving Our Country*).

4   White is broadly sympathetic to what I might call *The Baffler* backlash, as he makes amply clear in a chapter entitled "Such an Awesome Site of Resistance," basically a companion piece to Frank's chapter on cultural studies in *One Market Under God*, "New Consensus for Old."

5   This program for cultural studies would, however, follow Bourdieu with the crucial caveat raised by John Frow in *Cultural Studies and Cultural Value*, namely, that Bourdieu does not in fact succeed in showing a correlation between aesthetics and class location in *Distinction*: "the class fractions are ranked in each case by educational capital," Frow points out, "and this ranking establishes (as you might expect) reasonably neat correlations between educational capital and musical preferences" (1984: 40). This amounts to "the substitution of an educational for an economic hierarchy" (p. 40) – and, therefore, a somewhat circular argument to the effect that people with higher levels of education tend to have more recognizably educated tastes. Frow suggests that in the course of this "sleight of hand," Bourdieu's work charts a hierarchy that does not correspond directly with the economic: insofar as *Distinction* gauges class position by calculating a class fraction's distance from the realm of necessity, "something like an abstract concept of 'privilege' has been substituted for any more rigorous conception of class" (p. 43). Therefore, it may not be the case, despite Bourdieu's insistence, that the aesthetic serves as the marker by which the bourgeoisie distinguishes itself from the working class, as the cultural device by which the dominant and dominated fractions of the dominant class represent their structural remoteness from the grainy details of material production. But it is surely the case that questions about art, its uses, and its relative autonomy from "usefulness" are, as Frith insists, embedded in historical and material circumstances nonetheless, and that the system of cultural capital affects all decisions about cultural value – even if it doesn't do so in quite the way Bourdieu suggests.

6   I do not mean to suggest that there is a real core of academic cultural studies from which the degraded popular "bookstore" version must be distinguished. On the contrary, as Vincent Leitch (2003) argued in a paper delivered (ironically enough) at the founding conference of the Cultural Studies Association, cultural studies in the US has been notably disorganized and disaggregated. And while its disorganization has prevented US cultural studies from becoming routinized in college departments and professional associations (as evidenced by the fact that no one had even tried to create a Cultural Studies Association until the year 2003), it has also, for good and for ill, rendered cultural studies a random assortment of Stuff Studies. "Advocates of Birmingham cultural studies," Leitch writes,

> the relatively coherent earlier project coalescing during the 1970s, complain that US cultural studies has become merely a front for a wide range of

disparate enterprises. What most strikingly typifies this recent phase of disorganization is the rise of numerous discrete subfields more or less associated with cultural studies such as: media studies, science studies, subaltern studies, trauma studies, whiteness studies, fashion studies, food studies, disability studies, leisure studies, narrative studies, globalization studies, indigenous studies, border studies, urban and community studies, queer studies, visual culture studies, and body studies. And I see on the conference program girl studies and age studies. Add to this list more established fields such as film studies, American studies, gender studies, and postcolonial studies, plus indeterminate fields, for example, legal studies and cognitive studies, and you have a cursory inventory of today's US cultural studies, appearing an impossibly loose conglomeration of affiliated subfields.

Cultural studies, on this reading, is just a handy synonym for cultural criticism, albeit with the proviso that the cultural criticism in question should have something, anything, to do with the relation between culture and power.

7   Roman Jakobson's "Closing Statement: Linguistics and Poetics" (1960) is, I believe, the standard citation for the very-late-in-the-day structuralist insistence that there is a mode of language use that can be designated as "poetic" and a type of writing (i.e., literature) that can be defined intrinsically as a form of language use in which the poetic is dominant. Jakobson acknowledges that all language contains elements of the poetic (as well as elements of the other modes, namely, the referential, the emotive, the conative, the metalingual, and the phatic) and thus that even campaign slogans such as "I Like Ike" can be read with the attention ordinarily brought to bear on poems; one can say, for instance, that "both cola of the trisyllabic formula 'I like/ Ike' rhyme with each other, and the second of the two rhyming words is fully included in the first one (echo rhyme), /layk/-/ayk/, a paronomastic image of a feeling which totally envelops its object" (1960: 357). But he insists nonetheless that the question of whether the poetic is *dominant* in an utterance or a piece of writing is a question of intention rather than use: "a filibusterer may recite *Hiawatha* because it is long, yet poeticalness still remains the primary intent of this text itself" (p. 359). In so defining himself against the Wittgensteinian/pragmatist argument that the meaning of a word *is* simply its use in the language, Jakobson also repudiates Mukarovsky's insistence that the aesthetic is a function attributed to objects rather than an attribute possessed by objects by virtue of their creator's intent.

8   Williams closes "Base and Superstructure" with a section entitled "Objects and Practices" in which he writes that "the true crisis in cultural theory, in our time, is between this view of the work of art as object and the alternative view of art as a practice" (1977a: 47). Insisting that "we have to break from the common procedure of isolating the object and then discovering its components" (ibid.), Williams suggests that the idea of "practices" opens out onto the world in which art actually resides: "as we discover the nature of a particular practice, and the nature of the

relation between an individual project and a collective mode, we find that we are analysing, as two forms of the same process, both its active composition and its conditions of composition, and in either direction this is a complex of extending active relationships" (1977a: 48). It is of course to Williams's credit that he realized how very close to Mukarovsky's this position comes.

9 My point is that in parsing his own relation to Mukarovsky, Williams almost makes it sound as if Mukarovsky had managed to reject the idea of art as a "separate dimension" and the aesthetic as an "isolable extra-social phenomenon" in part by reading Williams's "Base and Superstructure" – or, more plausibly, by foregrounding the multiplicity of cultural practices. Although I am not an expert in Russian and Czech literary theory of the 1920s and 1930s, I think it more likely that Mukarovsky is drawing on Bakhtin and Medvedev's critiques of formalism in *The Formal Method in Literary Scholarship*, as well as Volosinov's *Marxism and the Philosophy of Language* (an important book for Hebdige's *Subculture* as well). For an overview of the intellectual history of Russian Formalism and Prague Structuralism, see Jurij Striedter, *Literary Structure, Evolution, and Value*.

10 Shklovsky's words are these: "art exists that one may recover the sensation of life; it exists to make one feel things, to make the stone *stony*. . . . Art removes objects from the automatism of perception" ("Art as Technique," 1965: 12–13); for a scathing critique of the deployment of the aesthetic as a cover for Pound's virulent anti-Semitism in the Bollingen affair, see Gerald Graff, *Poetic Statement and Critical Dogma*.

11 See Bürger, *The Theory of the Avant-Garde*.

12 Many of my interlocutors over the years, particularly those who know the history of Central and Eastern European literary theory better than I, have asked me why it is that most English-speaking scholars have not heard of Mukarovsky – particularly if he does, as I claim, bear fruitful comparison to the tradition of British cultural studies. I have no ready answer to this question, but I can suggest a few general factors. The Prague Linguistic Circle was represented to most English-language scholars in the 1950s and 1960s by émigrés Roman Jakobson and René Wellek, who were considerably more formalist than Mukarovsky and therefore considerably more assimilable into the then-dominant strains of English-language criticism. It did not help matters, of course, that Mukarovsky repudiated his earlier work after the Soviet crackdown in 1948, or that the English translation of *Aesthetic Function, Norm, and Value as Social Facts* appeared in 1970 from an exceptionally obscure publisher (the Department of Slavic Languages and Literatures at the University of Michigan), and has been out of print for many years. The strange reception history of Mikhail Bakhtin, with whose work Mukarovsky's has obvious affinities, might serve as a useful – and ultimately hopeful – point of comparison.

13 The similarity between Williams's argument about "practices" (see note 8 above) and Frow's concept of the "regime" will, I believe, reward further attention.

REFERENCES

Bakhtin, Mikhail and Pavel N. Medvedev. 1992. *The Formal Method in Literary Scholarship: A Critical Introduction to Sociological Poetics*, tr. Albert J. Wehrle. Baltimore: Johns Hopkins University Press. First published 1928.

Bérubé, Michael. 1998. *The Employment of English: Theory, Jobs, and the Future of Literary Studies*. New York: New York University Press.

Bourdieu, Pierre. 1984. *Distinction: A Social Critique of the Judgment of Taste*, tr. Richard Nice. Cambridge, MA: Harvard University Press.

Bürger, Peter. 1984. *The Theory of the Avant-Garde*, tr. Michael Shaw, foreword by Jochen Schulte-Sasse. Minneapolis: University of Minnesota Press. First published 1974.

Clark, Michael P., ed. 2000. *Revenge of the Aesthetic: The Place of Literature in Theory Today*. Berkeley: University of California Press.

Eagleton, Terry. 1990. *The Ideology of the Aesthetic*. Oxford: Blackwell.

Frank, Thomas. 2000. *One Market Under God: Extreme Capitalism, Market Populism, and the End of Economic Democracy*. New York: Doubleday.

Frith, Simon. 1996. *Performing Rites: On the Value of Popular Music*. Cambridge, MA: Harvard University Press.

Frow, John. 1995. *Cultural Studies and Cultural Value*. Oxford: Oxford University Press.

Graff, Gerald. 1970. *Poetic Statement and Critical Dogma*. Evanston, IL: Northwestern University Press.

Grossberg, Lawrence, Cary Nelson, and Paula Treichler, eds. 1992. *Cultural Studies*. New York: Routledge.

Hebdige, Dick. 1979. *Subculture: The Meaning of Style*. London: Methuen.

Heller, Scott. 1998. "Wearying of Cultural Studies, Some Scholars Rediscover Beauty." *Chronicle of Higher Education*, Dec. 4: A15–16.

Hunter, Ian. 1992. "Aesthetics and Cultural Studies." In Grossberg, Nelson, and Treichler 1992: 347–72.

——. 1988. "Setting Limits to Culture." *New Formations* 4: 103–24.

Jakobson, Roman. 1960. "Closing Statement: Linguistics and Poetics." In *Style in Language*, ed. Thomas A. Sebeok. New York: The Technology Press of Massachusetts Institute of Technology and John Wiley & Sons.

Jenkins, Henry. 1992. *Textual Poachers: Television Fans and Participatory Culture*. New York: Routledge.

Leitch, Vincent. 2003. "The Disorganization of US Cultural Studies and Theory." Paper delivered at the founding conference of the Cultural Studies Association, Pittsburgh, June 5.

Levine, George. 1994. *Aesthetics and Ideology*. New Brunswick, NJ: Rutgers University Press.

Michael, John. 2000. *Anxious Intellects: Academic Professionals, Public Intellectuals, and Enlightenment Values*. Durham, NC: Duke University Press.

Mukarovsky, Jan. 1970. *Aesthetic Function, Norm, and Value as Social Facts*, tr. Mark E. Suino. Ann Arbor, MI: Department of Slavic Languages and Literatures, University of Michigan. First published 1936.

Nelson, Cary. 1991. "Always Already Cultural Studies: Two Conferences and a Manifesto." *Journal of the Midwest Modern Language Association* 24 (Spring): 24–38.

Penley, Constance. 1997. *NASA/Trek: Popular Science and Sex in America*. London: Verso.

Radway, Janice. 1991. *Reading the Romance: Women, Patriarchy, and Popular Literature*, rev. ed. Chapel Hill: University of North Carolina Press. First published 1984.

Rorty, Richard. 1998. *Achieving Our Country: Leftist Thought in Twentieth-Century America*. Cambridge, MA: Harvard University Press.

Scarry, Elaine. 1998. *On Beauty and Being Just*. Princeton: Princeton University Press.

Schiller, Friedrich von. 1983. *On the Aesthetic Education of Man*, rev. ed., tr. and eds. Elizabeth A. Wilkinson and L. A. Willoughby. Oxford: Clarendon Press. First published 1795; this ed. first published 1968.

Shklovsky, Viktor, et al. 1965. *Russian Formalist Criticism: Four Essays*, tr. and intro. Lee T. Lemon and Marion T. Reis. Lincoln: University of Nebraska Press.

Smith, Barbara Herrnstein. 1988. *Contingencies of Value: Alternative Perspectives for Interpretive Theory*. Cambridge, MA: Harvard University Press.

Tomasky, Michael. 1996. *Left for Dead: The Life, Death, and Possible Resurrection of Progressive Politics in America*. New York: Free Press.

Volosinov, V. N. 1986. *Marxism and the Philosophy of Language*, tr. Ladislav Matejka and I. R. Titunik. Cambridge, MA: Harvard University Press, 1986. First published 1929.

White, Curtis. 2003. *The Middle Mind: Why Americans Don't Think for Themselves*. New York: Harper.

Williams, Raymond. 1977a. "Base and Superstructure in Marxist Cultural Theory." In *Problems in Materialism and Culture*. London: Verso, pp. 31–49.

——. 1977b. *Marxism and Literature*. New York: Oxford University Press.

——. 1983a. *Culture and Society: 1780–1950*, rev. ed. New York: Columbia University Press. First published 1958.

——. 1983b. *Keywords: A Vocabulary of Culture and Society*, rev. ed. Oxford: Oxford University Press. First published 1976.

1

The Role of Aesthetics in Cultural Studies

RITA FELSKI

Bashing cultural studies is a popular pastime. While critics often dismiss the field as mere fashion, nowadays it is attacks on cultural studies that are highly fashionable. But which cultural studies? I have a hunch that "cultural studies" has overtaken "postmodernism" as one of the most misused words in contemporary intellectual life. In the recent tidal wave of epitaphs, elegies, and jeremiads on what's happening to the humanities, cultural studies has a starring role as chief villain and scapegoat.[1] Only a few years ago, cultural studies was an obscure field that few American scholars knew or cared about. Now, it seems, everyone knows about cultural studies. But what exactly is it that they know?

In this chapter I discuss some recent complaints about cultural studies emanating from departments of literature. Two ideas come to the fore in these arguments. The first is that cultural studies had declared war on art and aesthetics. It is the implacable foe of all talk about beauty and pleasure, style and form. Cultural critics believe that such terms are nothing more than mystifying babble that distracts us from the coercive rule of hierarchies of taste. In their leveling zeal, they want to reduce text to context, poetry to propaganda, works of art to lumps of text churned out by a ubiquitous ideology machine. The second idea is that this anti-aesthetic has become the new norm. Practitioners of cultural studies have invaded and set up camp in English departments and are forcing everyone to think their way. "Cultural studies," mourns Marjorie Perloff, "currently dominates the arena of literary study" (2000: 24). The glittering prizes of tenure and publications, fellowships and invitations, now depend on knowing how to talk cultural studies talk. Pity the poor soul who still dreams of writing a monograph on the role of metaphor in Robert Frost. Cultural studies, its critics like to claim in a sly mimicry of their opponents' vocabulary, has become hegemonic.

It is the conjunction of these two ideas – cultural studies' sovereignty in the academy and its blithe disregard for language, beauty, and form – that lies behind the rallying cry for a return to aesthetics. In 1998, *The Chronicle of Higher Education* ran the headline "Wearying of Cultural Studies, Some Scholars Rediscover Beauty." The accompanying article drew attention to a growing backlash against cultural studies and its slighting of the aesthetic. There were quotes from disgruntled literary scholars fed up with the social agendas of contemporary criticism. They wanted to get back to talking about style and sensibility, the lilt of language and the play of form, the beauty of poetry and what makes Shakespeare a great writer (Heller 1998).

In the last few years, other voices have joined the chorus; rallying to the defense of the aesthetic has inspired a publishing mini-boom. Apart from James Soderholm's book, *Beauty and the Critic: Aesthetics in the Age of Cultural Studies*, prominently featured in the *Chronicle* piece, there is also Michael Clark's boldly titled collection *The Revenge of the Aesthetic*. In 1999, Elaine Scarry published her widely reviewed *On Beauty and Being Just*, followed by Wendy Steiner's *Venus in Exile: The Rejection of Beauty in Twentieth-Century Thought* and Denis Donoghue's *Speaking of Beauty*. And we should not forget the many recent books such as Alvin Kernan's *The Death of Literature* and John Ellis's *Literature Lost* that lament the current state of literary study in American universities. In such publications, as well as in the best-selling volumes of Harold Bloom's one-man publishing industry, it is simply taken for granted that the rise of cultural studies means the death of aesthetics.

I have no quarrel with those who want to defend the value of studying literature and high art, but I am growing weary of reading overwrought accounts of beauty under threat from the villainous machinations of cultural studies. This Beauty and the Beast scenario bears little relationship to reality. I want, then, to take issue with the two claims I have just outlined. Let us look at the first idea, the tyrannical sway of cultural studies in American universities. It is now so deeply entrenched as the new orthodoxy, its critics claim, that impatient scholars are itching for something new. In the above-mentioned *Chronicle* article, after a scathing dismissal of current trends in literary study, Heller quotes Marjorie Perloff as declaring: "people are really tired of the old cultural studies" (1998: A15).

The *old* cultural studies? On first reading this sentence I did a double-take. My own sense is that cultural studies is still a relative novelty whose impact on the day-to-day workings of literature departments has been modest. Of course, the *idea* of cultural studies is thrown around a great deal lately. There are more than a few card-carrying deconstructionists who are hastily tossing in a few references to shopping malls and Stuart Hall to meet the current trend. As a marketing category, cultural studies undeniably has a certain allure.

Nevertheless, I suspect that the key works of cultural studies are still largely unknown in most literature departments. How many scholars around the country are really up to date with the work of Kobena Mercer and Larry Grossberg, Meaghan Morris and Tony Bennett, Constance Penley and Ien Ang? Outside a few well-known centers for cultural studies, I wager not many. I often find that otherwise well-read graduate students are utterly unfamiliar with the central debates and methods of cultural studies. This is particularly true when it comes to the large body of scholarship that is written or published outside the United States. The number of academic jobs in cultural studies each year remains pitifully small. How can we reconcile these facts with the claim that English professors are wearying of the "old cultural studies," a phrase that suggests many years of relentless, numbing exposure? How can cultural studies be both old and new?

Perhaps we can solve this mystery by looking more closely at the second idea I've sketched out, that cultural studies wants to do away with aesthetics. Where does this idea come from? In many recent polemics, it is taken for granted that cultural studies is just another word for ideology critique. That is to say, doing cultural studies means looking suspiciously at works of art and debunking them as tools of oppression. It means reading them against the grain and denying the truth of art in favor of the truth of politics. It is another word for what Soderholm calls "inquisitorial criticism" (1997: 3) and what George Levine memorably describes as "seeing the text as a kind of enemy to be arrested" (1994: 3).

A good example of this view of cultural studies can be found in the epilogue of Richard Rorty's *Achieving our Country*. Rorty agrees that cultural studies is taking over departments of English. Its practitioners, he writes, can be identified by their dry, sardonic knowingness. They are suspicious of romance and enthusiasm and lack all sense of awe. They risk turning the study of literature into one more dismal social science and driving students away in droves. Rorty singles out Fredric Jameson as an example of this pernicious trend. He quotes Jameson's gloomy pronouncements on the death of the individual in postmodern culture as a way of driving home what is in store if departments of literature turn into departments of cultural studies. Instead of benefiting from the inspirational value of great works of literature, we will be left, says Rorty, with nothing but expressions of political resentment clothed in jargon.

There is one major problem with Rorty's argument: Jameson does not do cultural studies. His work is closer in spirit to Marxist aesthetic theory, especially the Frankfurt School and its gloomy vision of popular culture as a form of capitalist domination. In fact, cultural studies came about as a reaction against this very tradition. One of its goals was to question the standpoint of academic critics who pride themselves on their knowingness and superior political insight. But this discrepancy does not seem to bother Rorty, who cheerfully admits that his knowledge of cultural studies comes from friends like Harold Bloom. Cultural studies, for Rorty, is simply a handy label for all the bad things that have happened to literature departments in the last 30 years.

Rorty is not the only one to think this way. John Ellis, for example, also assumes that cultural studies is just another word for the invasion of English departments by hordes of what he calls "race-gender-class critics." Cultural studies, in recent American debates, is often just short-hand for political readings of literature. In particular, when used by hostile critics, doing cultural studies means focusing on content and context and paying no attention to form. It is synonymous with the crudest forms of sociological analysis. It means looking through a text as if it were a transparent vehicle for a simple political message. It means, quite simply, being a bad reader.

I want to leave aside, for now, the accuracy of this view of the political turn in literary criticism.[2] My question is simply: what does all this have to do with cultural studies? After all, such approaches to literature have been around in American universities for some time. Feminist, Marxist, and African American scholarship, for example, has been thriving since the 1970s. But critics in these fields, until recently, did not see themselves, and were not seen by others, as doing cultural studies. Indeed, not so long ago, this term meant little to the average professor. In 1987 Richard Johnson published an influential article called "What is Cultural Studies Anyway?" that introduced the field to an American audience largely unfamiliar with its main ideas.

What we're currently seeing, in other words, is a classic case of semantic drift. Cultural studies, once a name reserved for a specific intellectual tradition, is now being applied, often quite haphazardly, to any attempt to link literature, culture, and politics. A phrase that once identified a specific field of study originating in Britain is now being used as ammunition in America's own culture wars. History is being rewritten; those who once saw themselves as feminist literary critics or practitioners of New Historicism were, it seems, doing cultural studies all along. When people complain that they are tired of the "old cultural studies," this history is usually what they have in mind.

Let me be clear about my argument. I am far from suggesting that American cultural studies has no right to define its own goals and methods, that it should doff its forelock in deference to the British founding fathers. In fact, cultural studies has long since migrated from its Birmingham roots; Britain has no monopoly on an international field in constant flux. Much of the interesting work in cultural studies now comes from places like Australia, Canada, South Korea, South Africa, and indeed the United States, by scholars who are often deeply critical of the Birmingham tradition. It is widely recognized that this tradition paid scant attention to the politics of race, gender, and sexuality and that its research agendas focused on British examples that do not always translate into other contexts.

What distinguishes the new work in cultural studies, however, is a familiarity with the tradition that it criticizes, a sense of dialogue with a previous generation of scholars. Those working in the field, after all, expended considerable time and effort into hashing out basic issues of methodology. To see some scholars claiming to do cultural studies with no apparent knowledge of these debates is disconcerting. Both foes and fans of cultural studies often use the term in curiously careless and decontextualized ways. The field falls victim to a widespread amnesia, a studied indifference to its rich and contradictory history.[3]

Part of the problem, no doubt, has to do with the beguiling yet treacherous simplicity of its name. Cultural studies sounds like a synonym for studying culture, a convenient handle for anyone with interdisciplinary interests. Yet cultural studies is, of course, only one way of analyzing culture; there are many others, including anthropology, communication studies, American studies, cultural history, new historicism, cultural sociology, and other fields. The lines between these traditions are by no means hard and fast; indeed, some of them have cross-pollinated with cultural studies in fruitful ways. And yet they also have different names and distinct histories. One result of the diffusion of "cultural studies" is an increasing ignorance of the specific tradition it names. Scholars feel free to use the term without needing to learn anything about the field.

Against popular misconceptions, then, I want to stress that cultural studies started off not as ideology critique, but rather as a critique of ideology critique. It took left-wing intellectuals to task for their knee-jerk dismissal of popular culture, their airy assumption that mass-media forms were always aesthetically dreary and politically pernicious. From the standpoint of cultural studies, such attitudes revealed more about the professional blinkers of intellectuals than about the intrinsic qualities of popular culture. Cultural studies, then, did not seek to destroy aesthetics, but to broaden the definition of what counted as art by taking popular culture seriously. It was always as much about form as about content, as much about pleasure as about ideology. Cultural studies is as indebted to semiotics as it is to the work of Antonio Gramsci and the politics of new social movements. In retrospect, its emergence at a time when our everyday environment was becoming saturated with ever more sophisticated media images seems inevitable. Cultural studies provided a vocabulary for talking about the formal complexity of contemporary culture. It made a much wider variety of objects aesthetically interesting.

The work of Richard Hoggart and Raymond Williams, often seen as two of the founders of cultural studies, makes this commitment very clear. Neither of these scholars is particularly interested in arresting and strip-searching works of literature. For example, Raymond Williams's work spans a wide variety of subjects, from television to tragedy, from Welsh working-class culture to the more arcane works of the English canon. One of the first scholars to offer an eloquent defense of popular culture and ordinary life, Williams was also a scrupulous reader of literary works who argued strenuously against reducing such works to vehicles of ideology. In fact, as both Williams's supporters and his critics have pointed out, his vision of culture is powerfully influenced by the heritage of Romantic aesthetics (see Bennett's *Culture: A Reformer's Science* and Johnson's *The Cultural Critics: From Matthew Arnold to Raymond Williams*). Similarly, Richard Hoggart argued that the techniques of literary criticism would play a central part in the new field of cultural studies, allowing critics to attend to the specific formal qualities of popular culture. "Unless you know how these things work as art, even though sometimes as 'bad art,' what you say about them will not cut very deep" (quoted in Mulhern 2000: 96).

In the 1970s and 1980s, there was an intellectual shift in center of gravity as scholars turned in ever greater numbers to structuralist and poststructuralist theories. One result was a growing formalism in cultural studies, a concentration on the signifier rather than the signified. Scholars drew on semiotic theory to describe and analyze the patterns and conventions through which meaning was produced. An organic and romantic vision of culture gave way to an avant-garde sensibility that highlighted moments of rupture, contradiction, and ambiguity in popular texts. The aesthetic theories of the Russian formalists, the art of the European avant-garde, and the ideas of Bertolt Brecht all fed into the cultural studies project.

We can see this mélange of influences very clearly in Richard Hebdige's *Subculture: The Meaning of Style*, one of the classic works of cultural studies. Hebdige made a persuasive case for the parallels between the aesthetics of the European avant-garde and 1970s British subcultural style. Punks, for example, drew heavily upon experimental techniques of collage, bricolage, and surreal juxtaposition. They combined random mass-produced objects – dog collars, safety pins, garbage bags – in a perverse mimicry of consumer culture. Their manipulation of signs was knowing, self-conscious, and parodic. Clearly, it was no longer possible to draw a sharp line between the subversive experiments of the literary avant-garde and the mawkish tastes of the masses: intellectuals did not have a monopoly on formal sophistication and irony. Thus Hebdige wrote with the eye of an aesthetician as much as a sociologist, doing close readings of the multilayered meanings of subcultural styles.

In Hebdige's book, as in much cultural studies work, form was not incidental but essential. To confuse an interest in popular culture with a sociological stress on content is to mistake the essence of the cultural studies project. In a well-known essay, Peter Brooks argues for the continuing relevance of poetics, defined as a sense of "not only *what* a text means, but as well *how* it means" (Levine 1994: 161). It is precisely the curiosity about how things mean that lies at the heart of cultural studies. By training their eye on works once dismissed as aesthetically unworthy, cultural critics challenged the opposition between formally sophisticated high art and content-driven mass culture. It now seems obvious that many popular forms, from rap music to sitcoms, from science fiction novels to slasher movies, rely on a sophisticated manipulation of stylistic conventions. Can anyone sit through a Hollywood blockbuster that is orchestrated and marketed around the spectacular nature of its special effects and still believe that popular culture is primarily about content?

Of course, people in cultural studies also want to talk about politics, power, and ideology. In this sense, its opponents are right. Cultural critics do not believe that art is autonomous. They see it as embedded in the world rather than as transcending the world. They do not believe that aesthetic experience soars above the messy scrimmage of social relations. But this is a long way from saying that cultural studies has no interest in aesthetics. If by aesthetics one means looking at the "how" as well as the "what" of symbol-making and pondering the distinctive pleasures and meanings that arise from that "how," then any such claim is off the mark. There are, in fact, some interesting convergences between cultural studies and contemporary aesthetic theory. Even a cursory glance at the academic literature makes it clear that many philosophers of art no longer have much faith in an ideal of pure and contemplative detachment. Instead, they are moving, in Marcia Eaton's words, from a Kantian to a contextual aesthetic. Eaton writes:

> "pure," conceptless, valueless uses of "beauty" are rare. It has certainly been a mistake for aestheticians to take this sense of beauty as the paradigmatic aesthetic concept – to act, that is, as if by giving an account of it one automatically has given an account for all aesthetic properties. Many, I would wager most, aesthetic terms are "impure" – they reflect, even require, beliefs and values: sincere, suspenseful, sentimental, shallow, sensitive, subtle, sexy, sensual, salacious, sordid, sobering, sustainable, skillful... and that, of course, only scratches the surface of the s-words! (2000: 34)[4]

Certainly, when I first stumbled across cultural studies as a graduate student, it excited me not because it talked about politics – there were plenty of other approaches that did that – but because it made a compelling case for how rich and multifaceted works of popular culture could be. It forced me to look afresh at some of the assumptions that I had absorbed as an aspiring student of literature. Often, my professors spoke as if they were the sole guardians of the aesthetic sensibility, as if outside the hallowed walls of the academy there was only hideousness and horror. The problem with literature departments, I would argue, is not that they study literature, but that they often see themselves as having a monopoly on what counts as aesthetic experience.

There are various reasons for this belief, including the need to justify one's professional status and authority by laying claim to a unique form of expertise. In fact, the professionalization of aesthetics is not necessarily a bad thing. But it leads to problems when critics start to equate their own specialized techniques of reading with aesthetics *tout court*. In the heyday of New Criticism, scholars of literature were trained as technicians of language. They cultivated a reverence for words, assiduously poring over literary works that were rich in ambiguity, irony, and paradox. In spite of recent changes in the profession, things have not changed that much. Not surprisingly, literary critics still like works that reward their own professional prowess, that are satisfyingly indeterminate, that allow them to dig for obscure allusions to other literary works, that repay endless rereading.

Yet there are, one hardly needs to say, other aspects of art beside innovation, difficulty, and verbal pyrotechnics. For example, literature was once prized for its suspenseful plots and its powerful archetypal figures. But you will not get far as an English major nowadays by enthusing about an exciting story. If we look at the history of modern literature and professional criticism, we see a fastidious disdain for the well-made plot. Instead, storytelling continues to flourish in the popular fiction aisle, where it brings in stupendous royalties for Danielle Steele and Stephen King.

Again, while critics once enthused over novels that could freeze your blood, make your hair stand on end, or inspire copious tears, the professionalization of literary study has put an end to such talk. As an academic discipline, literary criticism teaches certain techniques of interpretation and ranks highly the works that reward such techniques. It teaches students to decode works according to accepted parameters and places a high premium on aesthetic difficulty. It leaves little room for attending to emotion, excitement, escapism, and other aspects of aesthetic response that cannot be evaluated, graded, and ranked. In fact, critics have often argued that such responses do not qualify as aesthetic at all. Thanks to modern ideas about the primacy of form and the linking of art to other artworks rather than to life, art is often defined as the province of specialists. Matei Calinescu is refreshingly blunt on this point: "true aesthetic experience may be rare to the point of being statistically irrelevant" (1987: 228).

This, then, is the real challenge posed by cultural studies. Not its denial of the aesthetic, but its case for multiple aesthetics. It insists that English professors and other cultural mediators do not have a monopoly on imagination, fantasy, playfulness, and delight in form. It struggles to unravel a longstanding distinction between the authentic art of the few and the mindless kitsch of the masses. John Frow underscores this point when he talks about regimes of value. "The concept of regime," he writes, "expresses one of the fundamental theses of work in cultural studies; that no object, no text, no cultural practice has an intrinsic or necessary meaning or value or function; and that meaning, value and function are always the effect of specific (and changing, changeable) social relations and mechanisms of signification" (1995: 145). In other words, the very appeal to aesthetic value presuppose a framework that defines certain properties rather than others as aesthetically valuable. Simon Frith puts the case more succinctly: "value judgements only make sense as part of an argument and arguments are always social events" (1996: 95). Cultural studies reminds us that there are other arguments, other values, other ways of appreciating and discriminating between works, than those that reign in the classroom.

It is, in fact, highly ironic that cultural studies now stands accused of neglecting beauty. It is not cultural studies that has outlawed beauty, but modern criticism and theory. Beauty, as Alexander Nehemas points out, is one of the most discredited ideas in contemporary philosophy. The history of aesthetics is the story of the ascendancy of the sublime over the beautiful. Modern art has been prized for being bleak, difficult, anguished, demanding – but certainly not for being beautiful. When Umberto Eco states that the timeless value of Beauty is "generally only a cover for the mercenary face of Kitsch," he is speaking for several generations of critics (1989: 216). Rather than agreeing that beauty is truth and truth beauty, critics have typically argued the opposite. Only the bleak, the ugly, the discordant, could do justice to the grim realities of modern life. Meanwhile our hunger for beauty, for harmonious, well-proportioned forms that are pleasing to the eye, is sated in popular culture, where we can feast our eyes on endless images of well-muscled Adonises and spectacular sunsets. But this is not a kind of beauty to which scholars of art have paid much attention.

In her recent book *On Beauty*, Elaine Scarry also averts her eyes from such questions. Instead, her archly archaic prose conjures up a genteel, inbred world, where we are all surrounded by exquisite *objets d'art*; a chance encounter with a flower begets a Rilkean moment of ineffable plenitude. Here is Scarry's list of beautiful things: a trellis of sweet pea; sonnets; mother-of-pearl poppies; Matisse paintings; Gallé vases; gods of both East and West; dances; birdsong; Phaedrus; Nausicaa; the daylit sky; mathematical proofs. It is a curiously rarefied account of beauty; Scarry's book blocks out the bustle of modernity, the hubbub of the marketplace, the voices of women, people of color, and others who have talked about art. It is as if Duchamp and Disney, camp and cyberpunk, muzak and MTV had never happened. The challenge, surely, is to think what beauty might mean in the light of this history rather than to push it out of sight.

Nor does Scarry's "we" ever consider differences, indeed clashes, of taste. Millions of Americans are enthralled by Thomas Kinkade's paintings of babbling brooks, forest glades, and ivy-covered cottages nestling in the twilight; indeed Kinkade himself has waxed eloquent on the life-affirming quality of his paintings in contrast to the ugliness, nihilism, and irrelevance of modern art.[5] Is the delight inspired by Kinkade's work akin to Scarry's own pleasure in Matisse? Is beauty simply in the eye of the beholder? Or are the 10 million consumers of Kinkade products being duped by the pseudo-harmony of kitsch, as some scholars would argue? Do perceptions of what is beautiful unite us or divide us? These seem like crucial questions, but Scarry never even attempts to answer them.

By contrast, cultural critic Simon Frith offers a more substantial engagement with questions of beauty and pleasure. His book *Performing Rites* is a wide-ranging exploration of popular music, its diverse styles and genres, its various audiences, and the complex and often inexpressible emotions that it arouses. As Frith points out, the appreciation of popular music is full of talk about aesthetic value. People feel passionately about the talents of particular artists and performers; and they often struggle to put into words the powerful effect that music has upon them. "We all hear the music we like as something special, as something that defies the mundane, takes us 'out of ourselves,' puts us somewhere else" (1996: 275). Transcendence, Frith concludes, is a crucial aspect of musical experience, even if it is less about independence of social forces than an alternative experience of them. While paying scrupulous attention to how musical response is framed by different expectations and contexts of reception, Frith adamantly refuses to see aesthetic experience as a mere mirror of social identity. Instead, he stresses the imaginative, emotional, and sensual power of music, its power to transport us, to create new registers of perception and feeling, to make us see the world differently.

Thus when Rorty argues that cultural studies means an end to aesthetic pleasure and romantic enthusiasm, he is dead wrong. Because he equates cultural studies with unmasking and debunking, he remains oblivious to its intense emotional commitments, its often buoyant mood, and its longstanding interest in desire and pleasure. Opposing romantic utopianism to the dryness of cultural studies, he seems unaware of the rich vein of utopian thought and romantic insurgency in writing on popular culture. Indeed, when scholars complain that cultural studies is rote sociology or one more dry social science, they are simply revealing their ignorance of sociology. Many sociologists hate cultural studies even more than English professors do, complaining about its lack of rigor, its retreat from politics, and its excessive reliance on aesthetic and textual forms of evidence. Much the same can be said about anthropology, history, and other neighboring fields, which often view cultural studies with considerable suspicion (see Morley 1998; Ferguson & Golding 1997; Nelson & Gaonkar 1996).

What, then, is the home of cultural studies? Where does it belong? I want to conclude with these questions because much of the controversy inspired by cultural studies has less to do with its intellectual content than with fights over turf. I have no objection to professors deconstructing Madonna videos, the argument goes, as long as they don't do it in my department. When I first voiced some of the arguments of this chapter in *The Chronicle of Higher Education*, English professor William Dowling wrote in to make precisely this point. "I have many colleagues," he observes, "who have come to loathe the empty trendiness of cultural studies." But, Dowling graciously concedes, "Not one of them is against studying the things that Ms. Felski wants to see studied – rap music, TV sitcoms, slasher movies – in the appropriate academic departments." In other words, "American universities are so structured that they already have departments – anthropology, sociology, history, communications – that study the sort of thing she's interested in" (1999: B10).

In fact, as I've just pointed out, Dowling is wrong. There is a great deal of disagreement about what the institutional location for cultural studies should be. One reason it has often taken root in English departments is precisely because its concerns are not identical with the traditional methods of anthropology, sociology, communication studies and the like. But what I want to address here is Dowling's assumption that my account of cultural studies is also a defense of the English department as its natural home. This belief is mistaken. I have tried to show that the study of culture is infused with aesthetic concepts, but it does not follow that cultural studies is the future of literary studies or that literary and cultural studies should become one.

This view is proving unfortunate not just for literary studies, as Dowling suggests, but also for cultural studies. When scholars trained in textual analysis decide to remake themselves as cultural critics, the results are not always salutary. Inevitably, old habits die hard. Cary Nelson (1999) comments on the sorry spectacle of scholars renaming or repackaging close readings of texts as cultural studies without bothering to learn anything of the field's traditions. Thus the influence of cultural studies on English goes along with a marked dilution of its features as a distinctive intellectual project. A complex interdisciplinary blend of social theory, anthropology, media studies, and textual analysis is slowly being turned into a subfield of English literature, often embraced by scholars far more familiar with Melville than with Marx or *Melrose Place*.

What defines cultural studies, moreover, is not just its object of analysis but its frameworks and methods. A long time ago, Raymond Williams argued that cultural studies was not about "isolating the object," but about "discovering the nature of a practice and its conditions" (1980: 47). What this meant was that cultural studies saw meaning as dynamic and interactive, forged under particular conditions, mobile and open to change. The pleasures, problems, and politics of texts were not etched for all time in the form of the texts themselves, but were created and recreated in the social flux of engagement and interpretation. Seeing culture as a practice meant shuttling between texts and institutions, aesthetics and social analysis, semiotics and power. The second term in these pairings is often shortchanged when the primary venue for cultural studies becomes the English department. Literary criticism gives us sophisticated ways of reading texts and signs, but it is a poor guide to the workings of structures, institutions, and systems.

A frequent stumbling-block here is the axiological dimension of literary criticism, its powerful attachment to the exemplary text. Critics often operate on the assumption that certain works, by dint of their formal properties, can give us unparalleled insight into how things really are. When this idea is translated into the register of cultural studies, it leads to poring over a popular text in the belief that a close reading of a metaphor or camera technique will unlock the secrets of the social system or the dominant ideology. A magazine or a movie becomes a magic conduit to the *Zeitgeist*. For example, it is not uncommon to see a reading of two or three films being used as evidence of pervasive anxieties (currently a much-favored word) about gender or race. Yet in at least some of these cases, picking a different sample might easily result in a dramatically different conclusion.

George Levine picks up on this point in discussing the relationship between aesthetics and cultural studies. He takes scholars like Stephen Greenblatt and Eve Sedgwick to task for spinning big stories about history and culture from a meager sample of literary works (1994: 5–10). Levine is right to point out the problems of trying to use close reading in this way as a source of reliable evidence about social phenomena. Textual skills are not a substitute for historical grounding and command of empirical detail. Literary critics who hold forth about politics, society, and economics need more than a superficial knowledge of how scholars in the social sciences have talked about such questions. Levine is wrong, however, in thinking that he has scored a point against cultural studies. What he clearly does not realize – and this is yet another example of the amnesia I have mentioned – is that scholars in cultural studies have been making similar arguments for a very long time. One of the ways in which cultural studies distinguishes itself from the politicized wing of literary studies is precisely by questioning the view that a single work can be treated as an allegory of social relations.

Let me summarize, then, what I see as the distinctiveness of cultural studies. First of all, it draws upon an anthropological as well as an aesthetic idea of culture, seeking to make sense of the full range of images, texts, stories, and symbolic practices. Such an approach does not exclude the analysis of literature and high art, but it does require an awareness of the relations and flows of interchange between different cultural spheres. Cultural studies also links descriptions of texts and practices to analyses of power. It does not believe that the making and getting of culture are free of social interests, needs, and struggles. But it is wary of grand theories of capitalism, patriarchy, or imperialism that look down on the patterns and practices of everyday life from a haughty distance. Cultural studies, at its best, is meticulously attentive to the local, the contingent, and the conjunctural: that is to say, the ways in which relations between texts, political interests, and social groups are formed, severed and realigned over time. Cultural studies, in this definition, involves a balancing act between the macro and the micro and between the competing claims of textual and social analysis.

What this suggests, then, is that any attempt to do cultural studies requires a more than superficial knowledge of different disciplines and traditions. It is not about collapsing aesthetics and politics into a general theory of textuality. Rather, cultural studies defines itself in relation to the tensions and competing pulls of different fields of knowledge. As Cary Nelson puts it, "if you only know one discipline intimately, and you operate securely within its principles, you cannot do cultural studies" (1996: 64).

The other side of this coin, however, is that cultural studies needs these other disciplines as intellectual resources on which to draw. This is one reason why I am opposed to any attempt to subsume literary studies into cultural studies. Such an encroachment threatens the integrity of an archive of important and enormously influential works and a longstanding body of commentary on those works as well as on general problems of hermeneutics and interpretation. Literary studies and cultural studies are related fields but they are also distinct fields. It makes as little sense to deny the differences between them as it does to think of them as implacable enemies locked in a struggle for supremacy.

Having chastised some literary critics for their ignorance of cultural studies, I must also, in all fairness, acknowledge the *bêtise* of some cultural critics on the subject of literature. Certainly, one influential trend within cultural studies has been to turn popularity into a new source of value. The worth of a text is measured solely by the status of its imagined constituency – young people, women, the working class, a vaguely defined notion of "the people." As some scholars in the field have pointed out, such a perspective soon runs into problems. There is more than an element of bad faith in an uncritical embrace of the popular. Some leftist academics seem to believe that such an embrace will absolve them of their role as intellectuals implicated in the hierarchies and distinctions of academic life. In fact, the opposite is true; romantic visions of the people as "more real," as standing for authenticity, spontaneity, and sexy, sweaty, nonalie-nated bodies, merely testify to the vivid fantasy life of intellectuals. Cultural studies means taking popular culture seriously and without condescension, but it should not lead to a flip-flopping of value, such that studying the popular becomes a sign of political righteousness, whereas high art is placed on the side of conservatism and reaction.

Such a view relies on a flawed understanding of the politics of literature as well as an overestimation of its influence. It is hard to make a convincing case that the values of canonical literature do much to shore up the political status quo or that there is much connection between knowing about Milton or Melville and running a country or a corporation. High art has a complex and often dissident relation-ship to social norms; in fact, modern literature is a major source of the bohemian, critical, antibourgeois sensibility that ultimately gave birth to cultural studies. Moreover, decrying high art as the culture of the ruling class reveals not just a poor grasp of aesthetics but also of politics and sociology. In contemporary Western societies, the relations between economic and political power and possession of cultural capital are hardly so straightforward. High culture and popular culture do not function as homogenous and mutually exclusive blocks that are closely tied to specific class interests. As John Frow points out, "'high' and 'low' culture can no longer . . . be neatly correlated with a hierarchy of social classes" (1995: 1).

Thus I find myself in the odd position of siding with both the old fogies and the young Turks. The forced marriage of literary and cultural studies is not good for either side; it will diminish the study of literature and blunt the cutting edge of cultural studies. That is not say that individual scholars cannot work productively on the cusp of the two fields, but any systematic attempt to merge them into a megadiscipline should be resisted. Those who claim that literature is defunct, that literary studies should give way to cultural studies, are engaged in the worst kind of disciplinary imperialism. It is as if the sociologists were to march over to the psychology department to inform its faculty that their discipline were now obsolete, that psychology would henceforth be a subfield of sociology. Do we really want to endorse such a corporate ethos of mergers and acquisitions? Tony Bennett (1998a) is surely right when he points out that, high-flown rhetoric to the contrary, the role of cultural studies is neither to subsume nor to replace the traditional disciplines.

What, then, is the place of cultural studies? Cultural studies is both like and unlike literary criticism, communication studies, sociology, anthropology, and history. By becoming too closely associated with any of these fields, it risks becoming lopsided and surrendering its distinctive identity. My own sense is that cultural studies continues to work best as an interdisciplinary major, where faculty and students are forced to confront the competing truth claims of different disciplines. Bennett puts it well when he describes cultural studies as an interdisciplinary clearing-house that stimulates intellectual traffic between various fields in the humanities and social sciences. It is out of such alliances and quarrels about the status and meanings of culture that the best cultural studies work emerges.

Of course, as an interdisciplinary enterprise, it is the permanent fate of cultural studies to be faulted by historians for not being historical enough, by sociologists for not being sociological enough, and by literary critics for not being sufficiently interested in literature. Moreover, people in cultural studies disagree passionately about its goals and methods, about the merits of textual versus social analysis, and about the meanings and merit of popular culture. Still, while cultural studies can mean many different things, there are limits to what it can mean. Cultural studies has become a term of abuse and a much-abused term in America's culture wars. I have tried to show that cultural critics are neither as beastly nor as insensitive to style and form as their detractors often make out. If we can arrive at a more careful and circumspect use of the term "cultural studies," – and a more careful and circumspect *practice* of cultural studies – then I, for one, will live happily ever after.[6]

NOTES

This chapter draws on some material first published in a short article in *The Chronicle of Higher Education*, entitled (not by me) "Scholars who Disdain Cultural Studies Don't Know What They are Talking About," July 23, 1999.

1 For a brief history of the American moral panic about cultural studies and an interesting discussion of cultural studies' "public relations problem," see Rodman 1997.
2 For an evaluation of this account as it applies to feminist approaches to literature, see Felski's *Literature After Feminism* (2003a).

3   A pertinent analysis of this phenomenon can be found in Cary Nelson's "Always Already Cultural Studies: Two Academic Conferences and a Manifesto" (1997).
4   A volume such as *A Companion to Aesthetics*, edited by David Cooper (1992), gives a clear sense of the changing register of much aesthetic theory. One good example of the convergence between aesthetics and cultural studies is of course Richard Shusterman's important *Pragmatist Aesthetics* (1992).
5   See, e.g., Orlean, "Art for Everybody" (2001).
6   I want to underscore that this chapter is intended as an attempt to clarify the meaning of the term "cultural studies." (For another such attempt, see my "Modernist Studies and Cultural Studies," 2003b). While I have some sympathy for the project of cultural studies, my point is not at all to make a case for the superiority of cultural studies *vis-à-vis* other critical methods, but to encourage a more clear-sighted recognition of their differences.

REFERENCES

Bennett, Tony. 1998a. "Cultural Studies: A Reluctant Discipline." *Cultural Studies* 12(4): 528–45.
——— . 1998b. *Culture: A Reformer's Science*. London: Sage.
Bloom, Harold. 1994. *The Western Canon: The Books and School of the Ages*. New York: Riverhead.
Brand, Peggy, ed. 2000. *Beauty Matters*. Bloomington: Indiana University Press.
Brooks, Peter. 1994. "Aesthetics and Ideology – What Happened to Poetics?" In Levine 1994: 153–67.
Calinescu, Matei. 1987. *Five Faces of Modernity: Modernism Avant-Garde Decadence Kitsch Postmodernism*. Durham, NC: Duke University Press.
Clark, Michael, ed. 2000. *The Revenge of the Aesthetic: The Place of Literature in Theory Today*. Berkeley: University of California Press.
Cooper, David, ed. 1992. *A Companion to Aesthetics*. Oxford: Blackwell.
Donoghue, Denis. 2003. *Speaking of Beauty*. New Haven: Yale University Press.
Dowling, William C. 1999. "Cultural Studies versus Literary Studies." (Letter to the Editor.) *The Chronicle of Higher Education*, Sept. 17, 1999: B10.
Eaton, Marcia. 2000. "Kantian and Contextual Beauty." In Brand 2000: 27–36.
Eco, Umberto. 1989. *The Open Work*. Cambridge, MA: Harvard University Press.
Ellis, John. 1997. *Literature Lost: Social Agendas and the Corruption of the Humanities*. New Haven: Yale University Press.
Felski, Rita. 2003a. *Literature After Feminism*. Chicago: University of Chicago Press.
——— . 2003b. "Modernist Studies and Cultural Studies." *Modernism/Modernity* 10(3): 501–17.
Ferguson, Marjorie and Peter Golding, eds. 1997. *Cultural Studies in Question*. London: Sage.

Frith, Simon. 1996. *Performing Rites: Evaluating Popular Music*. New York: Oxford University Press.

Frow, John. 1995. *Cultural Studies and Cultural Value*. Oxford: Oxford University Press.

Hebdige, Richard. 1979. *Subculture: The Meaning of Style*. London: Methuen.

Heller, Scott. 1998. "Wearying of Cultural Studies, Some Scholars Rediscover Beauty." *The Chronicle of Higher Education*, Dec. 4, 1998: A15–16.

Johnson, Lesley. 1979. *The Cultural Critics: From Mathew Arnold to Raymond Williams*. London: Routledge.

Johnson, Richard. 1986–7. "What is Cultural Studies Anyway?" *Social Text* 16: 36–80.

Kernan, Alvin. 1990. *The Death of Literature*. New Haven: Yale University Press.

Levine, George, ed. 1994. *Aesthetics and Ideology*. New Brunswick, NJ: Rutgers University Press.

Morley, David. 1998. "So-called Cultural Studies: Dead Ends and Reinvented Wheels." *Cultural Studies* 12(4): 476–97.

Mulhern, Francis. 2000. *Culture/Metaculture*. London: Routledge.

Nelson, Cary. 1996. "Literature as Cultural Studies." In Nelson & Gaonkar 1996: 63–102.

——. 1997. "Always Already Cultural Studies: Two Academic Conferences and a Manifesto." In *Manifesto of a Tenured Radical*. New York: New York University Press.

——. 1999. "The Linguisticality of Cultural Studies: Rhetoric, Close Reading and Contextualization." In Rosteck 1999: 211–25.

—— and Dilip Parameshwar Gaonkar, eds. 1996. *Disciplinarity and Dissent in Cultural Studies*. New York: Routledge.

Orlean, Susan. 2001. "Art for Everybody." *The New Yorker*, Oct. 15: 124–30.

Perloff, Marjorie. 2000. "In Defense of Poetry: Put the Literature Back into Literary Studies." *Boston Review* 24(6) (Dec. 1999–Jan. 2000): 22–6.

Rodman, Gilbert R. 1997. "Subject to Debate: (Mis)Reading Cultural Studies." *Journal of Communication Inquiry* 21(2): 56–69.

Rorty, Richard. 1998. "The Inspirational Value of Great Works of Literature." In *Achieving Our Country: Leftist Thought in Twentieth-Century America*. Cambridge, MA: Harvard University Press, pp. 125–40.

Rosteck, Thomas, ed. 1999. *At the Intersection: Cultural Studies and Rhetorical Studies*. New York: Guilford.

Scarry, Elaine. 1999. *On Beauty and Being Just*. Princeton: Princeton University Press.

Shusterman, Richard. 1992. *Pragmatist Aesthetics: Living Beauty, Rethinking Art*. Oxford: Blackwell.

Soderholm, James, ed. 1997. *Beauty and the Critic: Aesthetics in an Age of Cultural Studies*. Tuscaloosa: University of Alabama Press.

Steiner, Wendy. 2001. *Venus in Exile: The Rejection of Beauty in Twentieth-Century Art*. New York: Free Press.

Williams, Raymond. 1980. *Problems in Materialism and Culture*. London: Verso.

2

On Literature in Cultural Studies

JOHN FROW

The "desire called cultural studies" was formed in the principled rejection of the established aesthetic fields of literary studies, film studies, and, less cogently, art history.[1] This move, which we can somewhat arbitrarily date to the emergence of the Centre for Contemporary Cultural Studies as an autonomous satellite of the University of Birmingham's Department of English in 1964, was at once a defense against the institutional hold of the disciplines in which many of those who practiced cultural studies had been trained and, at the level of theory, a refusal of the unreflected discourses of value within which the aesthetic object had been conceptualized. Yet it is important to be clear that this was a refusal not of the object itself, nor even of the study of aesthetic value, but of the normative discourses within which the object and its "placing" were defined. As Grossberg, Nelson, and Treichler write:

> Cultural studies does not require us to repudiate elite cultural forms . . . Rather, cultural studies requires us to identify the operation of specific practices, of how they continuously reinscribe the line between legitimate and popular culture, and of what they accomplish in specific contexts. (1992: 13)

We can leave it to contemporary folkloric studies, à la Bowling Green, to define itself by the domain of the popular which it analyzes; cultural studies is concerned with the field of relations within which both "popular" and "legitimate" cultural forms (if that distinction can still be maintained – I think it probably can't and we need much more complex differentiations) are given shape and value.

In this, however, cultural studies is perhaps not as far removed as it believes from some currents in literary studies and art history (this is less true of the study of film). And the very force of its initial refusal of the normative has become a problem for it, since it occludes those questions of value which lie at the heart of the practices it seeks to theorize. In this chapter I address the concept of the literary, seeking not to redeem it but to account for its continued existence as an organizing category in the field of writing; and I speculate on whether cultural studies and literary studies might some day get back together again.

I

At the beginning of Joseph Roth's novel *The Radetzky March* a young infantry lieutenant, seeing the Emperor accidentally put himself in danger in the course of the battle of Solferino, pushes him to the ground and receives the bullet intended for the Supreme War Lord. Many years later, now a captain and ennobled, Joseph Trotta finds in his son's school reader an account of this incident. What he reads, however, is a quite different story, in which the Emperor

> had ventured so far forward among the enemy in the heat of battle that suddenly he found himself surrounded by enemy cavalry. At this moment of supreme danger a young lieutenant, mounted on a foaming chestnut horse, galloped into the fray, waving his sword. What blows he inflicted on the backs and heads of the enemy horsemen. (1974: 7)

This mythical lieutenant is then pierced by an enemy lance, but is protected from further harm by "our young and fearless monarch" (1974: 7). Reading this exemplary fiction, Trotta is outraged – perhaps particularly at his reassignment to the cavalry; he complains to the Emperor and retires from the army; the story is expunged from the textbooks, but not before Trotta has come to understand "that the stability of the world, the power of the law, and the splendour of royalty are maintained by guile" (1974: 10).

This incident repeats that moment in Part II of *Don Quixote* in which the hero discovers the existence of a spurious account of his adventures, and expresses his fears "that if the author of that history of my exploits, which they say is now in print, chanced to be some enchanter hostile to me [*algún sabio mi enemigo*], he has probably changed one thing into another, mingling a thousand lies with one truth, and digressed to narrate actions out of the sequence proper to a faithful history" (1950: 516). Two contrary movements are at play in these passages. On the one hand, by being opposed to the spurious fiction which misrepresents Trotta's or Don Quixote's life, the prior and encompassing fiction is raised to the power of truth. On the other, this "faithful history," now manifestly unable to control the penetration of (novelistic) life by secondary fictions, becomes even more intensely a fiction, fiction to the second degree, more true because more fictive; the narrative of a resistance to Literature has itself become a work of literature. When, later in this second part of the novel, Don Quixote discovers a spurious Part II (the really existing forged continuation of Cervantes's novel by Avellaneda), and indeed encounters characters from it, the novel's theme of the unreality of the literary is further undone: it is now only at a great ironical remove that this initial demystificatory step can be taken. It is in this double movement – merely adumbrated in Roth's novel, but worked out in its full complexity in Cervantes's – that the emergence of the literary can be traced: an emergence which is not only a punctual event (the initiation of "literature" as a category of modernity) but a repeated structure of thematized reflexive reference.

Now consider a second such moment of emergence. At a certain point in Balzac's *Lost Illusions* the provincial poet and man of letters Lucien Chardon (now calling himself Lucien de Rubempré) writes a review of a play in which a leading role is played by the actress Coralie, to whom he has offered "the virginity of my pen" (1971: 302). The review is a piece of puffery; Adorno describes it as "the birth of the feuilleton," and says of it that its " 'for the first time' quality gives that contemptible form a conciliatory charm" (1992: 34). Like the passages from Roth and Cervantes, this embedded text represents a moment of reflexivity, since it explicitly thematizes journalistic corruption. Adorno thus understands this feuilleton as "the work of art's reflection on itself. The work becomes aware of itself as the illusion that the illusory world of journalism in which Lucien loses his illusions also is. Semblance is thereby elevated above itself" (1992: 35–6). The literary text is at once like and unlike the piece of mass-produced journalism, sharing its commodified status but transcending it by virtue of its ability to recognize this status and to take a critical distance from it.

But another and less redemptive way of reading this moment would be to see it as the crystallization of a set of tensions that run through this novel, the first major European literary text to explore in a detailed and systematic way the commodity production of books. Two contradictory structures of value, centered on the relation between Lucien and his friend David Séchard, organize the book. In the first, the literary (exemplified by the poetry of Chénier and of Lucien himself, and by the historical novels of d'Arthez, a self-portrait of Balzac) is counterposed to the corrupt world of journalism and of the book trade to which it nevertheless belongs. This world is governed by the figures of prostitution and of commercial calculation. For the cynical Lousteau, the literary world is a place of bribery, of "spiritual degradation" (1971: 251), and of the buying and selling of reputations, a place in which venal journalists viciously attack work of merit and publishers treat books as short-term capital risks. As one "wholesale bookseller" puts it to an anguished author, "Walter Scott's novels bring us eighteen sous a volume, three francs sixty for the complete works, and you want me to sell your rubbishy books for more than that?" (1971: 200–1). But the category of literature is undercut not so much by its immersion in this world, to which it is at least morally superior, as by its merely honorific status in the text: all the intensity of writing is to be found in the nether world of venal prose, not in the higher realms of apparently autonomous literary production. And this focus of the novel's energy corresponds to the way in which, in a second structure of value, its fascination with David Séchard's ambitions is developed. David is an inventor seeking a process for making cheap, good-quality paper from vegetable pulp. At a time of rapid increase in the production and marketing of books and newspapers it was, says the anonymous narrator,

> vitally necessary to adapt paper-making to the needs of French civilization, which was threatening to extend discussion to all subjects and to take its stand on a never-ending manifestation of individual thought – a real misfortune, for the more a people deliberates the less active it becomes. And so, curiously enough, while Lucien was getting caught in the cogwheels of the vast journalistic machine and running the risk of it tearing his honour and intelligence to shreds, David Séchard, in his distant printing-office, was surveying the expansion of the periodical press in its material consequences. He wanted to provide the means for the end towards which the spirit of the age was tending. (1971: 489–90)

The contradiction is straightforward, but between that moralizing "real misfortune" and a "spirit of the age" [*l'esprit du Siècle*] driven by technological advance and capital investment, the novel's sympathies are fully engaged with the latter. The "literature" that emerges from this play of forces and values is neither the transcendent stuff of poetry and the "high" historical novel, nor the mere corruption of journalism, but a writing which is torn between the two and whose defining character is its status, and its dissatisfaction with its status, as a thing to be bought and sold.

Let me finally propose a third moment of emergence of the literary. I find it in one of the canonical sites of (post)modernist lyricism, Frank O'Hara's "The Day Lady Died," which is built around an opposition between two incommensurate temporalities. The first is the mundane time of a chronicle of disconnected events. This chronicle (O'Hara's "I do this and I do that" genre) sets up several different ways of describing what time it exists in, and veers between them since none seems satisfactory:

> It is 12.20 in New York a Friday
> three days after Bastille day, yes
> it is 1959

before then moving into the empty punctuality of a train timetable ("I will get off the 4.19 in Easthampton / at 7.15"). The "I" of the poem gets a shoeshine, buys a hamburger and malted, buys some books: this is what Marjorie Perloff calls a "flat literalism" (1977: 125), a recording of surfaces. The books that the speaker buys or thinks of buying – a copy of *New World Writing* ("to see what the poets / in Ghana are doing these days"), an illustrated Verlaine, Hesiod, Behan, Genet – are of the same order as the liquor and cigarettes he buys, packaged writing. It is only with the mention, five lines from the end of the poem, of buying "a NEW YORK POST with her face on it," a reference to the unspoken death of Billie Holiday (the "Lady Day" whose name is inverted in the singsong rhymes of the title), that the turn to the poem's other temporality begins. This turn is completed in the final quatrain:

> and I am sweating a lot by now and thinking of
> leaning on the john door in the 5 SPOT
> while she whispered a song along the keyboard
> to Mal Waldron and everyone and I stopped breathing

The sweat is because it's a muggy day (line 7), but it also perhaps accompanies the "thinking" that initiates the poem's second plane, that of a remembered time which breaks the episodic time of the previous stanzas and is their underlying reality. This is not the time of Holiday's death (that too belongs to the episodic present) but of the song "whispered...along the keyboard" so that everyone "stopped breathing," in a kind of death which does and does not resemble hers.[2] The lyrical stasis of this time is generated above all by the ambivalent syntax and rhythms of the final line, which reads in three different ways:

> to Mal Waldron and everyone | and I stopped breathing

or:

> to Mal Waldron | and everyone and I stopped breathing

or, in an unavoidable synthetic reading which, since the syntax is perfectly undecidable, combines the other two:

> to Mal Waldron | and everyone | and I | stopped breathing.

The first of these readings moves the song out along the keyboard from the pianist to the whole audience, and then rests on the isolated response of the speaker ("I stopped breathing"). The second, with its isolation of the pianist as the recipient of the song and its simultaneous immersion of the speaker in the audience and separation of him from it ("everyone and I") slows the line right down at the end as the speaker takes part in a shared experience. The third, which I think is the only possible way of reading the line, is a "torn" reading in which "everyone" goes both ways at once (and in which "I" perhaps functions ungrammatically both as a quasi-dative – the third recipient of the song – and as the subject of the verb). Again, this reading is slowed right down (we should probably add a further caesura between "stopped" and "breathing"), miming the loss of breath which meets the whispering of the song. The "emergence" of the literary that I find here is the effect of this shift of planes from the mundane to the epiphanic moment of memory, and from the book as packaged writing to the breathed authenticity of the voice as it intimates death and its transcendence.

II

Each of these three different modes of emergence of the literary – as epistemo-logical reflexivity; as sociological reflexivity; and as a shift from mundane time to the ecstatic moment – validly affirms a mode of its being (which is to say a mode of reading, and the forms of textual complexity that correspond to it). But the concept of literary emergence, as I have tried to indicate, specifies a dual temporality: on the one hand, it refers to the literary as an event that occurs within (or *as*) an act of reading; on the other, it refers to a structure of historical value which is variably consolidated in an institutional form. These two configurations of value are always potentially contradictory, since the stability of the latter threatens the status of the former as a momentary and always historically fragile achievement. It is surely clear enough that consolidated canonical formations are historically variable: the continuous reception of "Homer" or "Shakespeare" is a matter of constant reinvention within discontinuous frameworks of value and for changing social uses, rather than the constant recognition of a timeless worth. But it is equally the case that the sense of the literary as fleeting realization, with its ruptural relation to the ordinary time of writing, cannot be assumed to have a transhistorical force, since it is itself the achievement of a postromantic regime of reading. Thus when Thomas Keenan defines literature not as a collection of poems and novels but as "our exposure to the singularity of a text, something that cannot be organized in advance, whose complexities cannot be settled or decided by 'theories' or the application of more or less mechanical programs" (1997: 1), he ignores the extent to which reading is indeed always organized in advance by the institutions of genre and by norms of semantic determinacy (including norms of indeterminacy).

To posit "the literary" in these three rather different forms is not to posit a common structure, be it that of the self-awareness of language, of the embedding of social function in complex patterns of writing, or of a passage to redeemed authenticity; it is, rather, to pose the question whether there can be any ontological or functional unity to the category of the literary as I have used it here. The difficulty is not that the question "What is Literature?" cannot be answered, but that many perfectly valid answers are possible. In almost all cases these answers are normative: the literary constitutes a distinct, unitary, and special language game recognized contrastively in its relation to one or another nonliterary languages, or nonliterary uses of language, or nonliterary levels of organization of language, or indeed to canonical literary language itself. It is the opposite of scientific or philosophical statement (Richards, Lacoue-Labarthe), or the opposite of everyday language (Shklovsky); it is language of high intensity (Arnold) or of a high level of semiotic complexity (Eco); it is performative rather than constative language (Burke), language as aporia rather than communication; it is language aware of its own rhetorical status and its inherent liability to error (de Man), or a generalized principle of reflexivity, or it is its own impossibility. There is none of these definitions that does not embody a particularist structure of value (if only because of the assumption of literacy or of the ability to thematize formal structure). Any attempt now to define the literary as a universal or unitary phenomenon necessarily fails to account for the particular institutional conditions of existence which underpin its assumptions, and falls thereby into the fetishism of a culture of social distinction and of the marketing regime which it supports.

For, far from being a problem, Literature is alive and flourishing in the great world. Think of the John Keating character played by Robin Williams in *Dead Poets Society*, tearing pages of formalist and "official" criticism out of the poetry textbook in order to teach his boys that poetry is life, passion, authenticity, humanity. Think of *Educating Rita*, with its alignment of Literature with working-class feminist vigor pitted against a burnt-out academicism. Think of the valorization of the literary in *Shakespeare in Love*, or *Orlando*, or *Shadowland*, or any of the recent Jane Austen adaptations. Think of the way the full romantic concept of authorship continues to flourish in the brand-naming of popular authors or in the production of literary biographies or on Oprah, but also in the legal system, where authorship and originality continue to be the major support of copyright. In the café culture of upmarket bookshops, in the cultural promotion apparatus of festivals and chat-shows and prizes, and in Hollywood's version of the art movie, Literature remains a timeless product of genius and feeling, directly apprehended in the heart by the empathetic reader. None of this is at all far from Harold Bloom's reverential resuscitation of the Bard, or Lentricchia's profession of an untheorizable love of literature, or what Sedgwick calls "the organization of liberal arts education as an expensive form of masterpiece theatre" (1990: 51). Indeed, the literary canon never went away: it was always there as negative theology in deconstruction, and the *Norton Anthology* has simply gotten fatter. Literary criticism remains an important part of a marketing system and of a highbrow taste culture which it blindly serves.

III

There are no texts, readers, meanings, or values separate from the institutional framework that determines their place, their use, their very mode of being.[3] Texts and readers are in the first instance not entities but functions, values within a system, and texts and readings count as literary or nonliterary by virtue of protocols which govern this distinction and specify the processes (the routine recognitions and the leaps of the heart) by which it is ongoingly realized. These protocols may require the reader to apprehend a text (or rather certain kinds of text and not others) as revealed religious truth, or to scrutinize it for layers of allegorical significance, or to treat it as the basis for a practice of ethical self-perfection, or to actualize rather than restrict its full informational potential. Mircea Marghescou calls this semantic code regulating the informational poten-tial of the linguistic code the *regime* of a text, and writes that "only a regime designating the textual function through opposition to its linguistic function and above all to other possible semantic functions could give form to this virtuality, transform the linguistic form into information" (1974: 47; my translation). In adapting this concept I take it to designate a semiotic apparatus that inspires and regulates practices of valuation and interpretation, connecting people to textual objects or processes by means of normative patterns of value and disvalue.[4] But if it is not to be understood merely as a semiotic relation, the concept of regime must be more broadly defined as a social apparatus, the structured articulation of a set of knowledge institutions (the school, the church, the theater), a more or less professionalized custodianship of literary knowledge, a designated set of proper social uses, and a more or less supportive relation to hierarchies of caste or class, of gender, of ethnicity, and so on. Ontologically impure, the literary regime in this broader sense is composed at once of codes, practices, organized bodies of texts, physical spaces (libraries, bookshops, bedrooms), modes of authority, and people and things interacting (all at once) physically, semiotically, and socially.

In thus cutting the ontological knot, the concept of regime shifts attention from an isolated and autonomous "reader" and "text" to the institutional frameworks which govern what counts as the literary and the possible and appropriate manners of its use and valuation; it asks, not "what is this thing and what does it mean?," but "under what conditions and to what ends does this thing come into being, and what operations can be performed upon it?" It describes relations rather than substances. The danger is that in this shift of focus this purely relational concept can itself come to be objectified as a static and final cause – as though values and interpretations could simply be read-off from this prior and determinant structure as its necessary effects, and in such a way that the details of any textual engagement could be predicted in advance. It is against this kind of mechanical determinism that Keenan's argument that we should not understand reading as the *application* of a code or program is directed. The literary regime has no reality beyond the shape it gives to acts of reading. It can be "recognized" only by means of an interpretation; it must itself be read, and indeed its force resides entirely in its reinforcement (or its modification) in every act of reading. There is no "system" separate from its actualizations.

To speak of a literary regime is to posit that it is one regime amongst others, existing in a relationship of overlap and difference with regimes of popular reading, of film, of television, of visual culture, of all the domains of activity that make up the realm of cultural practice and cultural value. No special privilege attaches to a literary regime except insofar as such a privilege can be enforced by political means; although it may define itself as different and superior to the regimes of popular culture (for example), in fact it is only different. This difference is not, however, that of one social group from another (not, at least, in complex modern societies); cultural regimes are relatively autonomous of social groups, and do not represent them in the sense of bearing or expressing their essential interests. Although they may recruit preferred constituencies, they are normally not reducible to them. Nor – to make a final qualification to the model of relational difference that I have proposed here – should any of this be taken to imply an absolute relativism, such that no regime either overlaps with or contests the values of another; on the contrary, the principle of relationality requires that we think in terms of a relative relativism, an articulation not of pure differences between fully self-identical formations but of partial, incomplete, and constantly contested differences between formations which are themselves internally differ-entiated and heterogeneous. We ourselves are always positioned, and it is only as a necessary methodological abstraction that we can posit that all regimes should be considered to be axiologically equal. A literary regime is thus neither simply detached from other regimes, nor a homogeneous structure of value; it is a regulatory manifold which makes possible the free exercise of judgment within a limited but disparate range of interpretive possibilities.

IV

If this attempt to rethink the status of the categories of the literary, the text, and reading is to have any value other than as a taxonomic exercise, it will be to the extent that it can help to redefine and to redirect what goes on in a good practice of reading. What it suggests, I hope, is that an informed and reflexive reading will find it both possible and necessary to *notice* different kinds of structure: the plane of its vision will move from a focus on a "text" with "meanings" to the relation between a text and the set of framing conditions that constitute its readability. In this relation, the "text" is at once a closed aesthetic space, with lines of force radiating inwards from the framing conditions that establish its closure, and a space of opening which begins to merge with its edges, its borders with the nontextual or the heterotextual. This is not, however, a relation between an "inside" and an "outside" or between a "text" and its "context," since the framing conditions are rather the margin that at once carries and unsettles that distinction. As the literary regime changes in its interaction with other systems it constantly modifies the valency of the framing conditions and of the textuality they govern; conversely, new readings or uses of a text become incorporated as structural conditions in the textual regime and thus gradually alter the "context" of the text.

One way of imagining reading in this perspective is as a series of regressions, from "content" to "form" (at increasing levels of abstraction), to the level of "technique" determining the decision to read in this way, to the "literary" order that specifies these "technical" decisions and the objects on which they will work, to the structure of value within which this order is hierarchically ordered, and so on. A series of decisions about how and what to read is thus framed by this regression of frames, and it is this series itself that then becomes an object of attention. But it does not yield itself to a sociological or literary-historical description: the framing conditions of textuality are not to be thought of as general and objectively transposable structures which can be apprehended in their own right; they are extrapolations, from an act of reading, of a prior order that can be defined only *a posteriori*. Textuality and its conditions of possibility are mutually constitutive and can be reconstructed only from each other in a kind of hermeneutic bootstrapping which precludes conclusion and the perspective of a total understanding. This is the methodological implication of de Man's reminder that "what we usually call literary history has little or nothing to do with literature and that what we call literary interpretation – provided only it is good interpretation – is in fact literary history" (1971: 165).

"History" is the other major dimension of this interpretive focus on consti-tutive relations. I use the word here to designate very specifically the discrepancy between the conditions of writing and the conditions of reception of a text, either because of a temporal passage or because of translation from one regime to another. Any text which continues to be read over an extended period of time or beyond the bounds of its own culture will in some sense not be the "same" text; its value and standing, the interpretive possibilities it is seen to offer, its intertextual relations, its social or affective force and the uses to which it can appropriately be put all shift unstably in this passage. At least two sets of framing conditions must then be included in the act of reading, in such a way that interpretation is governed neither by a moment of origin nor by an unreflected application of contemporary relevances, but rather sets itself the task of mediat-ing these two moments. A reading of O'Hara's "The Day Lady Died," for example, would attend both to the moment of the New York "School" (itself however a retrospective construct), with its dual relation to high-modernist painting and to a camp aesthetic rooted in certain forms of popular culture, and to the canonization of that "third generation" of postwar American poetry (which I in turn would read in part through its influence on Australian poets like John Tranter and John Forbes) and its relation to the problematically marginal-ized place of poetry in contemporary culture. The mediation of these two moments would then give rise to a restricted set of thematic possibilities (is this a New York poem? A poem about the blues, about African-American culture, about gay culture? A poem about art and its relation to death?) and to choices between them governed by particular, partly definable structures of interest.

This model of a relational reading corresponds, I want to argue, to the project of cultural studies, which I define in shorthand as a concern with the social relations of textuality. The concept of regime expresses one of the fundamental theses of work in cultural studies: that no object, no text, no cultural practice has an intrinsic or necessary meaning or value or function; and that meaning, value, and function are always the effect of specific (and changing, changeable) social relations and mechanisms of signification. The exclusion of the literary from cultural studies in favor of the devalued practices of popular culture was a strategic delimitation of the field against an older and more prestigious discipline which was perceived to be deeply committed to a fetishized object of study. But there is no reason of principle why this exclusion should continue to be sustained, and the time has now perhaps arrived for a *rapprochement* in which literary studies would learn to attend in a more routine manner to the social relations of signification, and cultural studies would in its turn be reminded of the constitution of its major explanatory categories in practices of reading.

V

To attend to the specific historical, social, and semiotic conditions of existence of the literary is to open the way to the relativization of the literary to other cultural regimes. With this detachment from final grounds, the structures of value organizing each formation now lose their claimed universality: internally more or less coherent, they are nevertheless incommensurate and perhaps incommensurable with the axiologies governing other formations. In one sense what this aporia requires of us is an indefinite deferral of the moment of substantive engagement with literary texts as we seek, in a necessarily perpetual prolegomenon to literary studies, to define and account for those prior conditions governing the status, the relevance, the very possibility of the literary. In another sense, however, that moment has of course always already arrived, and it carries with it critical uncertainties about what can and should constitute literary study.

The moment of "theory" in Anglophone literary studies was, almost in the same breath, the promise and the undoing of the possibility of a systematic poetics. The poststructuralist complication of that project failed – for complex political and conjunctural reasons – to work as its continuation, and in its wake the discipline of literary studies has been split between a barely theorized "ethical" criticism, the idiot scion of the classical and neoclassical pedagogies of literary precept, which generates an endless stream of thematic commentary around the category of the (unified or disunified) "self"; a deconstructive criticism now enfeebled and demoralized since the disgracing of de Man – an event, however, which perhaps only confirmed an exhaustion that had already firmly set in; a "political" criticism whose routine practice is grounded in the category of identity and for which textuality is deemed to have an expressive or instrumental relation to race or gender or sexual preference; a historicist criticism, now more empiricist than Foucauldian, for which the literary archive has a merely documentary value; and a chattering bellettrism which has more to do with gossip than with the systematic study of texts. In one sense, the discipline of literary studies is flourishing as never before; in another, it has become lost in irrelevance.

These are not just issues about disciplines, of course; they have to do with the structure of socially valued knowledge, with hierarchies of cultural value in an era of mass visual literacy, and with the transformation of the ends of the University. At a mundane level, the most important questions for literary studies – the questions that go to the heart of its connection to the world – have to do not with research and the higher reaches of disciplinary development but with undergraduate teaching and the question of what might count as useful knowledge for a literary propaedeutics. The answer to that question is, I believe, less the imparting of systematic information than the teaching of a practice – of "reading" in the broadest sense – which would meet three conditions: it must be at once continuous with and richer than untutored practice; it must have a theoretical foundation which can be generalized; and it must be able to be extrapolated from "literary" texts to other discursive kinds. It would be at once a practice of intense scrutiny and intense connection, and it would be integrated with directly practical rhetorical skills of writing and arguing.

Those requirements for theoretical grounding and for a reach to nonliterary discourses of course suppose a certain model of disciplinary coherence. Yet, while literary studies has provided an enduringly powerful paradigm of the rhetorical analysis of texts, it continues to find itself in almost complete disarray over the principles that would constitute its integrity as what Northrop Frye called "an impersonal body of consolidating knowledge" (1957: 8). This disarray means that it is not possible to contemplate redeeming a sense of disciplinary wholeness and purpose by means of a theoretical program. Indeed, disciplinary coherence may not after all be as desirable a goal as the alternative values of theoretical openness and heuristic richness. It may be that the category of the literary itself is an obstacle both to the formation of a systematic knowledge of texts, and to that interdisciplinary dynamic and that sense of exploratory creativity that has characterized literary studies at its best in the decades since the "moment of theory."

It is for this reason that I have stressed the ambivalence of the notion of an emergence of the literary. If that emergence is at every moment a hard-won achievement of the text, it is also what most fully problematizes the category of the literary. Its dual temporality sets up a tension and perhaps a necessary contradiction between the interlocking dimensions of instituted value and of reflexive awareness. Take the case, first, of *The Radetzky March* and *Don Quixote*. In Roth's novel, the very order of the world [*der Bestand der Welt*] is maintained by a fiction, *Schlauheit* – "guile" or "cunning" – in which both the bureaucrats of the Ministry of Culture[5] and Education and the Emperor himself, a servant of that order, are complicit. In *Don Quixote* this order is two-fold. On the one hand, the order of life is above all a simulacrum of that of the book: if Sancho has happened to bestow on Don Quixote the title of Knight of the Sad Countenance, this is because "the sage [*sabio*] whose task it is to write the history of my deeds must have thought it right for me to take some title" (1950: 147); Don Quixote's deeds are governed by an already existent future for which the present has the closure of a past. On the other hand, the order of the world is an essence lying beneath the enchanted surfaces of reality; this enchantment is again the work of "sages" who turn giants into windmills. But what if this order and this false order are the same? This is the conclusion to which Don Quixote is forced when, learning that the history of his deeds is already in print, he surmises that "the author of our history is some sage enchanter" [*debe de ser algún sabio encantador el autor de nuestra historia*] (1950: 484, and 1970: 1497). We too, however, are drawn to reach this conclusion, since the disenchantments performed by Part I of the novel themselves become a myth to be disenchanted by a further act of literature. Writing never escapes enchantment; enchantment and guile transform it into a universal principle of untruth.

Similarly irreconcilable tensions inform the other two texts which I took to exemplify an emergence of the literary. *Lost Illusions* condemns the commodity production of literature at the very moment in which intellectual property rights – *droits d'auteur* – are becoming entrenched as the basis of the trade in writing, and it does so in a language whose rhetorical force is entirely engaged with the dynamics of contract and money. And "The Day Lady Died," moving between the packaged writing, the "little Verlaine / for Patsy with drawings by Bonnard," and the nameless song of the dying singer, reaches its breathtaking final moment in a line which cannot be read in a grammatically or rhythmically coherent manner. I would say that literature, "the literary," refuses itself, if this formulation did not repeat so closely the essentializing definitions that derive a general and ahistorical order from particular instances. These texts tell very different histories of the institution of the literary, but the refusal that is specific to each of them can be taken as a figure for the institution of a reading that would at once display and displace the literary regime and the relations of reading it enables.

NOTES

1   An alternative version of this essay appears in *The Question of Literature*, ed. E. Beaumont Bissell. Manchester: Manchester University Press, 2002.

2 Billie Holiday "whispered" because at the end of her life her voice had almost gone. For background on the poem, see Gooch 1993: 327–38.
3 The following section draws on concepts elaborated in my *Marxism and Literary History* (1986: 182–7), and *Cultural Studies and Cultural Value* (1995: 144–51).
4 Cf. Tony Bennett, "Texts in History" (1985: 7).
5 The word *Kultus* refers both to culture and to religious observance.

REFERENCES

Adorno, Theodor W. 1992. "On an Imaginary Feuilleton." In *Notes to Literature, Volume Two*, tr. Shierry Weber Nicholsen. New York: Columbia University Press, pp. 32–9.
Balzac, Honoré de. 1971. *Lost Illusions*, tr. Herbert J. Hunt. Harmondsworth: Penguin.
——. 1977. *Illusions perdues*, *La Comédie Humaine V.* Paris: Gallimard.
Bennett, Tony. 1985. "Texts in History: The Determinations of Readings and their Texts." *Journal of the Midwest Modern Language Association* 18(1): 1–16.
Cervantes Saavedra, Miguel de. 1950. *The Adventures of Don Quixote*, tr. J. M. Cohen. Harmondsworth: Penguin, 1950.
——. 1970. *Don Quixote de la Mancha, Obras Completas*, vol. II, ed. Angel Valbuena Prat. Madrid: Aguilar.
de Man, Paul. 1971. *Blindness and Insight: Essays in the Rhetoric of Contemporary Criticism*, 2nd ed. Minneapolis:Univeristy of Minnesota Press. Rpt. 1983.
Frow, John. 1986. *Marxism and Literary History.* Cambridge, MA: Harvard University Press.
——. 1995. *Cultural Studies and Cultural Value.* Oxford: Clarendon Press.
Frye, Northrop. 1957. *The Anatomy of Criticism: Four Essays.* New York: Atheneum. Rpt. 1965.
Gooch, Brad. 1993. *City Poet: The Life and Times of Frank O'Hara.* New York: Knopf.
Grossberg, Lawrence, Cary Nelson, and Paula Treichler, eds. 1992. *Cultural Studies.* New York: Routledge.
Keenan, Thomas. 1997. *Fables of Responsibility: Aberrations and Predicaments in Ethics and Politics.* Stanford: Stanford University Press.
Marghescou, Mircea. 1974. *Le Concept de littérarité: essai sur les possibilités théoriques d'une science de la littérature.* The Hague: Mouton.
O'Hara, Frank. 1972. "The Day Lady Died." In *The Collected Poems of Frank O'Hara*, ed. Donald Allen. New York: Knopf.
Perloff, Marjorie. 1977. *Frank O'Hara: Poet Among Painters.* New York: George Braziller.
Roth, Joseph. 1974. *The Radetzky March*, tr. Eva Tucker/Geoffrey Dunlop. London: Allen Lane.
——. 1990. *Radetzkymarsch.* In *Werke 5: Romane und Erzählungen 1930–1936.* Cologne: Kiepenheuer & Witsch.
Sedgwick, Eve Kosofsky. 1990. *Epistemology of the Closet.* Berkeley: University of California Press.

3

Excessive Practices: Aesthetics, Erotica, and Cultural Studies

JANE JUFFER

There is no question of an aesthetics of pornography. It can never be art for art's
sake. Honourably enough, it is always art with work to do.
— Angela Carter, "Pornography in the Service of Women"

Why has cultural studies so agonized over its relation to aesthetics when, as
Angela Carter suggests, the answer is quite obvious: "aesthetics" in its transcendent inclination doesn't really exist as it is often posited, in a vacuum – the kind of
aesthetics some cultural studies scholars have bemoaned. "Aesthetics" is always
doing some kind of work. The question – and perhaps also the reason for cultural
studies' angst – is in whose interests is aesthetics working?

For Carter, an aesthetics of pornography – what some would call erotica –
is working for women's sexual pleasures. For others, aesthetics works only
for the political right wing. As Tony Bennett argues, "To announce a requiem
for aesthetics *in toto* would, no doubt, be premature inasmuch as...it
still has undeniable political use value – but only for the right" (1990: 148).
Another sentiment of late, expressed by Edward Said and Elaine Scarry,
among others, is the need to return to "beauty" as an antidote to political
violence and human suffering; here, aesthetics works in the interest of the
marginalized.

The polemics characterizing the debate on aesthetics suggests as well that at the
heart of the issue is the role of the critic: who should be accorded the right to
determine how and for whom aesthetics works? Critics of aesthetics' influence on

cultural studies have condemned the literary critic as one who relies on ever-more-intricate readings of texts in order to prove one's superiority over readers/students who must be trained to read correctly. Questions of identity are neatly confined to texts and elide material conditions, including the institutional structures (such as English departments) that undergird aesthetic discourse as well as other sites where culture circulates. In "Aesthetics and Cultural Studies," Ian Hunter argues that:

> The problem with the aesthetic critique – and with cultural studies to the degree that it is still caught in its slipstream – is that it presumes to comprehend and judge these other cultural regions from a single metropolitan point, typically the university arts faculty. To travel to these regions though – to law offices, media institutions, government bureaus, corporations, advertising agencies – is to make a sobering discovery: They are already replete with their own intellectuals. And they just look up and say, "Well, what exactly is it that you can do for us?" (1992: 372)

Although cultural studies has several disciplinary locations, one important site, especially in the US, has been English departments, where cultural studies has at times been used to expand the kinds of texts considered worthy of study (film, television, stars, pornography) without moving beyond textual analysis as a methodology. Certainly, cultural studies in English has often maintained "culture" at the center of analysis, positing it as the primary site for understanding "society." In this model, the transformation of consciousness serves as the key to political change, with the catalyst being the readings of texts – whether these texts are interpreted to be hegemonic or resistant. Bennett, Hunter, and Lawrence Grossberg, among others, have argued that cultural studies must move away from a valorization of consciousness and toward a more spatial understanding of power. This methodology would, presumably, remove the critic from the position of moral superiority into the more objective position of "technician" (to use Bennett's term) – one who describes power and how it functions, in a Foucauldian fashion.

I agree in many ways with this anti-aesthetic position. From my position as a graduate student and now professor in the discipline of English, I would argue that aesthetic discourse as a relationship of moral critic to reader achieved through textual analysis continues to hamper the development of a cultural studies that effectively engages with power. However, the argument, made most directly by Bennett and Hunter, often relies on a fairly static understanding of aesthetic discourse, the assumption being that aesthetics, stripped of its claims to transcendence, can be predictably mapped and gauged; importantly, this mapping accounts for the material sites at which aesthetics are deployed, but in the relentless emphasis on the regularities of movement, this governmental approach to aesthetics dismisses the possibilities of irregularities, excesses, and unpredictable conduct – in part because the realm of consciousness is dismissed as one whose exploration puts the critic in the position of moral exemplar. Hence, even as it purports to be merely descriptive, a governmental position on culture assumes a position equal in moral superiority to the literary critic: the technician maps the body's movement without regard to consciousness, producing a very certain understanding of culture's effects.

I'll use women's erotica and its claim to aesthetic status (as a means of distinguishing itself from pornography) to first establish the importance of the anti-aesthetic critique – in other words, to argue, in the spirit of Bennett and Hunter, that the popularization of women's erotica rests on a series of suspicious claims about the relationship between critic, text, and reader that will ensue if the text is "read correctly." However, I will also argue that this relationship – one that purchases literary legitimation for erotica – is then immediately complicated by the multiple discourses intersecting with aesthetic discourse once the erotica begins to circulate – from the publishing companies to reviews in women's magazines to bookstores to the home as a site of consumption. The effect of aesthetic claims is to make women's erotica – even in its most explicit manifestations, when it is really no different from pornography – "safe" for domestic consumption within a context of governmental and religious norms that continue to posit "pornography" as antithetical to the home and especially to the role of mothering. We have, thus, competing and contradictory sets/sites of regulation; together, these produce spaces for excessive conduct (sexual fantasies, masturbation, s/m, etc.).

How, in other words, does aesthetic discourse increase women's sexual mobility in a manner not necessarily tied to the claims of whole subjectivity and transcendence made in the initial (moralizing) claim to aesthetic value? In pursuing the subject through her paths of sexual mobility, we understand both how culture is governed and how "freedom" resides in and *potentially exceeds* this very governance. By invoking "freedom," I do not return the notion of a Romantic aesthetics in which the subject transcends materiality, nor to the notion of aesthetics' "relative autonomy," in which aesthetics is still granted a privileged, albeit somewhat materially grounded, status. Rather, I locate the freedom of aesthetics in its dispersal across sites, sites through which a subject travels and occasionally defies the predictability of a governmental analysis of culture. This defiance is not necessarily intentional (although it may be); it occurs, rather, because the effects of aesthetics will be determined at multiple, often contradictory sites.

The effects of aesthetics are shaped as well by the realm of consciousness and affect that Bennett and Hunter disregard; my goal is not to "understand the meaning" of sexual fantasies but rather to work toward the expansion of the places and times where and when sexual fantasy can be explored. In turn, the freedom to practice sex as one chooses can lead back to a rearticulation of the initial sites of governing and regulation. The role of the critic here is both to map routes of access and to acknowledge that mapping does not capture all of culture's effects; in other words, there is indeed a realm of fantasy to which the critic does not have access, and it is important, tricky as it may be, to value this realm and the excessive practices it may generate.

THE CRITIQUE OF AESTHETICS

In choosing to focus on the work of Tony Bennett and Ian Hunter, I am perhaps overstating the influence of a certain strand of cultural studies. I do this in part to keep my argument historically and institutionally specific; given the widespread uses of the term "aesthetics," it would be frankly impossible to rehearse all the ways it has been deployed, even in relation to cultural studies. Bennett and Hunter were writing in Australia in the early to mid-1990s, and their arguments against aesthetics contributed to the debates about cultural policy studies that have continued since then. Both Bennett and Hunter made arguments against aesthetics and for policy studies at the influential 1990 Cultural Studies conference at the University of Illinois (out of which was published the book *Cultural Studies* edited by Grossberg, Cary Nelson, and Paula Treichler). Furthermore, I focus on Bennett and Hunter, and, to a lesser degree Lawrence Grossberg, because I think their work mounts the most serious and important critique of the legacy of literary analysis in cultural studies.

Bennett's *Outside Literature* was published in 1990; here, he lays the foundation for future arguments about culture and governmentality, so I'll begin with an analysis of some of the book's key arguments.[1] For Bennett, aesthetics purports to universality but is actually a discourse of discrimination, in which the subject (critic) who recognizes "universal value" then assigns a privileged status to others who similarly recognize the "universal value." Aesthetic discourse "is the form taken by discourses of value which are hegemonic in ambition and, correspondingly, universalist in their prescriptive ambit and which have, as their zone of application, those practices nominated as artistic. The position of universal valuing subject which is necessary to such discourse – and, invariably, such a position is produced by generalizing the attributes of the valuing subject associated with a specific discourse of value – can be refused *to* but not *by* the individual" (1990: 152). Interestingly, Bennett here assigns to aesthetic discourse a power not attributed to other discourses of distinction; the latter, he says, citing Bourdieu's *Distinctions*, function in regulated but alterable fashion to distinguish between classes: "such discourses are prescriptive, but only for those who occupy or take up the position of the valuing subject they construct, a position which may be refused since such valuing subjects are identifiably socially specific" (1990: 152).

Why this inevitability – the subject powerless to refuse aesthetic discourse? How does it function in such a totalizing fashion? Bennett can make this claim only by granting a significant power to the critic's ability to naturalize the relations of reading literature and subsequently to naturalize the distinctions separating those who read correctly from those who don't. He argues:

> while seeming to address literature as the object of a specialized knowledge, criticism in fact targets the literary text as a vehicle for the ethical organization of the reader by virtue of the relations between misreading and approved reading which it posits. For while criticism permits a means of identifying misreadings, those readings are not assessed as such in relation to any definite correct readings. Rather, they count as misreadings only in relation to a normatively prescribed correct way of reading – the literary or aesthetic mode – in which there is produced, for and within the literary text, that inexhaustible depth which can allow it to function as a device for the reader's self-improvement by means of the revision and correction of earlier readings." (1990: 183)

This process guarantees the job of the critic, as one for whom the text is always open to new interpretations.[2] This literary practice has informed cultural studies beyond literary analysis, argues Bennett, especially in relation to attempts to locate resistance in readings of popular culture. Citing de Certeau's work as an example, he says: "For the fathomless depths of the indecipherable reader allow the popular text to be pedagogically organized as a vehicle for inducting students into resistive readings which, with the assistance of the cultural studies teacher, can be corrected, revised and even assessed. It is, however, difficult to see how this amounts to anything but a form of licensed poaching performed under the watchful, tutelary eye of gamekeepers still in the employ of the literary apparatus (1998: 184).

In *Outside Literature*, Bennett shows how these relations are reproduced in Marxist criticism; the critic relies not on the romantic realization of self-knowledge but rather the Marxist understanding of how ideology shapes subjects – but the process still posits the critic as the one who leads the reader into full knowledge via a correct way of reading and elides material, institutional conditions (by not accounting for how the critic can see how ideology functions simply by reading a text as a reflection of either hegemony or marginality). The celebration of Raymond Williams as the father of contemporary cultural studies has had just such an effect, argues Bennett, in "Being 'in the True' of Cultural Studies." Williams combined his marginal status as Welsh working class with the role of literary critic of working-class culture to define a "whole way of life, positing an understanding of British culture as a whole in view of his lived experiences of the relations between the dominant and resistive elements" (1993: 218). The historical reliance of cultural studies on the personal qualities of the intellectual, such as Williams, produces a conflation of moral life and work that serves, Bennett argues, to legitimate cultural studies through "charismatic closure," which occurs when the moral authority of the intellectual supersedes material and institutional conditions. This reliance on personality helps to constitute cultural studies as a never-definable field that can heal the fragmenting effects of intellectual specialization; it reflects a nostalgic desire for culture as a whole way of life. As Hunter argues, "the limits of aesthetics are not to be transcended through the exemplary movement in which critique overcomes its inherent contradictions, subsuming it within a theory of culture as 'the way of life as a whole'" (1992: 365).

It is important to acknowledge the validity of these arguments, especially insofar as literary critics rely on moralisms to posit a correct reading that leads to an understanding of subjectivity. This practice has certainly occurred in the genre of women's literary erotica. Although an increasingly popular genre, literary erotica has its roots in academic criticism; many editors are literary critics and professors and use that position to distance the anthologies from the low-brow genre of porn. Furthermore, as I shall describe below, the distinction between erotica and porn derives largely from a long legal history based on aesthetic distinctions that were often testified to by literary experts. Contemporary erotica varies in the degree to which it retains the erotica/porn distinction, but many erotic women's texts invoke the written word as a legitimating strategy to disarticulate erotica from porn; the editors, then, become the moral exemplars who will help readers reconcile mind and body, reality and fantasy. The "correct way of reading," most often, is established as "not pornography/not masculine." Take, for example, the editors' introduction to *Pleasure in the Word: Erotic Writings by Latin American Women*, where they quote writer Luisa Valenzuela:

> Pornography is the negation of literature because it is the negation of metaphor and nuance, of ambiguity. It seeks a material reaction in the reader, a direct sexual excitement; eroticism, on the other hand, although it can be tremendously brazen and strong, goes through the filter of metaphor and poetic language. Pornography does not enter into literary disquisition. I think that as women, we have to rescue erotic language because in the final analysis it is dominated by male fantasies. Every one of us must tell one's own truth, trying to express the other's desires, because the last thing that wants to be expressed is desire. (Fernandez & Paravisini-Gebert 1993: 28)

The introduction attempts to set up a correct way of reading the collection's erotic stories based on a set of seemingly intrinsic literary qualities (ambiguity, metaphor, nuance). The editors position themselves as moral exemplars able to guide readers to the truth of their sexual subjectivity, a truth that stands in opposition to the lies that pornography tells about women's desires. Erotica expresses the power of liberation premised on the transformation of consciousness, the recognition of what it "truly means" to be a woman. Many feminists have noted the normalizing tendencies of the erotica/porn distinction. As Paula Webster describes in her critique of the group Women Against Pornography's attempt to distinguish between erotica and porn: "[Erotica] was good, healthy sexual imagery – the standard against which pornography and perhaps our own sexual lives were to be judged. . . . As feminists, we might question the very impulse to make such a rigid separation, to let a small group of women dictate the boundaries of our morality and our pleasure" (1986: 32).

The moral exemplar of aesthetic claims is thus linked to the moral exemplar of identity politics; the critic uses the text to make claims about the correct formation of identity, linked to a marginalized group who come to realize their oppression through consciousness raising. Both aesthetic claims and identity politics are in constant danger of claiming a position outside power and materiality – the position from which those on the margins are empowered to speak without, it seems, acknowledging their complicity in institutional practices. This leads me to the connection between the Bennett–Hunter arguments and Larry Grossberg's position. Much as Bennett and Hunter critique the privileging through marginalization achieved by Williams and its ongoing influence in cultural studies, Grossberg criticizes models of identity based on difference, which, quoting Kobena Mercer, he says invariably give rise to "the mantra of race, class, and gender" (1996: 89–90). These theories of identity are grounded in a politics of representation, which, for Grossberg, produce a notion of "identity as an entirely cultural, even an entirely linguistic construction" (1996: 90). For Grossberg, "the privileging of consciousness is the residual effect of a romanticism that survived poststructuralism"; it privileges time over space. Too much of cultural studies has relied on the idea that "identity is an entirely historical construction" with "subjectivity as internal time consciousness; identity as the temporal construction of difference; and agency as the temporal displacement of difference" (1996: 100). This formulation relies on "the principle of interiority or essentialism, which locates any practice in a structure of necessity and guarantees its effects even before it has been enacted. In such a structure, any event (including a cultural text) is assumed to already contain its own identity, and its place in a history of transformation can only involve spinning out the associations, relations, and correspondences already inherent within that identity" (1992: 52). This returns us, implicitly, to the role of the literary/cultural critic who turns to the interiority of the text, via interpretation, as a means of "spinning out" various political relations.

The alternative for Bennett and Hunter is not to disregard aesthetic discourse but rather to locate it – to take it from the realm of the universal to its deployment as a technique of subject formation. In his study of nineteenth-century British popular literary education, for example, Ian Hunter argues that practices of the aesthetic coincided with government's attempt to form good citizens. In his approach, there's nothing essential about aesthetics that guarantees its effects; however, Hunter's study suggests aesthetics' regularity, its operation as a kind of governance whose predictability can be gauged. He describes the conjuncture of aesthetics and administration in the nineteenth century as "one in which the exigencies of government led to the massive social dissemination of a sophisticated and powerful means for constituting the self as an object of ethical concern and labor" (1988: 363).

Their goal, then, is to chart the effects of culture rather than to rely, as does the literary critic, on the endless and indeterminate possibilities for rereadings and reformations. Here is the link to cultural policy studies, a field most forcefully articulated by Bennett. For him as well as for Hunter, aesthetics is a technique of self-governing, and the critic who acknowledges that culture is a form of governance is obviously better equipped to participate in policy studies than the critic who sees culture as opposed to governance. As Bennett says about his belief in the importance of policy studies, "My purpose is to detach the concept of culture as a way of life from the resistive credentials it has accumulated through its use within cultural studies and attach it to ones which accentuate both the governmental component which inevitably enters into the construction of the cultural field and the reformist disposition which this brings with it" (1998: 92). Culture always functions in a regulatory fashion, sympathetic with how power, under regimes of governmentality, is dispersed, in which the subject comes to govern him/her self in a manner coincident with yet not coerced by multiple sites of governance. As Bennett says in his study of the museum, describing governmentality as a "modality of power," "culture was increasingly thought of as a resource to be used in programmes which aimed at bringing about changes in acceptable norms and forms of behavior and consolidating those norms as self-acting imperatives by inscribing them within broadly disseminated regimes of self-management" (1995: 23). The scholar of governmentality is always able to map the subject's paths; indeed, for Bennett, there is no way to consider culture outside the realm of government: "A part of my concern has been to suggest how the history of culture might be written in ways that would see its modern constitution as inherently governmental, as a field of social management in which culture is deployed as a resource intended to help 'lift' the population by making it self-civilising" (1998: 128).

In somewhat sympathetic fashion, Grossberg proposes a spatial theory of subjectivity to replace a temporal model: "subjectivity describes the points of attachment from which one experiences the world" (1996: 101). In this model, subjects achieve agency through their ability to gain access to particular sites of empowerment:

> If subjectivity constitutes "homes" as places of attachment, temporary addresses for people, agency constitutes strategic installments; these are the

specific places and spaces that define specific forms of agency and empower specific populations. In this sense, we can inquire into the conditions of possibility of agency, for agency – the ability to make history, as it were – is not intrinsic to either subjects or to selves. Agency is the product of diagrams of mobility which define or map the possibilities of where and how specific vectors of influence can stop and be placed. (1996: 102)

Here, as do Bennett and Hunter, Grossberg emphasizes the material sites where subjectivity is shaped; identity, thus, is not a matter of consciousness but rather a product of the places through which subjects move. This passage also indicates, however, a greater concern with agency via mobility than is present in either of the other two critics; applying this theory to aesthetics and its effects suggests that aesthetic discourse, as it is deployed at various sites, can help produce agency insofar as its effects facilitate mobility.

Aesthetic discourse never operates by itself. If we see aesthetic discourse as dispersed, we also see how aesthetic discourse is always cut through with other discourses, functioning at different sites, with uneven effects on subjects' mobility. Furthermore, the very *claim* to whole subjectivity facilitates the subjects' movement across sites, while the movement across sites assures that no one site will determine subjectivity. In the process of studying a range of discourses that coincide and compete with each other, the critic's ability to map bodies and effects is made less certain; culture may act in accordance with one site of governance but in contradiction to another. What if aesthetic claims open up a realm of possibilities that are not predictably contained by governmentality, that are not only about good conduct but also about unruliness – shall we say bad conduct? This is not transcendence or transgression but rather unpredictability within the very routines that make such unpredictability possible. With erotica's aesthetic status, we find that the claim to a correct way of reading that distinguishes the female erotic from the masculine pornographic facilitates the proliferation of sexual practices – still legitimated under the sanctioned category "erotica" yet encompassing many practices previously deemed "pornographic."

Finally, we must ask, in terms of the role of the critic: is there really much difference between the critique of aesthetics as a universal discourse and its incorporation into regimes of governing – at which point its effects become regularized, put into the service of norms and predictable paths? Both methods posit the critic as able to fully understand the subject being studied. Although both Bennett and Hunter say they aren't engaging in whether people "actually experienced" things in the way planned, that claim is somewhat disingenuous. The exhaustiveness of their studies assumes that the institutions studied (e.g., the museum, the school) were successful in their governance; at the very least, governmentality disdains the possibility of dissent, excess, irregularities. In their understandable desire to distance cultural studies from moralistic claims to analyze power by standing outside it, Bennett and Hunter have suggested that the whole realm of consciousness, imagination, and fantasy simply doesn't matter; what matters for them is the body's movement through particular sites. Although it is not the critic's job to read consciousness off a text, I would argue that it is surely our job to work toward conditions of sexual freedom; in order to do so, we must acknowledge the importance of the realm of imagination and fantasy. It is, therefore, the critic's job to expand that realm which we do not know – without purporting to interpret it.

POPULARIZING AESTHETICS

Although literary erotica has been sanctioned through juridical proceedings for much of the twentieth century, only in the last 25 years have women used this safe space to create their own erotic texts in significant numbers, appropriating some of the cultural purchase granted to canonical works by authors such as James Joyce, Henry Miller, and D. H. Lawrence. Literary erotica has provided a way for women to explore, under the legitimating auspices of aesthetic discourse, the many different ways to reconcile reality and fantasy, the everyday and the erotic (with one possibility being the recognition of noncorrespondence between fantasy and reality). Women's erotica defines itself by a series of identity claims – not only gender but also sexuality, race, and ethnicity: African American, Latin American, Latina/o, Asian American, and Jewish collections, straight, gay, and bisexual, have been published. Aesthetic claims are most prominent in the realm of print, which has been the most easily accessible in terms of both production and consumption for marginalized groups; however, aesthetic claims also inform visual erotica as it distinguishes itself from porn.

The legal history of obscenity proceedings in the US was a primary site for the production of an aesthetic discourse that relied on the expertise of literary scholars to determine which sexually explicit works were "actually" works of art, with the courts gradually expanding the criteria for artistic and also social and political merit. Beginning with the 1957 Supreme Court case *United States v. Roth* and continuing into the 1960s, US courts gradually freed all but the most "hardcore" of pornographic materials. Although the court upheld the conviction of Samuel Roth for mailing a magazine containing nude pictures and erotic stories, Supreme Court Justice William Brennan ruled that only material "utterly without redeeming social importance" could be declared obscene. Legal scholar Edward de Grazia notes that Brennan's ruling "produced a significant crack in the country's century-old obscenity law"; during the next decade, it became very difficult for prosecutors to prove that a text was "utterly without redeeming social importance," leading to distribution in the US of all kinds of sexually explicit texts, ranging from *Lady Chatterley's Lover* to "blatantly pornographic pulp literature" (de Grazia 1992: 323–4). In 1964, the Supreme Court furthered the defense of artistic expression, in decisions authored by Brennan concerning Henry Miller's *Tropic of Cancer* and Louis Malle's film *The Lovers*. Lower federal and state courts "obediently put the Brennan doctrine to work in reversing obscenity findings in book, film, and magazine censorship cases throughout the country" (de Grazia 1992: 431).

This period of relative deregulation was not without its own set of norms; most obviously, the courts continued to preserve a category – the obscene – that, bereft of social value, potentially harms women, the potential victims of male pornography consumers. Also, the process of proving that a work "as a whole" does have "redeeming social value" and that it does not appeal to "prurient interests" – all defining characteristics of obscenity that emerge during this period – continued to uphold aesthetic distinctions between the erotic and the pornographic, or between soft-core and hard-core. As Ian Hunter et al. note, this aesthetic distinction set in motion a process of self-disciplining, emphasizing "individuals' ability to mediate and order their own sexual interests and to balance the excitations of erotica with an aesthetic appreciation of the work as a whole" (1993: 211). Although many kinds of texts were "freed" for fairly widespread circulation, the importance of artistic merit as a distinguishing factor between erotica and porn remained.

A number of factors converging in the 1970s paved the way for the development of a genre of women's erotica that built on this aesthetic distinction while making it specific to women's identity. Both the women's and gay/lesbian movements emphasized sexual freedoms; pornography entered the mainstream; a 1970 governmental commission on pornography produced the Lockhart report, which basically advocated pornography as a means of sex education (much in contrast to the 1986 Meese commission on pornography authorized by Ronald Reagan). In 1973, Nancy Friday wrote her groundbreaking book, *My Secret Garden*, recording and thus creating a nonjudgmental space of written expression for women's various sexual fantasies. By 1977, the climate was right for Anaïs Nin to publish the erotica she wrote in the 1940s under a pseudonym – erotica which she had been afraid to claim earlier for fear it would be declared pornographic, especially because she wrote it for money and was exhorted to "leave out the poetry and descriptions of anything but sex." In the 1977 introduction to *Delta of Venus*, however, Nin finds her suppressed woman's voice and uses this recognition of gender difference to make a literary claim about her erotic stories. To invoke Foucault's concept of the author function, it wasn't until 1977 that Nin's sexually explicit writings could be received as literary erotica – associated with her name, as an author of literature that must be received as literature, to be read in a particular way:

> the fact that the discourse has an author's name, that one can say "this was written by so-and-so" or "so-and-so is its author," shows that this discourse is

not ordinary everyday speech that merely comes and goes, not something that is immediately consumable. On the contrary, it is speech that must be received in a certain mode and that, in a given culture, must receive a certain status. (Foucault 1984b: 107)

Many editors of erotica anthologies published in the 1980s cite Nin as their foremother; through her didactic assertion of how to write/recognize erotica, Nin facilitated women's access to the production of literary erotica, erasing the shame in sexual expression because of its legitimation through both literary expression and a claim to define woman's true sexual identity. The production of women's erotica has thus also relied on the critic's claim to be able to discern both literary and erotic value in previously unremarked-upon texts – to construct a canon, so to speak, based on marginalized status. As Jeanette Winterson writes in the preface to *Erotica: Women's Writing from Sappho to Margaret Atwood*, "Erotica is a wild plunge into mostly overlooked territory. It accepts that women have not always been able to write directly about sex or desire but that they will have done so through nuance, suggestions, poetic device, and allegory" (Reynolds 1990: xxi). It takes a specially trained literary critic to recognize this erotic voice, which even the authors might not have recognized. Says Winterson about the book's editor, Margaret Reynolds, "Dr. Reynolds is not so simple-minded as to assume that the authors of her extracts will, in every case, have been aware of what they were doing. Most of us, even now, do not have that kind of self-knowledge" (Reynolds 1990: xxi).

This claim to produce self-knowledge through a correct way of reading is exactly the kind of aesthetic discourse critiqued by Bennett and Hunter. This moralistic position has offended some feminists; as Paula Webster suggests above, the positing of a correct way of reading erotica as indicative of the truth of sexual identity presents problems for women who find their "truth" in hard-core porn; are they victims of false consciousness? Furthermore, the aesthetics of erotica works in conjunction with the governmental regulation of porn in distinguishing between "good" and "bad" desires, reinforcing an essential conception of women's identity as less aggressive, more loving and egalitarian than men in their desires.

Yet this prescriptiveness is a condition of access; the category of "women's erotica" has been necessary for creating the conditions in which these regulatory tendencies may be violated. To understand how this works, we must pay attention to the particular historical and political conditions in which aesthetic claims are made. For example, in much erotica that links sexual desire to race and ethnicity, the editors connect the politics of representation to a broader politics of access; they describe the stories and authors in relation to the political situations in order to link gender and sexuality to class, race, and imperialism. Anthologies by people of color in the US counter stereotypes based on sexuality and race; these include *Pleasure in the Word: Erotic Writing by Latin American Women*; *Under the*

Pomegranate Tree: The Best New Latino Erotica; Erotique Noire/Black Erotica; On a Bed of Rice: An Asian-American Erotic Feast; Neurotica: Jewish Writers on Sex. In these anthologies, the editors assert aesthetic value as a way to distance their work from pornographic stereotypes based on race; the specifically literary nature of the writings legitimates the work for skeptical members of the identity group who fear that writing on sexuality could reinforce popular stereotypes. In the introduction to *Best Lesbian Erotica*, for example, Jewelle Gomez says, "This is a country where African Americans have fought to be allowed the right to read, where women of color are still routinely victimized by media misrepresentations, where our sexuality is used against us. The sexual stereotypes about women of color still abound and not just on television and movies . . . but also in lesbian bars, businesses, and activist organizations" (1997: 15). Gomez asserts the power of the aesthetic to reshape these social and institutional conditions; erotica helps produce alternative communities: Writing is about community. Telling our stories . . . to pass down history, to open up new paths for others" (ibid.).

Gomez may indeed act here as the "moral exemplar" of aesthetic discourse, yet the moralism must be seen for the specific work it does in facilitating erotica's circulation – at which point, the moralism disperses and becomes subject to different uses. The legitimation of women as writers of erotica, in part via aesthetic claims, contributes to the legitimation of women as consumers of erotica within the conditions of their everyday lives – that is to say, conditions that do not require them to see their sexual selves as hidden or shameful but rather as part of an openly defined community. Women's erotica has also popularized aesthetics; unlike the juridical legislation of erotica, which relied on the narrowing of access to a certain, educated class of readers, the aesthetic claims of women's erotica are intended to include as many women as possible, often with attention to the differences within the category "woman."

The question of the prescriptiveness of identity linked to aesthetics remains: does the erotica work toward the production of predictable conduct? Does erotica, by virtue of its insistence on a distinction from pornography, reinforce the very norms that have limited women's sexuality to a certain set of acceptable acts? I would argue, on the contrary, that the safe space granted to aesthetic claims has facilitated a wide variety of stories that simply cannot be contained under an essentialist woman's way of writing desire. The claims of the critic to represent a particular kind of women's writing that should be read in a particular way are contradicted by the stories, many of which experiment with gender roles, sex toys, rape fantasies, bondage, and other "pornographic" elements. The stories in the Reynolds collection, for example, range from an excerpt by s/m proponent Pat Califia to a nature piece by Dorothy Wordsworth.

The safe space generated by aesthetic/identity marketing categories has generated stories that make fun of identity politics, even as they are sold under the rubric of "identity politics." The *Herotica* series published by the feminist Down

There Press illustrates the expansion of "women's erotica" and yet the ongoing need to retain the category. When the first collection appeared in 1989, then-editor Susie Bright was quite insistent on the distinction between erotica and porn. From the start, *Herotica* contained a wide variety of stories that defied the attempt to categorize women's desire. And by *Herotica 4*, in 1996, stories were explicitly refuting the idea that pornography only speaks to men's desires. In *Porn Flicks*, two lesbians watch a straight hard-core porn video as part of a sex game: "Every time a woman gets something in her cunt, you get something in yours," says one lover to another (Tan 1996: 21). Another story in the same volume describes a woman's desire to be humiliated by two male lovers:

> They were being way too polite. I had to tell them to talk filthy to me. They started out pretty tame, but they ended up whispering things like, "Come on bitch, come for us. You know you want to. Let's hear you come. You like having two cocks in you, don't you? You like getting fucked by two dicks at once, you slut. Oh, you're such a little whore. What a sweet little snatch you have. Your ass is so hot and snug." (Reed 1996: 13)

The protagonist of this story, Madison, hardly speaks to the truth of a prescriptive female identity: "She dreamed that Jack would dissolve her identity, crush her faults, distill her down to a small pure lump he could slip into his pocket with his keys" (1996: 128). "Women's erotica" is a marketing category, and in that sense its aesthetic claims are part of a regime of governing subjects. However, the stories cannot be said to produce a singular kind of subject; the very regulation of aesthetics within governmentality may lead to excessive and unruly practices.

"RESPONSIBLE" PUBLISHING

The pornography industry in the US has become, by some estimates, a $12 billion industry; while there has been an increasing appeal to women consumers, men are still considered the primary market. The erotica/porn distinction continues to hold because of erotica's appeal to women; book publishing companies have clearly recognized erotica as a profitable genre. For example, Plume bought the marketing rights to the *Herotica* series in 1990 and has continued to publish it under basically the same marketing strategies.[3] The aesthetic claim to be producing a particular kind of subject – the healthy, sexual woman – coincides nicely with the publishing industry's desire to capitalize on the burgeoning market in sexually explicit materials while distancing the product from pornography as a still identifiable male genre. The appeal to erotica as a literary category works to normalize its production and circulation – to make it accessible within the terms of women's everyday lives.

The British erotic series for women, Black Lace, published by Virgin Publishing and marketed as "erotic fiction by women for women," illustrates this negotiation between the need to normalize erotica as a genre safe for women within the conditions of everyday life and yet not collapse erotica into the mundane. Editor Kerry Sharp describes the series as an example of "responsible publishing," which, she says, involves a negotiation between the liberatory realm of the sexual imagination and the regulatory realm of women's rights and antiporn censorship. For example, Black Lace guidelines for writers state that "all activities should be between mutually consenting adults – no matter what's happening, how kinky, or how depraved, it must be clear that the character is enjoying it, that it's being done with her consent." Yet Sharp disagrees with the notion that fantasy should be regulated by feminist criticisms of pornography: "A lot of feminist criticism of explicit works of erotica has been based on the old chestnut that it's demeaning to women. That denies the marvelous machine that is the human imagination. Whatever may be politically correct in real life, you can't really apply to fantasy." Finding the balance between "responsible publishing" and the erotic imagination is one key to mainstream distribution.[4]

Black Lace constantly reassesses the boundaries of the responsible, revising author guidelines as to level of explicitness. At the end of every novel is a reader survey that asks readers various questions about both content and packaging; for example, a series of questions inquires into the kinds of female and male protagonists readers find appealing. Sharp says most readers want sexually dominant but caring male characters. A recurrent theme is the professional woman who wants a safe space to explore her masochistic desires; for example, Frederica Alleyn's *The Bracelet* is a sort of rewriting of Pauline Reage's *The Story of O* (Reage is a literary foremother who rivals Anais Nin in number of cites in women's erotica, although usually with some apology, since O is unabashedly if self-reflexively masochistic). Yet unlike *The Story of O*, *The Bracelet* contains many more details of the protagonist's everyday life – her job, her friends, her boyfriend. This appeal to the everyday within the auspices of the literary consolidates the distinctiveness of the genre and contributes to mainstream circulation as well as to a comfortability about consumption. Hence, we see again the negotiation between regulation – everyday life, societal ideas about pornography and women – and freedom, or fantasy as a realm of deregulation and unruly conduct. The former in effect facilitates the latter but not in a fashion that can ultimately be "interpreted" (as in the "correct" reading of the story).

COFFEE AND EROTICA

In her introduction to *The Best American Erotica 2001*, Susie Bright simultaneously celebrates and laments the explosion in sexually explicit writing that has occurred since she first edited the collection in 1993, when, she notes, it was hard to even find enough "literary erotica" to comprise a collection. Now, by contrast, "there are thousands of erotica Web sites, stories, and compendiums; the bookstores that once feared the consequences of putting one erotic book on the shelf now have a whole section, from ceiling to floor" (2001: 7). But don't be misled, warns Bright; quantity doesn't necessarily mean quality: "the sad truth about most of what's sold as sex books, sex aids, and sex gurus is that it's fourth-rate slop" (2001: 8).

The need to invoke literary distinction as the hallmark of *Best American Erotica* is thus a product of the explosion that Bright herself helped instigate, and the distinction she attempts to accord *BAE* helps to sell it at the very sites she finds suspect – the superstore book chains that dominate US book retail, Borders and Barnes and Noble. Bookstores are critical sites for the production of aesthetic value – a value that, as in the publishing industry, reproduces certain class associations of literary pedigree even as it rearticulates those in a more accessible (of course, commodified) fashion. As John Frow comments, "There is no longer a stable hierarchy of value (even an inverted one) running from 'high' to 'low' culture... 'high' and 'low' culture can no longer, if they ever could, be neatly, correlated with a hierarchy of social classes" (1995: 1).

Barnes and Noble is a study in the contradictions of an aesthetic discourse that maintains a cultural purchase even as it seeks a wide audience. The bookstores with their indoor cafés function as quasi-public-sphere coffee houses, increasing access to books even as the superstore puts independent stores out of business. The bookstores' reputation for gobbling up independents has been duly noted, yet their appeal to a wide swath of consumers not served by independents has also been acknowledged, even by noteworthy critics of big capital including Doug Henwood, editor of the *Left Business Observer*. He "confessed" on the cultural studies listserv in June 2000 (responding to other queries about "big box bookstores") that though he felt "like a heretic in saying this,"

> the Barnes & Noble on Manhattan's Upper West Side (82nd & Broadway), which put Shakespeare & Co. out of business, is a pretty good bookstore. And Shakespeare, though nobly independent, wasn't: it had a small stock and non-helpful employees. The B&N has plenty of small press and university press books and even a cultural studies section.... I'd hate to see good independents... put out of business.... But chain doesn't necessarily mean bad and independent doesn't necessarily mean good, unless you've got a weakness for petit bourgeois sentimentality.

Barnes and Noble attaches middle-brow cultural capital to the practice of reading – great literature, that is. In the café where "Starbucks coffee is proudly sold," one sips lattes surrounded by drawings of T. S. Eliot, Virginia Woolf, James Joyce, and other canonical cronies – figures that also decorate the plastic bags of purchases.

Discriminating taste in coffee complements literary taste. Large comfortable couches and chairs are scattered throughout the store; unlike the more low-brow B. Dalton stores in shopping malls, the superstores are for people of leisure and hence intellect. "Canonical" also encompasses the *New York Times* bestseller list; books that make this indicator of literary value are discounted 30 percent. Literary value is diffused throughout the store; the reading of women's romance, for example, is elevated above the status it achieves at the supermarket by virtue of its shared space with "high culture."

The superstores bring this cultural capital into line with community values – counteracting the image of the large chain with local involvement. Both stores regularly sponsor appearances by local authors and artists, reading groups, children's story hours, and other events with community tie-ins. They are simultaneously cosmopolitan and local, literary and popular, leisurely and expedient. In terms, then, of women's access to erotica, the superstores represent a very safe space: large stores, easily accessible, with events for children, and aesthetic legitimation for any purchase. It is perhaps one of the few places where a mother can purchase a volume of explicit s/m fantasies for between US$8 and $12 and the latest book in the Magic Tree House series without feeling like a "bad mom."

The categorization of erotica differs between the stores. Barnes and Noble stocks erotica in three sections: literary anthologies, sexuality, and gay and lesbian literature; Borders adds to those possibilities a fourth section of directly marked "Erotica," usually next to the literature section. A wide variety of texts is available at both stores, although Borders clearly has the more explicit commitment to stocking erotica and making it easily accessible (however, for some women, going to the "Erotica" section may be more embarrassing than simply perusing the "Literary Anthology" section). Anthologies by major publishing houses, such as Bright's *Best American Erotica*, as well as books by independent houses, such as Masquerade Books, Cleis Press, and Carroll and Graf, are available, representing different kinds of fantasies and levels of explicitness. Precisely because of the legal history traced above that has more often granted legitimacy to print ("the literary") than film (more often "the pornographic"), these mainstream bookstores fear no legal consequences for selling even the raunchiest fantasies, such as *Letters to Penthouse*, that in other contexts have been labeled pornographic.[5]

These erotic books travel easily, much easier than adult videos – especially in a bag adorned with the face of Virginia Woolf. Many volumes have "tasteful" covers, suggesting they can be read in subways, left out on coffee tables; indeed, one of the questions on the Black Lace reader survey asks, "Would you read a Black Lace book in a public place – on a train, for instance?" We can thus connect aesthetic value to spatial mobility, applying Larry Grossberg's definition of agency as "relations of participation and access, the possibilities of moving into particular sites of activity and power, and of belonging to them in such a way as to be able to actually enact their powers" (1996: 99). Aesthetic value facilitates women's mobility between different sites – the bookstore and the home, for example. Returning home with a volume of erotica indicates a certain degree of sexual agency, one defined by everyday routines and yet hopefully exceeding them as well. Erotica begins with the aesthetic claim by a literary critic/editor, but this claim is both reinforced and redefined given the sites at which it circulates. The constant redefinition of aesthetic value at its sites of circulation and consumption produces the possibility of multiple sexual practices that contradict the editor's claim to a correct way of reading – even though, ironically, that claim facilitates the erotica's circulation at mainstream sites such as Barnes and Noble.

PREVENTING BOREDOM IN THE BEDROOM

Literary texts are never consumed in a vacuum; they exist in relation not only to the sites described above but also in relation to other media technologies in the home. In fact, women's literary erotica has helped spawn (although is certainly not wholly responsible for) a whole genre of women's erotica that includes film, video, the internet,[6] sex toys – all sexual/domestic technologies that depend in part on an aesthetic distinction from porn. Despite the growing acceptance of women's consumption of sexually explicit materials, there is still, in different geographical and generational groups, considerable fear and embarrassment about purchasing and/or renting erotica or porn – hence the ongoing marketing practice of distinguishing erotica from porn through the aesthetic relationship between critic and reader/viewer, across media. Often this relationship takes the form of an outsider of some sort – a storyteller, for example – introducing the representation as a fantasy, with instructions on how to read the fantasy so as to produce benefits for one's "real" sexual identity. As with the literary erotica, the narrator posits the discovery of some new truth – it is, again, the moralism exercised in prescribing a correct way of reading.

Such is the case, for example, with videos produced by Candida Royalle, a mainstream porn star who in 1984 decided to start her own porn production company, Femme Productions, with a focus on women's pleasures. Royalle's videos have been well received and even celebrated for their "explicit but tasteful" nature; as Royalle told an interviewer for *Elle* magazine, "I think a really raunchy fantasy depicted tastefully is where it's at" (Gould 1992: 148). Toward this end, many Femme videos are introduced with images of women in long, flowing dresses running across fields, with vaguely classical music and the words "Femme Productions" appearing in pink, cursive type across the screen (as a student in one of my classes noted, it reminded her of a feminine hygiene commercial). Royalle herself introduces one series, called *LOVERS: Intimate Portraits*, and she does so looking more like a fussy librarian than a former porn star. Her hair is pulled tightly back into a bun, and she wears a white blouse that buttons to the neck. Speaking in a calm, measured tone, she ensures viewers that adult entertainment "can foster a mood of intimacy and bring you closer together." Careful to distance the video from porn, Royalle explains that in the upcoming portrait, "Jennifer and Steve, two real-life lovers," will engage in "some acts of domination and surrender," but that these acts are "mutually consenting," done with "love and respect . . . there is no actual force or degradation of women or men." The video should help couples improve their sex lives at home, for, Royalle cautions, "It's up to us to prevent boredom in the bedroom." The correct way of reading is, again "not pornographic," but the represented practices would not seem out of place in mainstream porn (which has become increasingly concerned with women's pleasures).

Several erotic cable television series deploy similar strategies, with narrators functioning as mediators who provide the bridge between fantasy and reality; the fantasies are often legitimated by their association with the literary and with details of everyday life. In the Showtime series *Red Shoe Diaries*, for example, former *X-Files* star David Duchovny is the narrator; he is desperately seeking answers to his own lost love by running an ad in the newspaper that solicits erotic diary entries: "Women. Do you keep a diary? Have you been betrayed? Have you betrayed another? Man, 35, wounded and alone, recovering from the loss of a once-in-a-lifetime love. Looking for reasons why. Willing to pay top dollar for your experiences. Please send diary to Red Shoes . . . All submissions are strictly confidential." In a nostalgic rejection of such modern-day technologies as the internet, Duchovny receives the handwritten entries at various post-office boxes, accompanied by his loyal mutt Stella. He reads a few lines of the letter; the scene then shifts to the enactment of the sexual predicament, told in the woman's voice, as she struggles with how to negotiate love and sex. The episodes always contain a steamy sex scene, although rarely is it very explicit. As with women's print erotica, the episodes often integrate some details of "everyday life" with the sexual predicament. For example, in an episode that aired in June 2001, a woman washing clothes at a laundromat takes toys and other odds and ends out of the pockets of children's clothes; when a man starts coming on to her, she cautions him "I can't take you home, you know," because of the kids, and they go to a hotel. "Home" is thus posited as a site for child-rearing, even as women at home watch the episode, presumably after the kids have gone to bed. At the end of each episode, Duchovny returns us to the position of voyeur/moral exemplar, commenting cryptically on the dilemma, offering some final words to Stella, who obediently wags her tail.

While *Red Shoe Diaries* offers itself to heterosexual couples' erotic pleasures, Showtime's *Women: Stories of Passion* more directly targets women outside hetero relationships. Advertised as an "erotic anthology directed and written by women," it also draws on a history of aesthetic legitimation, with a literary narrator often framing the story. One episode, for example, begins with the narrator, a bisexual woman named Ellie, sitting next to a Nancy Friday-type figure on an airplane. She's writing a book about women's sexual fantasies and records Ellie's words as she begins to recount a recent sexual encounter with a younger man. The "reality" becomes a fantasy that is distributed to other women in a literary format; of course, it then becomes visual through the cable series.

Together, these sexual/domestic technologies have begun to transform the home into a site of potential erotic activity for women; the aesthetic and identity appeals of erotica have been necessary to this transformation because the home continues to be a site regulated by assumptions that women at home – especially mothers – aren't erotic and certainly don't consume pornography. Erotica's marketing success is premised on its upholding of these very norms: the label "erotica" (although not the content) is literary, it's not pornography, it retains the binary male/female upon which household relations/the family are based. Yet in the process of upholding those distinctions, erotica creates a space for their violation; in increasing women's sexual mobility in safe, easy fashion, materials legitimated as erotic facilitate care of the sexual self. The aesthetic relationship set in motion by literary critics and editors of erotica is indeed a kind of moral/ didactic mode of governance; however, as I have argued throughout this piece, the circulation of aesthetic value at multiple sites can lead to a different kind of aesthetics – one described by Foucault as a relationship of the self to the self:

> I am referring to what might be called the "arts of existence." What I mean by the phrase are those intentional and voluntary actions by which men [sic] not only set themselves rules of conduct, but also seek to transform themselves, to change themselves in their singular being, and to make their life into an oeuvre that carries aesthetic values and meets certain stylistic criteria. (1990: 10–11)

Aesthetics thus becomes a discourse of self formation; erotic texts are technologies that facilitate the transformation of the self. I take issue with Foucault's emphasis here on the "intentional" and "voluntary," for the rules of which he speaks are part of a broader social formation and never purely individualistic. Elsewhere, Foucault discusses these broader conditions of sexual/aesthetic freedom when he says he is trying to construct "an archeology of sexual fantasies." He says, "I try to make an archeology of discourse about sexuality, which is really a relationship between what we do, what we are obliged to do, what we are forbidden to do in the field of sexuality, and what we are allowed, forbidden, or obliged to say about our sexual behavior. That's the point. It's not a problem of fantasy; it's a problem of verbalization" (1982: 125–6). The aesthetics of erotica facilitate conditions in which women can verbalize – to themselves and to others – what is necessary in order to have the time and space in which to fantasize, masturbate, experiment. These practices will exceed the verbalization of the necessary conditions, but the verbalization is a necessary step toward the excessive practices – to what Foucault calls the practices of freedom: "Isn't the problem rather that of defining the practices of freedom by which one could define what is sexual pleasure and erotic, amorous and passionate relationships with others. The ethical problem of the definition of practices of freedom, it seems to me, is much more important than the rather repetitive affirmation that sexuality or desire must be liberated" (1984a: 283).

NOTES

1 I should also say that Bennett gave a series of lectures at the University of Illinois at Urbana-Champaign in the spring of 1994. Some of these lectures took place in Larry Grossberg's cultural studies graduate seminar, where I was a student.
2 Evan Watkins makes a similar point in *Work Time: English Departments and the Circulation of Cultural Value* (Stanford: Stanford University Press, 1989).
3 Deirdre Malane, the Plume editor in charge of the Herotica series, describes the anthologies' writing quality as one of their distinguishing characteristics (personal interview).
4 Personal interview.
5 The exception to legal challenges is anything that might be seen as child pornography.
6 The huge amount of sexual material in cyberspace is beyond the scope of this article, but it is worth noting that the erotica/pornography distinction is also operative across sexual cybersites.

REFERENCES

Alleyn, Frederica. 1996. *The Bracelet.* London: Black Lace.
Bennett, Tony. 1990. *Outside Literature.* London: Routledge.
——.1993. "Being 'in the True' of Cultural Studies." *Southern Review* 26(2) (July): 217–39.
——.1995. *The Birth of the Museum: History, Theory, Politics.* London and New York: Routledge.
——.1998. *Culture: A Reformer's Science.* London: Sage.
Bright, Susie, ed. 2001. *Best American Erotica 2001.* New York: Simon and Schuster.
Bukiet, Melvin Jules. 2000. *Neurotica: Jewish Writers on Sex.* New York: Broadway Books.
Carter, Angela. 1978. *The Sadeian Woman and the Ideology of Pornography.* New York: Pantheon.
Decosta-Willis, M., R. Martin, and R. P. Bell, eds. 1992. *Erotique Noir/Black Erotica.* New York: Anchor Books.
De Grazia, Edward. 1992. *Girls Lean Back Everywhere: The Law of Obscenity and the Assault on Genius.* New York: Random House.

Fernandez Olmos, Margarite and Lizabeth Paravisini-Gebert, eds. 1993. *Pleasure in the Word: Erotic Writing by Latin American Women*. New York: Plume.

Foucault, Michel. 1982. "Michel Foucault: An Interview with Stephen Riggins." In Rabinow 1997: 121–33.

——.1984a. "The Ethics of the Concern of the Self as a Practice of Freedom." In Rabinow 1997: 281–302.

——.1984b. "What is an Author?" In *The Foucault Reader*, ed. Paul Rabinow. New York: Pantheon.

——.1990. *The Use of Pleasure: History of Sexuality*, tr. Robert Hurley. New York: Vintage.

Frow, John. 1995. *Cultural Studies and Cultural Value*. Oxford: Oxford University Press.

Gomez, Jewelle. 1997. "Introduction." In *The Best Lesbian Erotica*, ed. Tristan Taormino. San Francisco: Cleis.

Gonzalez, Ray. 1996. *Under the Pomegranate Tree: The Best New Latino Erotica*. New York: Pocket Books.

Gould, Jodie. 1992. "Debbie Directs Dallas: Video Erotica Made by Women for Women." *Elle*, April: 144, 148, 150.

Grossberg, Lawrence. 1992. *We Gotta Get Out of This Place: Popular Conservatism and Postmodern Culture*. New York: Routledge.

——. 1996. "Identity and Cultural Studies: Is That All There Is?" In *Questions of Cultural Identity*, eds. Stuart Hall and Paul Du Gay. London: Sage, pp. 87–107.

Hunter, Ian. 1988. *Culture and Government: The Emergence of Literary Education*. London: Macmillan, 1988.

——.1992. "Aesthetics and Cultural Studies." In *Cultural Studies*, eds. Lawrence Grossberg, Cary Nelson, and Paula Treichler. New York and London: Routledge, pp. 347–72.

——, David Saunders, and Dugald Williamson. 1993. *On Pornography: Literature, Sexuality, and Obscenity Law*. New York: St. Martin's Press.

Kudaka, Geraldine. 1995. *On a Bed of Rice: An Asian-American Erotic Feast*. New York: Anchor Books.

Rabinow, Paul, ed. 1997. *Michel Foucault: Ethics, Subjectivity, and Truth*. New York: New Press.

Reed, Stacey. 1996. "Night Talk." In *Herotica 4: A New Collection of Erotic Writing by Women*, ed. Marcy Sheiner. New York: Plume, pp. 9–18.

Reynolds, Margaret, ed. 1990. *Erotica: Women's writing from Sappho to Margaret Atwood*. Foreword by Jeanette Winterson. New York: Fawcett Columbine.

Tan, Cecila. 1996. "Porn Flicks." In *Herotica 4: A New Collection of Erotic Writing by Women*, ed. Marcy Sheiner. New York: Plume, pp. 19–23.

Webster, Paula. 1986. "Pornography and Pleasure." In *Caught Looking: Feminism, Pornography, and Censorship*, eds. Kate Ellis, Nan D. Hunter, Beth Jaker, Barbara O'Dair, and Abby Tallmore. New York: Caught Looking, pp. 30–5.

4

The Burden of Culture

JONATHAN STERNE

With apologies to Hayden White

For the past few decades many writers in cultural studies have found it useful to employ a Fabian tactic against critics in related fields of intellectual endeavor.[1] It works like this: when criticized by literary critics or ethnographers for an insufficiently rich notion of culture, cultural studies writers reply that they are interested in the political dimensions of culture, rather than culture (or aspects thereof) as a thing in itself. If culture is always implicated in the very real social struggles of people's material existence, then we cannot simply pass aesthetic and political judgments about the meanings or implications of practices for all time. Or rather, we *can* make transcendental judgments, but they are by definition politically irrelevant. All this is to suggest that cultural studies is a resolutely political enterprise that uses its analysis of culture as an intellectual strategy; culture is a means to an end. At the same time, critics on the left decry cultural studies scholarship for lacking a radical political orientation and limiting political struggle to the domain of culture. Cultural studies writers in turn respond that culture is more complex than the left critics would have it. To seek out the liberatory or repressive aspects of cultural practices is not enough: culture is more than simply a means to political liberation or subjugation. These two arguments overlap in uncomfortable ways. One claims that the political dimension of culture is what matters to cultural studies. The other claims that culture has to be conceived as something more than an instrument of politics.

Of course, there are all sorts of details buried in the above paragraph. "Culture" and "politics" are heavily conflicted terms. They may mean different things to different parties in the discussion. But this Fabian tactic does reveal a fundamental contradiction at the heart of much of the best (and worst) of cultural studies scholarship. In order to do our work, we need an instrumental theory of culture. Through carefully contextualized and theoretically informed analyses, we show that cultural practices, texts, meanings, and events all point to something more significant inside or outside themselves. In a word, they are political, and politics is why culture matters in cultural studies. This is an instrumental theory of culture because it casts culture – whether conceived as texts, practices, or a whole way of life – as a means to an end. Stuart Hall's oft-quoted hope for cultural studies, that it would be "politics by other means," becomes cultural studies' hope for culture. Cultural politics become the privileged domain of political struggle for cultural studies scholars because it takes its place as that "other means" for political struggle. The field is organized around the premise that culture *matters* for politics, even if we cannot know in advance how it will matter.

At the same time, the political dimensions of culture are rarely enough to draw or sustain the passion of cultural studies scholars. In informal discussions, if not in formal writing and presentation, many of us are aware of a "something more" to culture than its political content. In fact, politics sometimes comes secondarily – scholars begin with aspects of culture for which they have an affinity and then seek to discover their political content. A great deal of the cultural studies literature on "popular culture" falls into this camp. Despite claims to reflexivity and promises to explain the author's own investment in a cultural practice, this move tends to bolster the instrumental theory of culture, at least when scholars try to justify their personal pleasures in political terms.

My thesis in this essay is that cultural studies occupies an uncertain terrain in part because of a primarily instrumental notion of culture, a notion of culture upon which the field depends for its intellectual and political vitality. As I will show, cultural studies' instrumental theory of culture is immensely useful for negative critiques of cultural practices and social relationships. In other words, culture conceived as a "means" is a very useful concept if you want to critique capitalism, colonialism, sexism, racism, homophobia, neoliberalism, and the various other "isms" to which most cultural studies writers are (or should be) in principle opposed. The "culture-as-means" concept allows all sorts of useful moves: we can criticize a cultural practice as furthering or reinstantiating some system of relations we oppose. We can also find cultural practices that challenge or even transform extant power relations. This is the familiar terrain of cultural Marxism and Gramsci-influenced cultural studies in the guise of "resistance/ recuperation" debates. It is also prevalent among cultural studies work influenced by other strains of Continental thought, like Saussurean semiotics and the various strands of thought broadly labeled as "poststructuralist." In the case of cultural studies writers who draw on Foucault (myself included), the resistance/

recuperation question has been displaced from a specific practice to the organization of relations of power. In other words, some writers have moved from the results of power relations to an analysis of their composition. But even transformed as a mechanics of power (or "microphysics," to use Foucault's term), the idea of culture as a means to a political end persists.

So why write another commentary that criticizes the critical stances of cultural studies? The answer is simple: the instrumental notion of culture needs supplementation. For cultural studies, it is necessary but not sufficient. Alone, it is a political dead end: it carries with it a reactive notion of politics and a deferral of social and political imagination. It reduces what ought to be to what is. The instrumental notion of culture falls down when we begin to articulate our political project in positive terms: criticizing "what is" in terms of what "ought to be." In and of itself, the instrumental notion of culture contributes nothing to the project of conceiving a culture or society in which people would want to live. It's actually a kind of negative faith: "if we turn culture into politics, maybe things will get better." Where the culture industry looks to each possible text or practice as a means to revenue generation, cultural studies considers each text or practice in terms of its possible and actual political uses. As Lawrence Grossberg and others have pointed out, this idea of culture as a political tool has been appropriated by the right as well; it is not a uniquely left-wing idea (Grossberg 1992; Bertsch 1994).

"Culture" in cultural studies is an entity that always points to things outside itself. This is an immensely powerful tool of critique, but as a political program it descends into politico-pragmatic managerialism. Though we cannot know ahead of time the effects of any given cultural practice, the underlying logic appears to be that we should seek out cultural practices that have the right effects. This is a useful pragmatics (which is not the same thing as pragmatism), but it is not a compelling political program in and of itself. Nobody (at least nobody I know) wants to live in a world where his or her every action is a means to a political end. Political pragmatics assume that some other debate about the good will happen or has happened. We can either enter into cultural studies with a pre-given political program, like socialism, feminism, environmentalism, antiracism, queer politics, and so forth, or we can defer our political judgments to "the last instance," which, like the Althusserian moment of determination, never arrives for the cultural studies scholar – at least not in writing. As it stands, compared to the vast amount of writing dedicated to explaining what we in cultural studies should be *against*, comparatively little writing exists in cultural studies about what we should be *for*.

This is not a call for Habermasian proceduralism or grounding cultural studies in other branches of "normative" philosophy. Rather, it is to argue that we always already carry with us implicit visions of the good in our writing – a point demonstrated at some length by Amanda Anderson. By attending to, and even debating those visions of the good, we will be better able to understand politics in proactive as well as reactive terms, and therefore more strategically – which, after all, is supposed to be the goal of cultural studies. We need a more vigorous political imagination.

This is a very difficult position to argue, since outside of normative philosophy, explicit "should" questions are rarely seen as legitimate scholarly activities. It sounds unduly grand, pompous, elitist, even vanguardist to argue that academics should have debates about the social good. After all, who are we to dictate to others? But in principle, there is no reason why Stuart Hall's call for modesty in cultural theorizing couldn't also be applicable here: the point isn't to theorize "the good" and "the should" once and for all for everyone, but rather to simply think about how those kinds of conceptions already inform our writing, and to orient our writing toward those visions of the good that we find most appropriate or beneficial. The need for theory is as pressing at this level as it is at the level of cultural description: we need to fashion concepts to interrogate and rethink the obvious, the thinkable, the possible (on this point, see, e.g., Hall 1978; see also Fraser 1989 and McClure 1992). Cultural studies has long taken as gospel the idea that cultural objects, texts, and practices are not synonymous with their surface appearances. Why should we arbitrarily give up the intellectual vocation at the point of "is" before asking questions of what should be? If questions of political vision weren't so often taken for granted in cultural studies writing, this point would be too banal to be worth an essay.

Following C. Wright Mills (1959), our task is both to provide compelling and useful explanations of social and cultural life, and to create and debate alternatives to these existing ways of life. Our relative institutional independence from social movements is a double-edged sword – we can and do descend into navel gazing, but it also affords us the necessary luxury of sustained speculation and theorizing. This speculation is a luxury because not everyone is afforded the opportunity. But it is a necessity because as context changes, so too must our questions.

This chapter explores cultural studies' instrumental definition of culture in two contexts. Using the work of and around Stuart Hall as its anchor, the next section shows how cultural studies has come to rely on an instrumental definition of culture. Using the debates around the work of John Fiske (and "resistance theory" in general), the subsequent section shows how instrumental definitions of culture limit the possibilities for positive political vision, regardless of what position one takes within the debate. The conclusion explores some way in which we might usefully supplement instrumental notions of culture in cultural studies. Let me be clear from the outset: I am not attacking in any universal way the idea of an instrumental notion of culture. It is certainly necessary for the kinds of work done in cultural studies. I am simply arguing that an instrumental theory of culture is not sufficient. I should add that much of the scholarship discussed in this piece may be considered as "dated" in the sense that most of the authors have moved on to other questions: Hall has moved into questions of race and global-ization (among other things), and late in his career, Fiske significantly qualified the populist position for which he is famous. The point is not to freeze these scholars in time but rather to argue that their earlier writings are still relevant because contemporary cultural studies – especially in the United States – is still very much concerned with the issues raised in this earlier work. So perhaps this essay carries with it a sense of canonicity in referring back to a set of core texts or at least a preoccupation with continuity, since I continue a conversation that cultural studies scholars have been having for over 40 years – and wish to point out that its longevity is itself worthy of critical reflection.

STUART HALL, BRITISH CULTURAL STUDIES, AND THE INSTRUMENTALITY OF CULTURE

In perhaps the most succinct-yet-compelling definition of the vast cross-discip-linary mangle of scholarship known as cultural studies, Tony Bennett has written that cultural studies is "a term of convenience for a fairly dispersed array of theoretical and political positions which, however widely divergent they might be in other respects, share a commitment to examining cultural practices from the point of view of their intrication with, and within, relations of power" (1992: 23). For Bennett and others, that "intrication" or entanglement is actually more of a deployment – culture is a way of working out power relations. Though it is not necessarily the case, historically, the assertion that culture is political has led cultural studies scholars to consider it as a means to a political end. As Cary Nelson, Paula Treichler, and Lawrence Grossberg have written, "cultural studies cannot be used to denigrate a whole class of cultural objects, though it can certainly indict the uses to which those objects have been put" (1992: 13). The term "uses" is the key hinge of the sentence. The example of culture here is objects, and cultural studies is less concerned with the objects in themselves than their existence as means – the uses to which they are put. The same could be said for culture conceived of practices, "formations" or any of the other metaphors used in cultural studies. This instrumentality is built into the history of the field. After all, one of the earliest cultural studies books is entitled *The Uses of Literacy*.

This section briefly explores the instrumental status of "culture" in the writings of Stuart Hall (and in a few writings in Hall's intellectual neighborhood). Regardless of whether Hall is "representative" of cultural studies in a sociological sense, he certainly "represents" cultural studies because of his role in the field's development. Hall's work explicitly thematizes and develops an instrumental notion of culture for the purposes of political analysis and critique. His Grams-cian politics of culture is still very influential across disciplines, and many writers still analyze culture in Gramscian terms. Hall's contribution to this approach to culture is singular, and in that sense, he may very well be descriptively representative of the field. So if I may hedge for the moment on questions of who speaks as or for cultural studies, a consideration of Hall's work and its intellectual neighborhood will usefully illustrate my point.

Hall's interest in culture has always been directly political. His famous passage in "Notes on Deconstructing the Popular" succinctly summarizes his view of culture's significance: "Popular culture is one of the sites where this struggle for and against a culture of the powerful is engaged: it is also the stake to be won or lost in that struggle. It is the arena of consent and resistance. It is partly where hegemony arises and where it is secured. It is not a sphere where socialism, a socialist culture – already fully formed – might be simply expressed. But it is one of the places where socialism might be constituted. That is why popular culture matters. Otherwise, to tell you the truth, I don't give a damn about it" (1981: 239). These are strong words, and leaving aside whether Hall is exaggerating for polemical purposes, the point is clear: politics is the reason to care about popular culture. In fact, politics is the reason to care about culture at all. For Hall, culture is to be conceived as a political tool. This is its ultimate value: if you can't *do* something with popular culture, then there's no point to it.

Culture is of course a central term in the history and mission of cultural studies both before and after Hall. Hall's scholarship clearly builds on the works of earlier scholars like Richard Hoggart, Raymond Williams, and E. P. Thompson. Williams, especially, was preoccupied with the concept of culture. His oft-cited line that it is "one of the two or three most complicated words in the English language" (1975: 76) probably says more about the valuation of culture in cultural studies than the actual complexity of the term. There is no doubt that culture is a dizzyingly complex concept for the field, but plenty of other words exhibit similar complexity and slipperiness in their own disciplinary milieus. Williams's career was built around a singular obsession with the concept and status of culture, so his evaluation comes as no surprise. But this quote from *Keywords* also speaks directly to an investment in culture as a privileged object of thought and practice. It carries forth a sense that culture matters, but also a sense that culture *should* matter.

For his part, Williams bears a strong debt to conservative cultural critics like F. R. Leavis and T. S. Eliot. Eliot, especially, influenced the notion of culture as a "whole way of life" as Williams developed it in *Culture and Society* (1958) and *The Long Revolution* (1961). But as Hall writes, Williams was a kind of "lone Marxist" at this point in his career. Though he understood culture as a field of struggle, he had not articulated an explicit theoretical vocabulary for describing that struggle (Hall 1980: 59–60). This was also one axis of E. P. Thompson's critique of *The Long Revolution*: Williams's history is heavily depersonalized. Thompson writes of Williams's "determination to de-personalize social forces and at the same time to avoid certain terms which might associate him with a simplified version of the class struggle which he rightly believes to be discredited" (1961: 26). Thompson's complaint is that through depersonalizing history – talking about large-scale processes rather than in terms of specific historical actors – Williams deemphasizes struggle, bracketing questions of winners and losers and shifting accounts of the ways in which "men have made history" toward accounts of how "history happened" (ibid.).[2]

Williams's depersonalization of culture, however, was part of his larger reevaluation of it. As a socialist, Williams sought to rescue culture as a singular term, properly owned by the elite and widely believed by that elite to be in decline. This is one reason why Eliot is one of Williams's influences: while Eliot believed culture was a whole way of life that belonged to the few, Williams argued that culture was ordinary – it was indeed a whole way of life, but a way of life that belonged to the many. He challenged "this extraordinary decision to call certain things culture and then separate them, as with a park wall, from ordinary people and ordinary work" (Williams 1958).

So descriptive depersonalization was a kind of universalizing move in Williams. His was a project of validation, something that many later cultural studies scholars – especially Hall – would continue. The idea was to examine everyday practices as valid and important expressions of cultural life, and through that, to see the working class as a valid producer and agent of culture. At the same time, the aim was supposed to be realistic: rather than idealizing working-class culture by acting as if it necessarily embodied a socialist sensibility, Williams and his contemporaries sought to consider it for its political potential, and through the consideration of that political potential, contribute to the project of social transformation. As Hall would put it, popular culture became a site where socialism *might* be constituted.

Among other things, Hall's contribution was to build on Williams's culture concept but to foreground and thematize conflict. If Hoggart (1957/1992), Williams (1958, 1961), and Thompson (1964) aimed to democratize the concept of culture and in the process politicized it, if they moved it from a singular "practice" to a domain of practices, Hall highlighted the dimension of "struggle" as the most important axis for cultural analysis. For Williams, Hoggart, and Thompson, culture is "interwoven with all social practices"; culture is "*both* the meanings and values which arise amongst distinctive social grounds and classes, on the basis of their given historical conditions and relationships, through which they 'handle' and respond to the condition of existence; *and* the lived traditions and practices through which those 'understandings' are expressed and in which they are embodied" (Hall 1980: 63). Hall argued that this "culturalist" mode of cultural studies existed in useful tension with a "structuralist" mode of cultural studies. In fact his own career represents something of an attempt to synthesize these approaches. Hall says that he parts company with the poststructuralists when they say that society *is* language, but that the metaphor "structured *like* a language" has been immensely useful to him because it provided a way to conceptualize the circulation of meaning within a determinate system (see Hall 1986; 1988a).

In particular, Hall's advocacy of the conceptions of hegemony (via a reading of Antonio Gramsci) and articulation (via a reading of Ernesto Laclau) illustrate his commitment to an instrumental theory of culture as a tool of political critique and his particular combination of culturalism and structuralism. They also show us the flip-side of the commitment: the need to show that culture is about doing something. Hegemony usefully conceptualized the role of struggle in cultural life for Hall. Culture was the site where social groups fought for political control of a society. In Gramsci's idea of hegemony, writes Hall, "we discover the beginnings of a way of conceptualizing how classes, constituted at the fundamental level of production relations, come to provide the basis of the social authority," the political sway and cultural domination a "class alliance on behalf of capital" without a narrowly conceived "class interest" driving historical relations and social forces (1977: 66). In other words, hegemony enables some of the theoretical concepts dearest to British cultural studies: negotiated power blocs among fractured social groups instead of a dominant class; competing worldviews and articulations of "common sense" rather than a single top-down conception of ideology; and meanings and practices as *negotiating* power relations instead of simple subordination of nondominant groups. In Hall's vision of hegemony, culture and the superstructure become vital sites through which the base might be transformed.

Since the goal of cultural analysis *via* hegemony is clearly the production of a political analysis, culture becomes the means to the political end. If hegemony requires consent, and is manufactured in the cultural domain, then the cultural domain is of primary interest because it is a means toward maintaining or transforming social power. Hegemony played an important theoretical role in two of the major collaborative projects that Hall undertook during the 1970s. In the introduction to *Resistance Through Rituals* (Hall & Jefferson 1995), John Clarke, Stuart Hall, Tony Jefferson, and Brian Roberts use hegemony as a grounding framework for the related studies in the collection. For them, youth subcultures are interesting as alternative means to political ends. They are tools for negotiating working-class identity, for working out youths' relations to the dominant culture:

> There is no "sub-cultural solution" to working-class youth unemployment, educational disadvantage, compulsory miseducation, dead-end jobs, the routinization and specialization of labour, low pay, and the loss of skills. Sub-cultural strategies cannot match, meet or answer the structuring dimen-

sion emerging in this period for the class as a whole. So, when the post-war sub-cultures address the problematics of their class experience, they often do so in ways which reproduce the gaps and discrepancies between real negotiation and symbolically displaced "resolutions." They "solve," but in an imaginary way, problems which at the concrete material level remain unsolved. Thus the "Teddy boy" expropriation of an upper class style of dress "covers" the gap between largely manual, unskilled, near-lumpen real careers and life-chances and the "all-dressed-up-and-nowhere-to-go" experience of Saturday evening. Thus, in the expropriation and fetishization of consumption and style itself, the "Mods" cover for the gap between the never-ending-weekend and Monday's resumption of boring, dead-end work. (Hall & Jefferson 1995: 48)

Subcultural theory is a particularly powerful example of the politics-by-other-means sensibility, since it is primarily interested in youth culture, and oriented around activities that had hitherto been understood as deviant, aberrant, or otherwise antisocial. Subcultural theory reconstructed these practices as deeply social and politically significant. From this point forward in subcultural theory, there would be an enduring need for cultural practices to be "doing something." Even when they were self-consciously "doing nothing," working-class youth were doing "something" politically through their actions and stances. This "doing somethingness" in turn bolstered an instrumental theory of culture because it construed youth subcultures as means to political and social ends. The essays in *Resistance Through Rituals* do not present a strictly a functionalist analysis in Durkheim's sense (contrast with, for example, the discussion of mechanical solidarity in Durkheim 1933), because of the key element of struggle within social relationships. The above quote reads subculture as a way of "working out" or "working through" class-based oppression even as the subculture itself cannot possibly "solve" the problems of class oppression. Though as Angela McRobbie (1991) has pointed out, the options for "working through" and "working out" class position are heavily shaped by gender as well. But if culture is not functional, it is instrumental because the subculture struggles "by other means" – the means in this case being cultural expression. So even when they are hanging about "doing nothing," subcultural youth are doing something because cultural activity is itself an arena of struggle. In this classic cultural studies text, subculture becomes a means to a political end.

As a response to law-and-order discourses about youth on the one hand and sociological "deviance" literature on the other, *Resistance Through Rituals* aimed to do for youth culture what Williams had done for culture in general: to show that culture is an arena of struggle, to argue that it mattered – to validate it in an academic context – and to take it seriously as a political problem. Dick Hebdige's subsequent *Subculture: The Meaning of Style* (1979) takes this even further, essentially doing for aesthetics what *Resistance Through Rituals* had done for culture. As Raymond Williams writes in *Keywords*, the idea of the aesthetic

> at once emphasized and isolated subjective sense-activity as the basis of art and beauty as distinct, for example, from *social* or *cultural* interpretations.... Like one special meaning of the word *culture*, [aesthetic] is intended to express a human dimension which the dominant version of society appears to exclude. This emphasis is understandable but the isolation can be damaging, for there is something irresistibly displaced and marginal about the now common and limiting phrase "aesthetic considerations," especially when contrasted with *practical* or *utilitarian* considerations, which are elements of the same basic division. (1976: 28, emphasis in original)

Hebdige brought aesthetics back into the domain of culture and society, and in so doing, aimed to more fully politicize aesthetic activity. In his analysis of youth culture, he effectively collapsed the distinction upon which common uses of the idea of the aesthetic were premised: all aesthetic activity was always already practical and utilitarian. Aesthetics, like the domain of culture in general, became a means to an end.

To be absolutely clear, these approaches made a great deal of sense at the time. They were significant and radical analyses at the moment they developed. But in their instrumentalization of culture, they carried with them a prejudice that cultural activity *should* be about doing something more than the activity itself would at first indicate. In subcultural analysis, the "is" and the "ought" of cultural practice were collapsed around the question of culture, as if to say, *culture is politics by other means, and it ought to be.* To be sure, this has something to do with the history of the term "culture" itself. To return to Williams in *Keywords*, culture has roots in an agricultural metaphor: one cultivates plants, and eventually this idea of cultivation was grafted onto persons as well. Cultivation is primarily an instrumental activity: one cultivates something else to a particular end (and even if one cultivates plants for beauty or hobby, the cultivation may still just be a means to an end). This cultivation metaphor makes up only one of three possible modern uses, according to Williams; the other two are "a particular way of life" and "works and practices of intellectual and artistic activity" (1975: 80). Whether it is necessary, I do not know, but I would argue that in cultural studies, the instrumental sense of the first usage of culture has fertilized the other two: ways of life, and intellectual and artistic activities become politics by other means. For cultural studies, they become entry points into politics.

In a certain sense, this is taking aesthetics at its face value. Lots of people committed to aesthetics have argued for aesthetic practice as a form of personal improvement: whether we are talking about Friedrich Nietzsche or Matthew Arnold, aesthetic creation and contemplation are keys to creating a better self.

For its part, cultural studies simply expands the domain of what counts as aesthetics and the ends to which the aesthetic can be put – for instance, in fostering collective consciousness rather than atomized individual improvement. So to treat culture, especially in its aesthetic dimensions, as a means to an end is not an abandonment of aesthetic approaches to culture but rather an extension and generalization of those approaches.

Of course, the "politics of culture" argument extends far beyond subculture theory. To return to Hall's work, his appropriation of the "by other means" motif is perhaps most powerful in his work that deals with politics in the more narrow sense of states and governments. In *Policing the Crisis* (Hall et al. 1977), we have a familiar understanding of the news media as a "field of ideological struggle" where competing interests fight to create and assign meaning to events – very similar to youth subcultures. Hall's later work on Thatcherism (e.g., Hall 1988a and 1988b) would also make use of Gramscian theory to locate culture as a site of struggle where hegemony must constantly be rebuilt and rewon. In fact, this usage is much closer to Gramsci's original conceptualization of hegemony, since he was talking about the state and civil society and clearly had in mind a parliamentary model of politics as part of that state. Of course, Hall's work on Thatcher, though arguably a more seminal application of Gramscian political theory, has not translated as well in the United States. Many writers have noted that while the writings on subculture have enjoyed an enthusiastic reception in the United States, the writings on British politics and the state are less widely read across the Atlantic. This is probably, in part, a result of Americans' ignorance of British politics, but also the different situations of British and "American" cultural studies (insofar as there is such a thing): while Hall and the other major cultural studies figures were (and continue to be) actively involved in left party politics, fewer cultural studies scholars writing in the US have maintained the same level of political involvement, or at least reflected it in their work. This can be attributed to many factors – for instance, the absence of a clearly "left" major political party in the United States, the differing positions of American academics versus their British or Australian counterparts, etc. But for my argument, the effect is perhaps more important than the cause: on this side of the Atlantic, "hegemony" has seen lots of play as a term to be applied to cultural politics more often than it is applied to political culture or what Meaghan Morris (1988) calls the politics of politics.

So Hall uses hegemony as a wedge to talk about the mechanics of cultural politics. His use of "articulation" is similarly instrumental: in fact the very definition of articulation casts it as an instrumental theory of culture that enables us to talk about the ways in which cultural politics can happen. As he explains:

> In England, the term has a nice double meaning because "articulate" means to utter, to speak forth, to be articulate. It carries that sense of language-ing, of expressing, etc. But we also speak of an "articulated" lorry (truck): a lorry where

the front "cab" and back "trailer" can, but need not necessarily, be connected to one another. The two parts are connected to each other, but through a specific linkage, that can be broken. An articulation is thus the form of the connection that *can* make a unity of two different elements, under certain circumstances. It is a linkage which is not necessary, determined, absolute, and essential for all time.... Thus, a theory of articulation is both a way of understanding how ideological elements come, under certain conditions, to cohere together within a discourse, and a way of asking how they do or do not become articulated, at specific conjunctures, to certain political subjects. (1986: 53)

To drive the truck metaphor a little further, Hall is saying that whatever is in the trailer and whoever is in the cab doesn't necessarily matter, and if it does matter, it matters conjuncturally, situationally. *In theory*, then, any cab can be hitched to any trailer – though you may need a special adapter to hook some pairs together. Once hitched, they can be sent on all sorts of delivery routes. A classic example for articulation theory would be populism: it has "no necessary belongingness" (Hall borrowed this phrase from Laclau 1977), and at different times has been appropriated as a political strategy on the left or the right. But the theory of articulation itself is an instrumental theory of culture: it asks how a particular cultural form, practice, or idea gets attached to others, and then how that attachment gets used politically. That is the very goal of articulation theory: not to consider the in-itself or for-itself of a cultural practice, but rather to discover how it is used in any particular situation. Hall's is a "Marxism without guarantees" in which "history is the struggle to produce the relation within which particular practices have particular meanings and effects, to organize practices into larger structures, to 'inflect' particular practices and subject-positions into relation with political, economic, and culture structures of domination and resistance" (Grossberg 1997: 179). This is why cultural studies can condemn the *use* of a cultural practice or artifact, but it cannot condemn the cultural practice or artifact in itself: it could later be articulated within a wholly different formation.

As I intimated above, I believe Hall's instrumentalism is typical of cultural studies work. More recent incarnations of cultural studies work also depend on the idea that culture is a means to a political end. For instance, the cultural policy studies movement is premised on this very idea. Tony Bennett, in challenging the dominant notions of culture in cultural studies, winds up arguing for a *more* instrumental and pragmatic theory of culture: drawing on Michel Foucault's theory of governmentality, Bennett and other cultural policy studies scholars seek an account of culture as the conduct of conduct, as a modality of person formation and social ordering (e.g., Bennett 1992, 1995, 1997; Hunter 1988; see also Miller 1998 and Sterne 2003). It seems that the commitment to the politics of culture almost demands an analysis of culture as a means to an end. But this is not exactly the case.

THE IMAGINATIVE IMPASSE OF INSTRUMENTALISM: FISKE WARS

Perhaps the most extreme version of cultural studies' instrumental approach to culture appears in John Fiske's work. Fiske was widely popular in the United States (and Australia, I hear) for some time in the late 1980s and early 1990s, and he worked the culture-as-politics-by-other-means thesis until it broke. In this section, I show that the instrumental theory of culture – which reached a sort of natural limit in Fiske's work – is also at work in left criticisms of cultural studies. Fiske the populist argued that culture was valuable because people (audiences, fans, etc.) were active agents in their participation, interpretation, and use of that culture, and more importantly, because that culture was put to political ends. Rather than contesting Fiske's conception of culture altogether, critics of cultural studies' populism – themselves often outside the field – have wholly accepted the instrumental notion of culture. Their criticism is that culture isn't as political as Fiske says it is. But most of them still argue from the position that culture should primarily be understood as a means to a political end. Instrumental theories of culture promoted by cultural studies thus still hold a great deal of significance among the intellectual left.

Because of Fiske's stridently populist position, he has been a favorite whipping post both inside and outside cultural studies. My purpose here is not to criticize (or defend) Fiske's populism, since that's been done to death. In fact, I would venture to argue that at this point it is even more cliché to offer a critique of populism in cultural studies via a reading of Fiske's work than it is to offer a reading of cultural practices as resistance. But before we consider Fiske's detractors, let us for a moment dwell on what the man actually says.

There is no doubt that Fiske identifies himself as a populist and an unrepentant optimist: "I believe the popular forces to be a positive influence in our society and that failing to take proper account of their progressive elements is academically and politically disabling" (Fiske 1989a: 194). Fiske sees his work as continuing the long-term project of validation in cultural studies, where previously denigrated cultural objects are considered for their political potential, and where audiences are considered as active agents rather than cultural "dupes."

But Fiske is also politically programmatic in ways that other cultural studies writers are unwilling to be: he is clear that his is a politics of reform, a progressivism rather than a radicalism. This is because he sees a split between macro- and micro-level social and political processes: there is no simple homology or identity between large-scale social forces and small-scale experience (and here we should hear echoes of Hall's articulation theory). Fiske writes that "we are wrong to expect popular culture to be radical (and thus to criticize it for not being so)" because "popular" motives for social change are different than theoretical or radical ones. For Fiske, this also means that if academics fail to consider popular culture on its own terms, they will be unable to harness popular energies and affective investments for the project of social change. "This does not mean, however, that when historical conditions produce a radical crisis the media and popular culture cannot play an active role in the radical change that may occur: what it means is that symbolic or cultural systems alone cannot produce those historical conditions" (1989a: 188).

Clearly, there's some truth to Fiske's position. Particularly strident political content rarely becomes popular entertainment, both because of the prevailing practices in media industries (something Fiske admittedly does not talk about) and because audiences are not looking for political instruction in their entertainment. That audiences get this instruction anyway is irrelevant to Fiske's point: ideological positions that nudge the status quo call much less attention to themselves than those calling for total social transformation. For Fiske, many cultural texts and practices are popular precisely because they retain some political ambiguity. This is not an ontological condition, but a condition of the capitalist culture industry and a condition of widespread consumption practices in industrial societies.

So if radical messages aren't going to work in the media system, Fiske reasons, then we need to start thinking more incrementally in terms of ground gained or lost in a Gramscian war of position. This is the theoretical basis for his readings of popular culture: it's not that Madonna fandom makes teenage girls into revolutionary feminists but rather that Madonna offers a representation of semiotic and social power to some of her fans and that these "in turn, may empower the fan's sense of self and thus affect her behavior in social situations" (1989b: 113). Clearly, we could dispute Fiske's research methods, his findings, or his orientation – many have. But for the sake of argument, let's take him at his word. All Fiske is really saying here is that Madonna fandom may make some incremental difference in fans' lives. The point strikes me as uncontroversial.

Fiske's work follows logically from the subculture work done 15 years prior – since fans cannot simply transform the material conditions of their lives on their own, they look for ways to deal with their conditions of existence. But here again, we have an instrumental theory of culture at the center of cultural studies practice: popular culture is politics by other means, a means to an end of self-empowerment, making do, and coping. Fiske's instrumentalism becomes its own kind of aesthetics: he prefers texts that are open to interpretation because they allow for audience agency and negotiation. In other words, Fiske explicitly values cultural texts and practices that can be put to political ends (within his particular brand of micropolitics).

Of course, there's much more to it than that. I've chosen not to "go after" Fiske because so many others have, but he clearly offers lots of fodder for hostile readers, occasionally slipping from a more modest reading of making-do to a full-on politics of popular cultural resistance. Fiske is clearly a populist more than he is a committed leftist – though he names capitalism, racism, and patriarchy as oppressive systems, he offers no theory of – or even hope for – systematic change. Instead, he argues for an explicitly reformist platform and then follows through on that political project.

If everyone in cultural studies were doing what Fiske was doing, we would be open to the accusation of a monomaniacal interest in popular culture as resistance. But subculture theory came under criticism inside and outside cultural studies well before Fiske was a significant figure in the field. Shortly after Dick Hebdige's *Subculture* hit the shelves, Gary Clarke (1982) published a substantial critique of subculture theory calling for more attention to political transformation and economic conditions. Judith Williamson attacked consumptionist studies in a 1985 *New Socialist* article. Meaghan Morris criticized Baudrillardian dystopianism and Fiskean populism in an essay that appeared in 1989 – the same year that Fiske's two major textbooks appeared in print. Jim McGuigan's well-researched and carefully reasoned *Cultural Populism* appeared in 1992. That same year, the introduction to the massive conference-based anthology *Cultural Studies* approvingly cites criticisms of populist and affirmative strains in the field, and several essays in the volume take potshots at populist cultural studies. In fact, the discussion following Fiske's essay in that volume consists of the most sustained and hostile audience reaction printed in the whole book – it is astounding to read. A variety of cultural studies scholars repeatedly attack Fiske on theoretical and political grounds: for his theorization of "habitus," his characterization of academic life, his distinctions between the abstract and concrete, his collapsing of everyday practices and great art, his misreading of Marxism, his gender politics, his oppositions between intellectuals and the underclass, and his use of single individuals to describe whole social formations (Fiske 1992: 165–73). In fact, Fiske's later work would modify somewhat the position for which he became famous (see Fiske 1993), though his central interests and concepts remained in this later work. So there is no paucity of critiques of populism within the discourse of cultural studies and Fiske's populism is not representative of the field.

I make this rather mundane point because Fiske-bashing has become a fashionable sport in some sectors of the academy. Leaving aside for the moment more serious and well-informed critiques of populism by writers sympathetic to the cultural studies project, a whole industry of "critiques of cultural studies" has sprung up in History, American Studies, English, Communication Studies, and a host of other fields. As Meaghan Morris wrote of resistance theory in 1989, so we could today write of critiques of cultural studies' populism: I get the feeling that somewhere in some publisher's vault there is a master disk from which thousands of versions of the same article about cultural studies, populism, and left politics are being run off under different names with minor variations (rephrased from Morris 1990: 21). This work exploded quantitatively in the mid-1990s and continues – showing no signs of relenting – to the present day.

These articles and talks all share a set of basic features and they generally follow a Jeremiad form. They begin by hailing the achievements of Hoggart, Williams, Thompson, Hall, and whomever else they like in the British Cultural Studies canon. Having – often in bad faith – established their commitment to classic cultural studies, they then lament cultural studies' subsequent decline into bland populist affirmation of various kind of consumption as political resistance (this is often combined with a discussion of Americanization). The article or talk then concludes with a program for cultural studies to return to its former greatness. With surprising regularity, these critiques refer only to the work of John Fiske in specific (if they refer to any specific works at all), claiming that it represents a "general trend" in the field. There are clearly questionable intellectual ethics in lambasting an entire field on the basis of a trend which it has itself criticized. But this is not my main point. Rather, I believe that while critiques of cultural studies' populism make their stance on the basis of some broadly leftist principle, they often fall into an instrumental description of culture that mirrors the tendency within cultural studies. In other words, despite their greater willingness to make explicitly normative claims, these critics have an equally instrumental description of how culture works and thus built their own aesthetics on the basis of this instrumentality.

I will offer a brief example of external criticisms of cultural studies' populism to illustrate my point about instrumental theories of culture (though others, like McGuigan 1992, Garnham 1995, Czitrom 1995, McChesney 1996, and Gitlin 1997, would also work). My example is drawn from an essay entitled "The Affirmative Character of US Cultural Studies," published in 1990 by Mike Budd, Robert Entman, and Clay Steinman. Their main criticisms would become stand-ard fare over the next decade: cultural studies loses "much of its critical edge" because it overestimates the freedom of media audiences, minimizes the economic dimensions of cultural life, fails to distinguish between mass advertising and specialized media, and confuses active reception with political activity. Addition-ally, these authors counterpoise cultural studies to political-economic approaches, arguing that what is missing is an analysis of production and a contextualization of consumption. To their credit, they read the work of Lawrence Grossberg and several other cultural studies scholars as well. It is somewhat atypical in that the authors attempt to be responsible scholars and read beyond Fiske into the cultural studies literature. Though it is from 1990, I believe that it speaks to contemporary concerns. But here, let me concentrate on their responses to Fiske.

One of their key arguments is that alternative readings aren't necessarily political. To do so, they return to Fiske's Madonna example, arguing that "we should not make too much of the significance of alternative readings":

Women who find in Madonna's image the sexual independence they admire may do so without actually altering their personal relationships with men, let alone joining feminist organizations. They may admire Madonna and still believe that patriarchal sex roles are natural, resolving internal conflicts in favor of the external forces that they confront. If this were not so, we should see one subversive belief becoming linked to others, leading to visible confrontations with power, especially when subversive readings are as widely available as they are in the realm of feminism. (1990: 178)

Here, they are criticizing Fiske for overestimating the political efficacy of these interpretations, but crucially, they uphold an instrumental model of cultural practice. There's a strong "should" that sits like a pink elephant on the surface of their argument: women who find pleasure in Madonna *should* get more politically active as a result, *but they don't*. Their point is made clear a few sentences below, where they argue that analyses of media need to account for the widespread acquiescence to conservative politics prevalent in America at that time (though they may not have known this, Grossberg was writing on that very question at about the same time their article appeared – see Grossberg 1992). Again, the presumption is that media content and cultural practice does play an important role in political life, and that it should be judged as a means to a political end.

To be fair to Budd, Entman, and Steinman, there's not much to disagree with in their assessment of the political efficacy of alternative readings; though to be fair to Fiske, he already made the point that subversive readings and political action are two different things and that subversive readings do not necessarily lead to organized political action. But the larger point is that both Fiske and his critics want to understand culture as a means to an end – more importantly, they think it *should* be a means to an end.

This becomes explicit a little further along in the article. Budd, Entman, and Steinman posit a zero-sum game between television-watching and subcultural practice: "Further work may well show that one of the most important effects of television has been its theft of time from subcultural experience in favor of exposure to the mass audience programming and advertisements rooted in the 'discourse through and about things'" (1990: 179). The theft metaphor is particularly important here because it suggests that by right of origin (or some other unspecified divine conjuring), leisure-time properly belongs to subcultural practice – and television is stealing that time. Not surprisingly, they also happen to like subculture more as a possible site of political resistance: "we suspect that rootedness in a subculture that organizes the lived experience of a community usually provides a firmer basis for critique of the dominant than the deracinated consciousness promoted by the political economy and the culture of mass advertising" (1990: 180). Descriptively speaking, they may be right (though they also may not – as they say, we really don't know). But normatively speaking, we again find an insistence by left intellectuals that culture matters because it can be put to progressive political ends. The aesthetics are purely instrumental.

For Ben Franklin, time was money. For Budd, Entman, and Steinman (and Fiske too) leisure time is political capital. In a strange way, both the political economists and populists have thus mirrored the very capitalist logic they seek to criticize. Political economist Dallas Smythe (1994) used the phrase "all non-sleeping time is work time" to describe culture industries' orientations to their audiences. Audiences' attention to media texts could be "put to work" as broadcasters converted it into a product and sold advertising time. The same could be said for critics in cultural studies and political economy: insofar as we have an instrumental theory of cultural practice, we judge practices on the basis of whether they contribute to the project of social change or don't. Some of our biggest inter- and intradisciplinary fur-fights have been around the question of exactly how much and under what conditions cultural practices do contribute to social transformation. But there is a tacit agreement that they should.

Certainly, Fiske's forfeiture of any hope for significant social change in exchange for a very limited war-of-position will not do. But neither will Budd, Entman, and Steinman's zero-sum game. One reason that Americans watch so much TV is that it's easy to do after a long and draining day of work. Instead of criticizing the paucity of leisure time left over after the ever-extending workday (as Schor 1991 would later show, leisure time was in significant decline as Budd et. al wrote), Budd, Entman, and Steinman want to put their subjects right back to work for social change. Sure, that would be nice, but I suspect that many of their subjects are tired and drained, and not particularly in the mood to foment revolution in their sparse evening hours. Though Fiske has given up on significant political changes, he at least builds affect into his theory of culture: people watch TV or listen to music because it brings them pleasure. Given that so many people hate their jobs, we ought to take that seriously. To take it seriously, we need to treat "doing nothing" as a worthwhile practice in itself. We must let go of the idea that all cultural practices can or should be converted to politically productive labor. Otherwise, we are no better than ratings companies like Arbitron.

CONCLUSION

For all of cultural studies' inversions and critiques of traditional aesthetics, we have basically carried forward Matthew Arnold's "sweetness and light" program, where culture would be used to transform the philistine masses, replacing Arnold's hope for personal redemption with our hope that culture will lead the way to social transformation. For cultural studies, the burden of culture is to matter. "If it isn't political, then I don't give a damn!" Stuart Hall's polemic has become a kind of manifesto for the field. Not only *is* culture political, it *should be* political.

What if – for just a moment – we imagined that the decades-long project of validation of audiences and ordinary culture could be taken for granted? Perhaps they cannot; perhaps today there is a backlash against cultural studies' valorization of ordinary culture. But let's continue along this hypothetical line of reasoning for a moment. What if cultural studies actually "won" the "culture wars"? What would we do if we didn't have to demonstrate that cultural practices, texts, and audiences mattered politically? The quick answer, of course, is that we still have to deal with the question of *how* they matter, how they work. Many of the recent trends in the field, such as cultural policy studies, performativity as a theory of gender, the turn to Deleuze and Guattari, postcolonial theory, and so forth are precisely concerned with developing an account of the mechanics or physics of power via the analysis of culture. Cultural studies aims to explain, rather than explain away, the intrication of culture and power. But if you'll allow me a can of paint and an inordinately large brush, I believe these approaches still carry around a pink elephant they don't want to talk about: the normative assumption that culture should matter politically.

Should culture matter politically? To say that it does matter in our lived world seems utterly uncontroversial. But as I argued above, this instrumental theory of culture leaves something to be desired as a political and aesthetic program. In transforming all culture into political action, we are essentially putting our subjects to work. In our scholarship, at least, they perform the work of politics by other means. But I know of very few people who want to live in a world where their every action is considered instrumentally. This is not to say that such an analytic approach inaccurately describes the world as it is, only that it provokes the question of what should be. To put it another way, if we really believe in articulation, then it cannot be taken for granted that culture does matter in every circumstance, and there may in fact be circumstances in which it doesn't matter.

The reasons for our prescriptive ambiguity are simple enough to understand: cultural studies is still very much caught up in the project of validation. We validate cultural texts and practices as meaningful – if they cannot be given a generous formalist reading (though many in fact can), at least we can point to their political relevance. If audience members aren't political activists or explicitly criticizing dominant power relations, they're also not simply passive and stupid: people negotiate the texts they're given and make sense of their worlds in complex and contradictory ways. But in the process (and to offer another giant generalization), cultural studies has developed a distaste for making judgments. Perhaps this is because we rightly distrust the kinds of judgments made by our aesthetician predecessors, who excluded most of humanity from the domain of culture, properly conceived. But a theory of articulation should tell us that judgment in and of itself is not a dirty word: even aesthetic judgment can be articulated in new ways that differ markedly from more traditional aesthetics. Of course, like any articulation, it's not simply a matter of saying that it can be done. It would require a great deal of work on our part – but it is also an important next step.

An interesting corollary to cultural studies' own brand of political sweetness and light is the concurrent deemphasis of another notion of culture that might be equally useful under some analytical circumstances: culture as debasement. Culture is not just about building up, increasing, improving, striving. Culture can also be about ritual destruction, desacralization, and general mayhem. I don't mean to suggest Bakhtin's carnival, which is largely a functionalist concept, but rather a sense of culture as meaningless, nondirected activity that nonetheless uses human energy, effort, and creativity. It is not a choice between one or the other, but rather a belief that culture goes both ways. As cultural practice builds up, so it destroys. This need not be conceived as a zero-sum game or a form of stasis (one step forward, one step back). But just because a cultural practice lacks cultural studies' own particular brand of political goodness, truth, and beauty, does not necessarily make it less worthy of existence or a less essential part of human life (though I will grant that it might be less significant for a given political analysis). To put it another way, a humane society would allow for meaningless, nondirected activity that nonetheless uses human energy, effort and creativity. The alternative is to put our subjects to work day in and day out, which leaves them to a rather dim social fate.

If we fail to consciously engage with more programmatic concerns, then for all our self-congratulation at creating politicized scholarship, we will have accomplished only a reactive politics, one that can intervene only after the terms of the debate have been set. For all our reflexivity, we will be accepting pre-given political programs formed by others who dare to ask difficult questions about the difference between what is and what should be. As a loosely coherent field of scholarship, cultural studies' strengths have historically lay in its contextualism and its ability to look beyond texts to practices, and in turn to look beyond practices to their social and political horizons. The next step is to begin redescribing those horizons. As Raymond Williams (1961) put it, "the moral decline of socialism" – and to this we could today add feminism, antiracism, queer politics, postcolonial thought, environmentalism, and other left movements – "is in exact relation to its series of compromises with older images of society and to its failure to sustain and clarify the sense of an alternative human order."

Today, when cultural studies writers want to get polemical about politics, more often than not they get pragmatic: "all this utopian dreaming is not strategic; we need a political pragmatics!" This has authorized countless cultural studies in the past. But I want to make the opposite move: we cannot get pragmatic without doing a little dreaming. If you don't believe in social transformation then we have little to discuss – and frankly I have no idea why you'd want to do cultural studies. But if you believe that societies have radically changed over the past few centuries or eons, perhaps you believe they can change again. If this be the case, then it is worthwhile to think about what kind of world we should want to live in. Perhaps we should want a world in which people are not only free of the burdens of oppression, but where they are free of the burden of culture as well. Imagine how much better life would be if cultural practices did not need to be mapped on a grid using a political compass. Perhaps a better world would include a way of life where all nonsleeping time is *not* work time, whether that work is for sustenance, trade, or politics. I have no doubt that in our current cultural and political world, culture is very much a means to an end; it is very much politics by other means. But it should not always be so.

NOTES

1 Many thanks to Carrie Rentschler for her help and suggestions on this essay.
2 Granted, Thompson would not necessarily have been satisfied had Williams made use of a Gramscian vocabulary (and *certainly* not if he had used an Althusserian or other poststructuralist vocabulary – see Thompson 1995) to describe cultural politics. However, that Williams didn't do so is an enabling condition of Thompson's critique.

REFERENCES

Anderson, Amanda. 1992. "Cryptonormativism and Double Gestures: The Politics of Post-Structuralism." *Cultural Critique* (Spring): 63–95.

Bennett, Tony. 1992. "Putting Policy Into Cultural Studies." In *Cultural Studies*, eds. Lawrence Grossberg, Cary Nelson, and Paula Treichler. New York: Routledge.

——. 1995. *The Birth of the Museum: History, Theory, Politics.* New York: Routledge.

——. 1997. *Culture: A Reformer's Science.* Thousand Oaks, CA: Sage.

Bertsch, Charlie. 1994. "Gramsci Rush: Limbaugh on the 'Culture War.'" *Bad Subjects no. 12* (March). Available online at http://eserver.org/bs/12/bertsch.html.

Budd, Mike, Robert M. Entman, and Clay Steinman. 1990. "The Affirmative Character of US Cultural Studies." *Critical Studies in Mass Communication* 7(2): 169–84.

Clarke, Gary. 1982. "Defending Ski-Jumpers: A Critique of Theories of Youth Sub-Cultures." Stencilled Occasional Paper no. 7, Centre for Contemporary Cultural Studies, University of Birmingham.

Czitrom, Daniel. 1995. Paper presented on the panel "Philosophical and Historical Critiques of Cultural Studies." Across Disciplines and Beyond Boundaries: Tracking American Cultural Studies, Urbana, IL, Nov. 1.

Durkheim, Emile. 1933. *The Division of Labor in Society,* tr. George Simpson. Glencoe, IL: The Free Press.

Fiske, John. 1989a. *Understanding Popular Culture.* Boston: Unwin Hyman.

——. 1989b. *Reading the Popular.* Boston: Unwin Hyman.

——. 1992. "Cultural Studies and the Culture of Everyday Life." In *Cultural Studies*, eds. Lawrence Grossberg, Cary Nelson, and Paula Treichler. New York: Routledge.

——. 1993. *Power Plays, Power Works.* New York: Verso.

Fraser, N. 1989. *Unruly Practices: Power, Gender and Discourse in Contemporary Social Theory.* Minneapolis: University of Minnesota Press.

Garnham, Nicholas. 1995. "Political Economy and Cultural Studies: Reconciliation or Divorce?" *Critical Studies in Mass Communication* 12(1): 62–71.

Gitlin, Todd. 1997. "The Anti-political Populism of Cultural Studies." In *Cultural Studies in Question,* eds. Marjorie Ferguson and Peter Golding. Thousand Oaks, CA: Sage.

Grossberg, Lawrence. 1992. *We Gotta Get Out of This Place: Popular Conservatism and Postmodern Politics.* New York: Routledge.

——. 1997. *Bringing It All Back Home: Essays on Cultural Studies.* Durham, NC: Duke University Press.

Hall, Stuart. 1977. "Re-Thinking the 'Base-and-Superstructure' Metaphor." In *Class, Hegemony, and Party,* ed. John Bloomfield. London: Lawrence and Wishart.

——. 1978. "Marxism and Culture." *Radical History Review* 18 (Fall): 5–14.

——. 1980. "Cultural Studies: Two Paradigms." *Media Culture and Society* 2: 57–72.

——. 1981. "Notes on Deconstructing the Popular." In *People's History and Socialist Theory,* ed. Ralph Samuel. Boston: Routledge and Kegan Paul.

——. 1986. "On Postmodernism and Articulation." *Journal of Communication Inquiry* 10(2): 45–60.

——. 1988a. "The Toad in the Garden: Thatcherism Among the Theorists." In *Marxism and the Interpretation of Culture,* eds. Cary Nelson and Lawrence Grossberg. Urbana: University of Illinois Press.

——. 1988b. *The Hard Road to Renewal: Thatcherism and the Crisis of the Left.* New York: Verso.

—— and Tony Jefferson, eds. 1976. *Resistance Through Rituals: Youth Subcultures in Post-war Britain.* New York: Holmes & Meier.

——, Charles Critcher, Tony Jefferson, John Clarke, and Brian Robert. 1977. *Policing the Crisis.* New York and London: Macmillan.

Hebdige, Dick. 1979. *Subculture: The Meaning of Style.* London: Methuen.

Hoggart, Richard. 1957/1992. *The Uses of Literacy,* with a new intro. by Andrew Goodwin. New Brunswick, NJ: Transaction Publishers.

Hunter, Ian. 1988. *Culture and Government: The Emergence of Literary Education.* London: Macmillan.

Laclau, Ernesto. 1977. *Politics and Ideology in Marxist Theory: Capitalism: Fascism, Populism.* Atlantic Highlands, NJ: Humanities Press.

McChesney, Robert. 1996. "Is There Any Hope for Cultural Studies?" *Monthly Review* 47(1) (March).

McClure, Kirstie. 1992. "The Issue of Foundations: Scientized Politics, Political Science, and Feminist Critical Practice." In *Feminists Theorize the Political,* eds. Judith Butler and Joan W. Scott. New York: Routledge.

McGuigan, Jim. 1992. *Cultural Populism.* New York: Routledge.

McRobbie, Angela. 1991. *Feminism and Youth Culture: From Jackie to Just Seventeen.* New York and London: Macmillan.

Miller, Toby. 1998. *Technologies of Truth: Cultural Citizenship and the Popular Media.* Minneapolis: University of Minnesota Press.

Mills, C. Wright. 1959. *The Sociological Imagination.* New York: Oxford University Press.

Morris, Meaghan. 1989. *The Pirate's Fiancée: Feminism Reading Postmodernism.* New York: Verso.

——. 1990. "Banality in Cultural Studies." In *Logics of Television: Essays in Cultural Criticism,* ed. Patricia Mellencamp. Bloomington: Indiana University Press.

Nelson, Cary, Paula Treichler, and Lawrence Grossberg. 1992. "Cultural Studies: An Introduction." In *Cultural Studies,* eds. Grossberg, Nelson, and Treichler. New York: Routledge.

Schor, Juliet. 1991. *The Overworked American: The Unexpected Decline of Leisure.* New York: Basic Books.

Smythe, Dallas. 1994. *Counterclockwise: Perspectives on Communication,* ed. Thomas Guback. Boulder, CO: Westview Press.

Sterne, Jonathan. 2003. "Bureaumentality." In *Foucault and Cultural Studies: Governing the Present,* eds. Jack Bratich, Jeremy Packer, and Cameron McCarthy. Albany: SUNY Press.

Thompson, E. P. 1961. "The Long Revolution." *New Left Review* 9–10: 24–39.

——. 1964. *The Making of the English Working Class.* New York: Vintage Books.

——. 1995. *The Poverty of Theory: Or an Orrery of Errors.* London: Merlin.

Williams, Raymond. 1958. *Culture and Society 1780–1950.* New York: Harper and Row.

——. 1961. *The Long Revolution.* Westport, CN: Greenwood Press.

——. 1976. *Keywords: A Vocabulary of Culture and Society.* New York: Oxford University Press.

Williamson, Judith. 1985. "Consuming Passion." *New Socialist* (Feb.).

5

Cultural Studies and Questions of Pleasure and Value

DAVID SHUMWAY

This essay began as a response to the question, posed as the title of an MLA Convention session, "does cultural studies have bad taste?" In order to answer that question, I have to ask another: "why ask this question?" Perhaps the answer is obvious, but it is important to my argument to spell it out. We are asking this question because cultural studies as theory and practice seems to ignore, to reject, or, perhaps, to mishandle the very issues that since the rise of the New Criticism have seemed to be central to literary studies. It is the element of criticism known as judgment, central to aesthetic theory since Kant, which is apparently absent from cultural studies. As Simon Frith has argued, although popular culture is now the subject of much academic attention, "the aesthetics of the popular continues to be at best neglected and at worst dismissed" (1996: 11). Like the New Criticism, cultural studies has focused its efforts on interpretation, or close reading, of texts – a fact lamented by some practitioners more oriented toward the social sciences. It has not had much to say, however, about the quality or value of the objects it interprets. The question may imply that this lack of judgment results in poor judgment, the taking up of "bad" art. To decide this, of course, you would need to be able to answer persuasively questions of taste. In other words, you would have to offer something that heretofore has not existed, an aesthetics that can yield widespread agreement about critical judgments.

Now, to answer the original question in light of these considerations, we can't claim that cultural studies has bad taste since we can't agree on what bad taste is. What I think we can say is that cultural studies has an aversion to questions of taste. The aversion to such questions results from the desire to avoid reproducing bourgeois ideology. Raymond Williams has argued that the concept of taste emerged as a marker of bourgeois class affiliation in the same social transformation that produced both "literature" and "criticism" as we know them. "Literature" had previously been associated with "learning," the knowledge that was embodied in written works. Taste differs from learning in that it cannot be acquired by study. Taste is for Williams a name for the habits of the dominant class rendered as inherent qualities. As Williams describes their function, "taste" and its twin, "sensibility," served chiefly to help unify the bourgeoisie and "could be applied over a very wide range from public and private behaviour to (as Wordsworth complained) either wine or poetry" (1977: 48). Criticism developed together with literature as a means by which its distinction was promoted and defended. The emergence of the term "Criticism" reflects the increasing specialization of "literature" (ibid.). A new term in the seventeenth century, "criticism" shifted from the practice of commentary on learning to the "conscious exercise of 'taste,' 'sensibility,' and 'discrimination.'" In the nineteenth, it becomes "the only way of validating [a] specialized and selective category. It was at once a *discrimination* of the authentic 'great' or 'major' works, with a consequent grading of 'minor' works and an effective exclusion of 'bad' or 'negligible' works, and a practical realization and communication of the 'major' values" (1977: 49–51).

Pierre Bourdieu has shown in great detail how taste functions in the ways Williams's argument says it does. In *Distinction*, Bourdieu shows that taste in France during the 1960s is more strongly correlated with class than with any other factor. But Bourdieu also recognizes that taste is not a simple extension of bourgeois hegemony. Not only do other classes have their own tastes, but within the dominant, the role of taste is also related in complex ways to other sources of value. In order to represent such relations, Bourdieu makes use of the term "symbolic capital": "economic or political capital that is disavowed, misrecognized and thereby recognized, hence legitimate, a 'credit' which, under certain conditions, and always in the long run, guarantees 'economic' profits" (1993: 75). Symbolic capital is thus fungible prestige or authority, the fungibility of which depends upon its being not recognized as such. One species of symbolic capital is "cultural capital," which is best understood as a sort of savoir-faire. Cultural capital is not disciplinary or scholarly knowledge (*connaissance*), but a familiarity that entails the ability to understand cultural products. "A work of art has meaning and interest only for someone who possesses the cultural competence, that is, the code, into which it is encoded." (1984: 2). To acquire cultural capital is to learn the various codes that permit art to be read and judged. Since such codes are modes of perception, they are most effectively taught in the household, where early access permits the denial of the existence of a code in favor of natural taste or genius. Taste, it turns out, is learned, but, like language, it is easily learned at a particular age and as part of one's environment.

Given what both Williams and Bourdieu show about the social function of discrimination and the distinctions it produces, it is not surprising that cultural studies would avoid engaging in arguments about taste. These two theorists, however, point cultural studies in different directions. For Bourdieu, culture is nothing more than a field of distinctions. The content of culture is irrelevant. Williams's model, which may seem less materialist than Bourdieu's, does take into account these various fields of which literature has been a part. For Williams, culture does more than mark status: it is the medium of social reproduction. What is represented in the texts of culture in part explains and in part represents the society at any historical moment.

If Williams is right, then cultural studies must do more than simply analyze the way culture functions. If the democratic values that drive cultural studies are to be reproduced, then the field must promote texts that embody such values. In the past, the only judgments cultural studies typically has offered have concerned political effects; specifically, whether the text is affirmative or subversive of hegemony. What is needed is a much broader range of judgments. But on what grounds can we make these judgments? Does cultural studies need an aesthetics? Has the philosophical project of aesthetics historically served to ground the actual practice of critical judgment? As Eagleton (1990) argues, the rise of aesthetics is coincident with the rise of the bourgeoisie; but as he also notes, this alone should not stigmatize the project. Williams shows that the idea of taste has been disparaged by generations of British critics starting with Wordsworth. The aesthetic in the late Victorian period came to be associated with a particular attitude toward art, rather than with the project of grounding judgments of it. The problem rather is that aesthetics has hit a dead end. As Barbara Herrnstein Smith (1988) has convincingly argued, there are no grounds for believing that we can arrive at a universal foundation for judgments of taste. A theory of artistic value can only be predicated on particular cultural assumptions. The pleasure we take in texts certainly can be interpreted in a general way on the basis of human constants, but such constants cannot account for the fact that people even in the same society predictably disagree about art, much less explain cultural and historical differences.

So far, cultural studies has been preoccupied by explaining such differences and it has often done this impressively. It has exponentially increased our knowledge of the historical and cultural relativity of taste. Cultural studies cannot abandon this knowledge, but it needs to move beyond it. The realm of culture is of limited interest as an objective entity. Cultural productions derive their meaning from the judgments of pleasure and value that audiences make of them. To refuse to make such judgments is to remove oneself from the domain of culture and to place oneself in the domain of science. Rather than return to aesthetics, cultural studies must ask culturally specific questions of pleasure and value, and it must make them as central to its project as questions of subversion and affirmation have been.

The theme of pleasure is, of course, a common one in recent theoretical writing. What its use often amounts to in cultural studies is the proclamation of an identity. While I don't wish to reject that usage, I think we need to assert more generally that pleasure is a significant element of the experience of art. In a sense, my move here is to try to embrace the wide application of "taste" that Wordsworth rejected. Of course, in doing so I'm also appealing to the more literal meaning of "taste" as a particular kind of sense experience. To put it perhaps too crudely, cultural studies should be interested not in art that is in good taste, but in art that tastes (or looks or feels or smells or sounds) good. My hypothesis is that if you want to understand the longevity of art, its entertainment value is among the most important factors. So, if we want to know why people have read Homer and Shakespeare over the years, the place to start is with the guess that their works have tended to yield pleasurable experiences. These experiences certainly differ depending on the context of reception. As Lawrence Levine showed, Shakespeare could yield different pleasures for nineteenth-century American audiences of different classes.

In aesthetic terms, what I am arguing here is that Kant's distinction between the "agreeable" and the "beautiful" is untenable. Here is how Kant makes the distinction:

> As regards the *agreeable* everyone acknowledges that his judgment, which he bases on private feeling and by which he says that he likes some object, is by the same token confined to his own person. Hence, if he says that canary wine is agreeable he is quite content if someone else corrects his terms and reminds him to say instead: It is agreeable to *me*. . . . It is quite different (exactly the other way around) with the beautiful. It would be ridiculous if someone who prided himself on his taste tried to justify [it] by saying: This object (the building we are looking at, the garment that man is wearing, the concert we are listening to, the poem put up to be judged) is beautiful *for me*. For he must not call it *beautiful* if [he means] only [that] *he* likes it. (1987: 213)[1]

This distinction is usually regarded as the basis upon which art may be distinguished from other, less elevated sources of pleasure. Yet, readers of Kant have disagreed about the nature of the distinction. Is it essentially one of the subjective and contingent versus the objective and absolute? Or, is it mainly a matter of the sort of pleasure that each experience yields, brute, simple sensory pleasure – most often exemplified by sex – as opposed to refined, distanced, intellectual appreciation?[2] Or, finally, as Bernard Gendron has suggested, is it merely the distinction between that which can be argued about, and that which cannot be (2001: 9–10)? Gendron's conception has the effect of relativizing the distinction, thus defeating the chief purpose for which it has been typically invoked. He notes that we now may regard some objects as worthy of argument that were not so regarded in Kant's time – for example, the pleasures of wine and food. Such pleasures are usually held to be precisely what the idea of the aesthetic is meant to exclude. Yet, Gendron's observation that we do argue about such tastes is accurate. Food and wine critics and their readers don't believe that such criticism merely expresses private preferences. Indeed, the language of wine criticism today is arguably more precise and makes a stronger case for intersubjective validity than does most literary criticism. While literary scholars have tended to regard poetics, the descriptive analysis of literary works, as a dead end, wine writers make use of a shared vocabulary that describes the tastes and aromas of a wine in terms of those associated with other familiar objects: citrus, pear, tar, chocolate, herbs, etc. Moreover, the common use of numerical ratings claims a precision in judgment seldom claimed by literary critics in or out of the academy. No one, of course, believes that these ratings are objective, but a great many people find them to have enough validity to be basis for their own decisions about what wine to purchase. Is there a literary critic who commands anything like the authority of wine critic Robert Parker? His *Wine Advocate* often strikes fear in the hearts of wine producers from Bordeaux to the Napa Valley.[3]

Another argument that might distinguish "base" sensual pleasures from those "higher" mental ones is that the latter require training while the former do not. We are all born with the capacity for the sensual pleasure, but in order to aesthetically appreciate *Beowulf* one must not only learn to read, but learn to read a dead language and appreciate its distinctive qualities. But tastes for food, wine, and even sex are not innate. While our senses equip each of us to experience these pleasures, they do not guarantee we will actually experience a particular thing as pleasure. Consider the typical American's response to thought of eating such Chinese delicacies as sea slug or the typical East Asian reaction to the idea of consuming the congealed spoiled milk known as cheese. Americans drink much less wine than the French or Italians because Americans are much less likely to learn to drink it at home. Universities in the United States often offer wine-tasting courses, and the international advocacy group Slow Food has developed a curriculum for use in primary schools to teach children an appreciation for the traditional foods threatened by American fast-food's expansion. While the West has largely lacked a tradition of *ars erotica*, other cultures have long regarded sexual pleasure as something worthy of cultivation. All pleasures are learned, and all may be increased by further learning.

Since neither objectivity nor susceptibility to reasoned argument seem to explain the distinction between the agreeable and beautiful that founds aesthetics, the explanation must be located in the desire to distinguish among pleasures. The way in which the idea of the aesthetic is most often used is to maintain that pleasure in beauty is fundamentally different from the pleasures of the senses, or the "lower" pleasures. If it might be conceded that food and wine could perhaps reach the level of art, most would argue that there remain sensuous pleasures that could not be so elevated. Thus, pornography might seem to be the utter antithesis of the aesthetic. Unlike a great meal or an exceptional bottle of wine, the pornographic work is a representation. It is in this sense more like the aesthetic object than other, literally consumable sources of immediate pleasure. But, unlike those objects considered aesthetic, the pornographic work is designed to elicit immediate sexual stimulation. If it distances the audience in any way, its success as pornography is inhibited. Yet, pornography often comes in the guise of some kind of aesthetic form: pornographic movies have plots; the pictures in skin magazines borrow all manner of convention from the fine art of photography; Anaïs Nin's stories in *Delta of Venus* make use of figurative language typical of highly valued poetry and prose.

Clearly, pornography is regarded as the lowest form of pleasure because the specific pleasure it yields is regarded as evil, either because sexual pleasure itself is evil or because vicarious sexual pleasure is. The desire to segregate some pleasures from others is a basic motive for the maintenance of the distinction between the agreeable and beautiful. I propose that we drop the overt or covert moral judgment that renders those pleasures we call aesthetic better than other pleasures. Accepting this proposal does not entail the reductionism that it may seem to at first. That all pleasures are valuable does not mean that all pleasures are the same. That one's liking for Shelley and one's liking for a particular sexual position do not have different epistemological foundations doesn't mean that we can't distinguish between the two.

So far, I've been arguing that Kant illegitimately created a special faculty for the appreciation of the beautiful as distinguished from the merely agreeable. By dismissing this distinction, I may seem to be devaluing art by rendering it merely pleasurable. But as Philip Sidney pointed out (in his "Apology for Poetry") several centuries before Kant, poetry instructs and delights. The instructive value of art corresponds to a third form of liking discussed by Kant, the "good." This term can be glossed as referring to an object's moral value, its positive or useful effects. Kant holds that the good and the agreeable have interestedness in common, while the beautiful is disinterested. "We call *agreeable* what GRATIFIES us, *beautiful* what we just LIKE, *good* what we ESTEEM or *endorse*" (1987: 210). Kant's distinctions have been used to justify the notion of art for art's sake, which holds that true art is by definition what we "just LIKE," and not something that we like because of its moral, political, or other useful content. Thus, aesthetic theory in the twentieth century could be said to be founded on the opposition of instruction and pleasure. In finding an aesthetic suitable to its own ends, cultural studies would do well to go back to Sidney and reject this opposition. The field's interest in works with "subversive" power, and its focus on determining the precise political message of the texts it reads, would suggest that it takes for granted that art instructs.

Of course, there are theoretical objections to the idea that works of art "instruct," a conception that may be seen as a version of the theory that such works function in culture by causing or influencing behavior. While this theory is opposed by those who would emphasize the agency of the audience in the reception of the work, cultural studies has not been able to reject it. Indeed, it would be hard to imagine a theory of the political import of art that did not accord works some kind of influence. Sometimes this influence is said to function at a less than conscious level: for example, interpellating the subject rather than instructing the rational mind. Even those commodities that audiences have been able to appropriate for their own oppositional ends must be assumed to have a primary and contradictory influence that the empowered audience is refusing. The Birmingham School emphasis on audience usage does, of course, diminish the importance of the objects used, yet it does not necessarily render them noninstructive. The punks whom Dick Hebdige argues appropriated the detritus of postindustrial capitalism made such objects teach new lessons. "Instruction," in the broad sense I'm using the term, is entailed in most conceptions of works of art and representation found in cultural studies. To say that a work instructs is not to say anything about what is learned, so the term should not be understood to imply a theory that denies agency to audiences.

Historically, however, when works of art were explicitly judged, it was most often on their moral or political value, and not on their pure formal beauty or their success as entertainment. It is only in the twentieth century that art for art's sake has become widely accepted. And even in this century, it is hard to argue that purely formal criteria in fact account for the dominant cultural judgments. As Jonathan Arac has argued, "the main line of academic and public discussion of literature in the English-speaking world since the nineteenth century has not been primarily or fundamentally aesthetic" (1999: 769). Consider the New Criticism. While this movement seemed to make aesthetic judgment an accepted part of academic literary study for the first time, the practice that followed from the triumph of New Critical theory was not mainly devoted either to purely formal analysis or to aesthetic judgment. It was, in fact, typically devoted to interpretation of texts that were already regarded as having formal excellence, and such inter-pretation tended to emphasize the moral value of the work being read. Such reading amounted to an implicit judgment of the work's moral worth. Arac believes that twentieth-century American critics perpetuated a Victorian concep-tion, the "moral aesthetic," deriving from Matthew Arnold but found even in Walter Pater, that "baldly mixes realms to which Kant had devoted separate critiques. For the main traditions of philosophical aesthetics, a moral aesthetic is no aesthetic at all..." Arac goes on to quote Frith, who argues that for pop music fans "aesthetic and ethical judgments are tied together: not to like a record is not just a matter of taste; it is also a matter of morality" (1999: 774–5).[4] In other words, the most typical practice of criticism – whether by fans, journalists, or academics – seems to follow Sidney or Arnold rather than Kant, though without necessarily invoking the particular Christian or humanist morality they assumed.

Academic New Criticism seldom engaged in explicit aesthetic discrimination. In this respect, the New Criticism perpetuated the status quo in literary studies, for the philologists and literary historians who had previously dominated the discipline also dealt with literature that others had judged to be great. English professors' arguments didn't canonize Chaucer, Spenser, Shakespeare, and Milton, and their arguments didn't canonize Eliot, James, or Melville either. However, this is not to say that professors had no role in the construction and perpetuation of the canon. It is rather to say that that role was not mainly one of explicit aesthetic judgment. Rather, the major professorial influence on the canon was the attention paid to certain works.[5] Texts that critics repeatedly interpreted in new ways – each scholarly article depended on a new interpretation – accrued value simply by being frequently and rewardingly discussed. The second of those terms is crucial. The first point is simply a variant of Smith's maxim that "Nothing endures like endurance" (1988: 50). The second one is meant to allow that texts that are repeatedly reinterpreted have qualities that enable such performances. Some of those qualities are formal: for example, complexity. Some of them are moral or political; the texts either raise important issues of moral or political conflict, or they effectively support a particular position in such a conflict. These qualities are relative; they depend on the context of reception to be realized. But they are also intrinsic in the sense that they exist in the texts and not merely in the minds of critics.

It is perhaps obvious where I am going with this historical excursus. Cultural studies has already begun to create its own canon by virtue of the attention it has paid to particular objects. Whether many of these choices will long endure is not a question that interests me. What does concern me is the typical reaction with cultural studies to the realization of this more or less inadvertent canon formation. The resistance to judgment within cultural studies is so strong that any selection is immediately treated as an ideological symptom. I want to argue that cultural studies must accept the inevitability of selection. There is too much produced for all of it to be noticed, and, for reasons I have just suggested, random notice is not likely to engage readers or critics. My argument is that cultural studies needs to be more conscious of the project of canon construction, engaging in ethical-aesthetic criticism on its own terms.

The reality of inadvertent canonization should lead us to wonder about the long-term effects of cultural studies' tendency toward symptomatic readings. It might be argued that practitioners of cultural studies find texts that are surreptitiously infected by pernicious ideology more interesting and attractive than those which seem to explicitly endorse or represent the political and moral values on which cultural studies is founded. Some clearly take Marx's call for a "ruthless criticism of all that exists" to mean that we shouldn't find anything good under capitalism – except that which is subversive of capitalism. Hence, the one value cultural studies has sought and found is "opposition," which seems to be so common that it is hard to understand how the status quo could stand up in the face of it. More curiously still, such subversion is most often found in the most seemingly mundane and apolitical works of mass culture. Explicitly left-wing artists have seldom been the focus of cultural studies.

But why shouldn't cultural studies, as a discipline committed to the idea that knowledge is inherently political, champion works that openly express its democratic values? If art instructs and delights, then what a work instructs is always a relevant concern. Perhaps cultural studies has failed to champion work on this basis because its practitioners are as much put off by didacticism as were the New Critics. In the interpretation of the latter, moral lessons had to emerge from art organically, out of "tensions" and qualified by "irony." Explicit teaching was a flaw that usually condemned the work to a status below that of art. One would think that cultural studies would not share this criterion, but its persistence may explain the reluctance of the movement to embrace explicitly political art. Consider, for example, the treatment (or lack of it) of filmmaker John Sayles. Sayles's films, from *The Return of the Secaucus Seven* (1980) to *Sunshine State* (2001), have consistently expressed progressive political positions on issues that cover virtually the entire range of concerns addressed by cultural studies: race, gender and sexuality, class, and disability. Yet a search of the usual databases finds very little scholarly writing devoted to Sayles. Of the 10 or so articles and book chapters, only a few are recognizably related to cultural studies. Given this fact, it is a bit risky to use this essay to try to understand the field's response to the filmmaker. Nevertheless, I believe we can find some clues there.

Sayles's most traditionally left-wing film, *Matewan* (1987), was trashed for failures of historical authenticity and "truth status" in *Radical History Review*, while an article in *Appalachian Journal* made virtually the opposite argument in praising the film (Brier 1988; J. Williams 1988). The film tells part of the story of the Stone Mountain Coal War, which took place in West Virginia in the spring 1920, with a focus on the "Matewan massacre." In this incident, union workers and their allies, including local lawmen, won a shoot-out with Baldwin-Felts agents hired by the mine owners. The film's story ends with this victory, which helped to spur a brief period of union militancy but which also ended in defeat at the Battle of Blair Mountain in August 1921. Sayles tells the story from the miners' point of view, and he chooses to emphasize the value and valor of their struggle, and to play down its unsuccessful outcome. One of the film's chief concerns is the multiracial and multiethnic make-up of the union. It thus addresses explicitly the way in which the ruling class used race and ethnicity as wedges that would divide workers, a tactic that temporarily failed in the face of union solidarity. Why has cultural studies ignored this film that advances the very sort of race and class analysis the field itself conducts?

The similar fate met by Sayles's later film *Lone Star* (1994) is even more perplexing. The old-left class politics at the center of *Matewan* have never been the central concern of cultural studies in the US, but *Lone Star* is mainly a film about identity politics. One would have thought that cultural studies would have embraced it, since it might be argued that the film itself is a work of cultural studies. As Rosa Linda Fregoso observes, "*Lone Star* reads like an application of Chicana/o borderlands theory" (1999: 139). Yet only two articles have appeared, neither of them in locations one might regard as central to cultural studies (Fregoso, Limón). Both of these articles agree that the film deals explicitly and progressively with race and class issues, although they disagree about whether its gender politics are progressive. For my purposes, this disagreement is less important than the fact that some discussion of the film is taking place. But why is it so little and so marginal?

I can't provide the definitive answers to these questions, but several alternatives come to mind. One is that Sayles's films fail to attract the attention of those in cultural studies because of their traditional forms. *Matewan* takes its basic structure from Westerns such as *Shane* and *High Noon*, while *Lone Star* also borrows from the Western but is fundamentally a murder mystery. *Matewan*'s narrative is chronological and uncomplicated, while *Lone Star*'s story is Faulknerian in its complexity, but both films end with what can easily be read as closure. Since cultural studies has typically been drawn to formal innovation, Sayles's explicitly progressive politics may not be enough to overcome this bias. If so, cultural studies would seem to be held hostage to an aesthetic invented by those it otherwise regards as its enemies. It was an article of faith among the proponents of High Modernism that progressive politics and formal innovation must go hand in hand. Thus, critics in the *Partisan Review* circle believed that T. S. Eliot was a revolutionary, but naturalists like Theodore Dreiser or the proletarian writers were not, whatever their stated political positions.

The critical debates of the 1930s also suggest another explanation for the failure of Sayles's films to capture the imagination of cultural studies. My conversations with a number of people in the field revealed dislike for *Lone Star* precisely because it was so explicit. Clearly, reviewers in the popular press do often respond this way to Sayles. For example, a reviewer for the *Village Voice* (an organ one might expect to be friendly to Sayles's politics) found *Matewan* to be a "'union snooze,' full of ideological pieties, improbable heroes and 'hissable villains.'" Another review called it a "dime-store morality play." The *Washington Post* found it incredible that the good guys could be so good and the bad guys so bad (quoted in J. Williams 1988: 346). If practitioners of cultural studies share theses responses, it would suggest the lingering power of the tastes formed by modernism and art for art's sake according to which didacticism is the worst sin. If so, it would be ironic that, while the right accuses cultural studies of political correctness – that is to say, a very crude form of didacticism – cultural studies lacks the courage of its own convictions and behaves much as the right does. If either formal conservatism or didacticism were indeed behind cultural studies' response to Sayles, it would reveal the degree to which questions of pleasure can trump questions of instruction even in an audience apparently devoted to politics and explicitly opposed to taste.

However, the negative response to Sayles may not be to his didacticism *per se*, but rather to what might be called his "pedagogy." Instead of objecting to the explicitness of the film's politics, the objection would be rather to the epistemological implications of the way in which the message is presented. It could be argued that any instruction carries with it assumptions about the character of knowledge itself. Those assumptions can range from the rigid absolutism entailed in much theology to the mindless relativism typical of college sophomores. Since cultural studies is informed by theories that tend more toward relativism than absolutism, we might guess that it would favor works that teach questions rather than answers. To some extent, this corresponds to the field's interest in "subversive" or "oppositional" works, which need not propose anything positive. The issue may again be one of pleasure rather than theory. A work that is explicit in its politics may seem to leave nothing for the audience to figure out, thus frustrating the desire to actively read the work. I don't agree that this charge is accurate of Sayles's films, but it could be plausibly made of *Matewan* and *Lone Star*.

Didacticism or rigid pedagogy cannot account for all of the omissions that have characterized the work of cultural studies. Whole fields of artistic production have been ignored. Indeed, with the partial exceptions of literature and the visual arts, cultural studies has excluded most of the traditional arts. There is little analysis of classical music, dance, or theater. This suggests that cultural studies has been too willing to accept the categorical distinction between high and low culture that John Frow has shown to have become untenable by the late twentieth century (1995: 23–6). As Frow notes, the privileging of the "low" does not solve this problem, but merely reverses "the distribution of value between the two poles" (1995: 27). Instead of restricting itself to popular or mass culture, cultural studies should be about reading cultural production in general, not only to criticize the ideology of the dominant, but also to endorse and explicate works that themselves challenge that ideology.

As an example, consider playwright Robert Myers, whose work represents a useful point of comparison with Sayles's films. Myers's plays might be described as archival, in that they incorporate not just the facts of historical events, but the very language of historical documents. Like many of Sayles's films, these plays address themselves explicitly to political questions. Unlike Sayles's films, they do so without preaching – or least without seeming to preach – since the meaning of the work must be discovered by the audience in the pieces of archive the playwright gives us. Myers's first produced work, *Atwater: Fixin' to Die*, tells the story of Republican political consultant Lee Atwater, relying mainly on Atwater's own words. The play offers so little overt judgment of its protagonist that it was as popular with Atwater supporters in South Carolina as it was with his detractors in New York. The very genre of the play seems to depend on the viewer's perspective. Atwater's early death from a brain tumor is a tragedy to those who revere him, but poetic justice to his opponents, who would see the play as a satire. Atwater's contradictions make him an interesting character to audiences regardless of their politics. The brain behind the notoriously racist "Willie Horton" attack ad against Michael Dukakis in the 1988 presidential campaign, Atwater was a devoted fan and amateur performer of blues and soul music. This devotion is unlikely to redeem Atwater in the minds of those victimized by his politics, and it raises the important issue of the difference between personal affection (or prejudice) and institutionalized racism. The lessons this play teaches may be too subtle to reach everyone, but they may be more intellectually satisfying as a result.

If the playwright's politics are ambiguous in *Atwater*, the title of *Dead of Night: The Execution of Fred Hampton* makes Myers's position in that work as plain as day. Here Myers used the FBI's own files, obtained under the Freedom of Information Act, that show the Bureau to have planned the Chicago Black Panther leader's murder in 1969. But if that is the most striking historical interpretation that the play offers, it is not its dramatic focus. The central character is neither Hampton nor one of his government antagonists, but William O'Neal, the FBI informer who infiltrated the Panthers and helped the feds to arrange the attack. O'Neal told the bureau of a weapons cache at an apartment used by the Panthers, and that provided a pretext for the raid in which Hampton was shot. Events are presented within the frame of the last two hours of O'Neal's life, immediately before he commits suicide by running into traffic on an expressway. This device succeeds on a number of levels. As a structural element, it connects the worlds of the Panthers and the police, so that we experience the events from both perspectives. In terms of dramatic impact, O'Neal provides a complex point of identification for the audience. We experience his tortured responses to the events, making them emotionally powerful. It might be said that O'Neal's personal experience is a distraction from the political facts, but if so it is a strategic distraction. Because the facts are so clear, we do not need to have them as our constant focus. By fixing our attention on O'Neal, Myers allows the historical truth to emerge out the events to which the character was witness, thus avoiding the appearance that the playwright is preaching.

In the aesthetic theory I have been developing here, a work of art that fails to delight – that is, to provide pleasure – fails as art. Thus, a purely didactic work – one we might be inclined to label "propaganda" – might have value for the lessons it teaches, but not as art. Conversely, a work of art that delights but does not instruct is trivial. Wallpaper is the proverbial example. A work that gives pleasure, but gives bad instruction, qualifies as flawed or even pernicious art. Why try to distinguish propaganda from other forms when we know that all art instructs? I want to argue that propaganda usually fails to achieve the status of art because in it instruction overwhelms pleasure, and/or because of the absolutist character of the instruction. Propaganda has its place, of course, but a political understanding of art needs to be able to insist that art is more than simply propaganda dressed up to go out. Such insistence does not deny the political character of art, but rather specifies the way in which art is political. I would argue that neither Sayles nor Myers are propagandists despite the explicitly political character of their work. Their work teaches us history – new interpretations of past events – and implicitly advocates a politics for the present. Their work also provides the pleasure of well-executed and innovative narrative and dramatic form. Form in this sense is not sugar coating for the politics, but a way to embody the abstraction of political theory in the details of everyday life. Such embodiment must qualify and complicate the politics, but that is what makes the teaching of art different from the teaching of the party platform. Myers may do this more successfully than Sayles, whose films may be less pleasurable because they are leave less to the viewer's judgment.

I've mentioned the films of John Sayles and the plays of Robert Myers as examples of the kind of politically invested art that cultural studies has neglected. Both artists provide pleasure and both help us to better understand the past and its relation to the present. Or at least that is my argument. I don't expect everyone in cultural studies to agree with my judgments of Sayles and Myers. Thus, while it may seem I am assuming that we in cultural studies can agree on which artists are the ones all of us should endorse, I am in fact arguing that we in cultural studies need to discuss our many differences on this question. What I hope is that when these discussions occur, they will not boil down to whether the artist's politics are "correct," or to the artist's gender, race, class, or sexuality.[6] Both are relevant concerns, but they should not be the only concerns. Art that is politically flawed may still be politically valuable. Correcting the unrepresentative character of the canon is itself a political necessity, but it is also politically limited. We in cultural studies should be arguing more about what works we think are valuable and less about what pernicious effects other works may have.

NOTES

1 I use the standard pagination for the Kant corpus.
2 Smith's critique of Kant treats the distinction mainly as a matter of the subjective and objective, but my sense is that objectivity has not been the main issue in the typical application of the distinction since the mid-twentieth century.
3 For an account of Parker's influence, see Langewiesche 2000.
4 Arac attributes the phrase "moral aesthetic" to Buckley (see e.g. his 1969). The quotation is from Frith 1996: 72.
5 On the role of academics in the formation of the American canon, see Shumway 1994.
6 I am using "correct" here in the sense invoked on the left prior to the right's "political correctness" smear campaign of the early 1990s. The earlier meaning identified a tendency, probably derived from the pretensions to science of some Marxists, to measure all discourse by its degree of approximation to a specific political line. This has some validity perhaps in dealing with theory or critique, but it cannot allow for the messiness of art.

REFERENCES

Arac, Jonathan. 1999. "Why Does No One Care about the Aesthetic Value of Huckleberry Finn?" *New Literary History* 30(4): 769–84.

Bourdieu, Pierre. 1984. *Distinction: A Social Critique of the Judgment of Taste*, tr. Richard Nice. Cambridge, MA: Harvard University Press.

——. 1993. *The Field of Cultural Production: Essays on Art and Literature*, ed. Randal Johnson. New York: Columbia University Press.

Brier, Stephen. 1988. "A History Film Without Much History." *Radical History Review* 41: 120–8.

Buckley, Jerome Hamilton. 1969. *The Victorian Temper: A Study in Literary Culture*. Cambridge, MA: Harvard University Press.

Eagleton, Terry. 1990. *The Ideology of the Aesthetic*. Oxford: Blackwell.

Fregoso, Rosa Linda. 1999. "Imagining Multiculturalism: Race and Sexuality on the Tejas Borderlands." *Review of Education, Pedagogy, and Cultural Studies* 21(2): 133–48.

Frith, Simon. 1996. *Performing Rites: On the Value of Popular Music*. Cambridge, MA: Harvard University Press.

Frow, John. 1995. *Cultural Studies and Cultural Value*. Oxford: Oxford University Press.

Gendron, Bernard. 2001. "Pop Aesthetics: The Very Idea." In *The Aesthetics of Popular Art*, ed. Jostein Gripsrud. Kristiansand, Norway: Nordic Academic Press.

Hebdige, Dick. 1979. *Subculture: The Meaning of Style*. London: Methuen.

Kant, Immanuel. 1987. *Critique of Judgment*, tr. Werner S. Pluhar. Indianapolis, IN: Hackett.

Langewiesche, William. 2000. "The Million Dollar Nose." *The Atlantic*, Dec.: 42–70.

Levine, Lawrence W. 1988. *Highbrow/Lowbrow: The Emergence of Cultural Hierarchy in America*. Cambridge, MA: Harvard University Press.

Limón, José E. 1997. "Tex-Sex-Mex: American Identities, Lone Stars, and the Politics of Racialized Sexuality." *American Literary History* 9(3): 229–45.

Myers, Robert. 1997. *Atwater: Fixin' to Die*. Dir. by George Furth. MCC Theater, New York.

——. 1999. *Dead of Night: The Execution of Fred Hampton*. Dir. by Jonathan Wilson. Pegasus Players Theatre, Chicago.

Sayles, John, dir. and writer. 1987. *Matewan*. Cinecom Pictures.

——. 1996. *Lone Star*. Castle Rock Entertainment, Columbia Pictures.

Shumway, David R. 1994. *Creating American Civilization: A Genealogy of American Literature as an Academic Discipline*. Minneapolis: University of Minnesota Press, 1994.

Sidney, Philip. 1952. "An Apology for Poetry." In *Criticism: The Major Texts*, ed. Walter Jackson Bate. New York: Harcourt.

Smith, Barbara Herrnstein. 1988. *Contingencies of Value: Alternative Perspectives for Critical Theory*. Cambridge, MA: Harvard University Press.

Williams, John Alexander. 1988. "John Sayles Plays the Preacher." *Appalachian Journal* 15: 344–52.

Williams, Raymond. 1977. *Marxism and Literature*. Oxford: Oxford University Press.

6

"I Give it a 94. It's Got a Good Beat and You Can Dance to It": Valuing Popular Music

DAVID SANJEK

WHERE THE ACTION ISN'T

At the end of the year 2000, statistical reports of popular music sales gave investors in the entertainment industry reason to rejoice. Sales of CDs rose 4 percent over the previous year, from 754.8 million to 785.1 million units (Christman 2001). However, this lively level of domestic consumption led to little applause in the corporate boardroom. The further one looked, the more fissures appeared in the public's fascination with popular music. Even though 2000 was the fourth year of sales growth since the dramatic slump of the mid-1990s, the rate of increase in the consumption of recorded music has been on a downward spiral ever since 1997. Whereas the acquisition of CDs increased a whopping 9.1 percent between 1997 and 1998, it dipped to a growth of only 5.9 percent between 1998 and 1999. Furthermore, the public's interest in configurations other than the CD was particularly weak. The sale of singles declined a precipitous 36.6 percent. Cassettes experienced a comparably significant loss of 26.6 percent from 105.1 million units the year before to 77.2 million. Purchase of deep catalog – albums that have been available for three years or more – accounted for 23.8 percent of all album sales, yet that was virtually 3 percent below the figures for 1997 (Christman 2001).

These statistics challenge the widely held assumption that the entertainment business is an impregnable industrial monolith. Indeed, dedication to a particular artist or group appears nowadays to be as transient as the typical adolescent infatuation. The public no longer appears to take an interest in performers over the long term. Whereas in years past a debut album rarely reached the No. 1 position on the US *Billboard* charts, it has become a commonplace occurrence. In 1997, three of the top-selling releases of the year – the Spice Girls, Jewel, and Puff Daddy – were first-time records (Strauss 1998). Six years later, only Puff Daddy/P. Diddy retains any hold on the public consciousness, more for his appearances in court, on the society pages, or in the New York City Marathon than as a performer or producer. Loyalty to artists has been replaced by a more or less overnight obsession with a particular song or a sound. In the process, the record industry's willingness to invest in the development of a career is being redefined: the financial return on a label's dedication to an act must be immediate, not incremental. That does not mean, however, that the number of recordings being released has diminished. In the 1960s, an average of 45 albums appeared each week, whereas the current figure is 710. The vast majority of them fail to register on the public's radar. A study indicates that 80 percent of the customers at US record stores make their choices from only 25 percent of the available material (Strauss 1998). Patterns of consumption on-line are more diverse, ranging across a wider number of genres and incorporating a larger number of performers. Nonetheless, one can only imagine how many artists – good, bad, and indifferent – disappear without a trace, lost in an unstoppable surfeit of recorded music.

With these considerations in mind, let us turn to an examination of the US sales data for the most popular recording artists of the year 2000. They not only offer a striking illustration of the sudden emergence of new performers but also demonstrate an unusual division at the core of American society. Topping the bestseller list was the mainstream harmonizing of the boy band 'N Sync (10 million copies) and the incendiary ranting of the rapper Eminem (7.9 million copies). Appearing close behind was the female equivalent of 'N Sync, Britney Spears, followed by the Christian metal band Creed and two holdovers from the rock and roll pantheon of years past, Santana and the Beatles. The Fab Four were, in the view of many retailers, the only artists on this list that appealed to adults. Santana's success was due not so much to the group's established fans as to the attraction of the younger artists, like Rob Thomas of Matchbox 20, who appeared as guest performers with the group.

The coexistence of these disparate artists on the bestseller list certainly indicates a long-noted gap in taste between adults and their descendants. Most striking is how the presence of 'N Sync and Eminem at the top of the charts draws attention to an even more substantial chasm amongst the younger record-buying public. One cannot imagine that many fans of the boy band are also aficionados of the rapper; the evocation of heterosexual romance espoused by 'N Sync and numerous similar groups (Backstreet Boys, 98°, and LFO) has little in common with the taboo-breaking practices of Eminem. The differences are stark, and more than one commentator has compared this fissure in taste among the broad scope of American consumers of popular music to the ideological chasm revealed by the 2000 presidential election. The antithetical relationship between the romantic idealism of the boy bands and the social realism of rappers bears a remote resemblance to the national split in voting patterns between the long-standing Democratic bastions of the industrial North and Midwest as against the Republican strongholds of the Sunbelt and Far West. We seem to inhabit a nation divided against itself, culturally and politically – divided not only between red states and blue but between (in both red and blue states) ballads and bellicose ranting.

Unpredictable as our national sensibilities might be, examining the question of why individuals prefer one form of music over another is potentially more illuminating than enumerating sales figures. We do not purchase recordings simply because many other people have done so. A variety of factors – some conscious and many unexamined or unacknowledged – govern our attachment to a particular performer or group. The fact that we are but one among a legion of fans provides ample satisfaction, even if the community we join bears an unflattering resemblance to that entity the art critic Harold Rosenberg called the "herd of independent minds." Passion is an overwhelming emotion, regardless of whether we share that sentiment with a body of other individuals or pursue it on our own. In the end, "Popular cultural arguments," as Simon Frith has written, "are not about likes and dislikes as such, but about ways of listening, about ways of hearing, about ways of being" (1996: 8).

The basis on which we choose to be led by our passions is, therefore, a complicated affair. To press this point further, I will examine a body of materials that appeared during the course of 2000 that address the compelling attraction of popular music. They illustrate a range of positions on how the public values what it listens to, and what ability, if any, individuals have to determine what they consume and how it influences their lives. First, I will discuss the work – first published in *The New Yorker* – of John Seabrook and Malcolm Gladwell. Both writers are obsessed, by and large uncritically, by the force of the "buzz" – that "hierarchy of hotness," in Seabrook's phrase, that lends credibility to some forms of culture more than others (2000: 28). Then, I will consider the resurrection of the late rock critic Lester Bangs, and his elevation in Jim DeRogatis's biography and Cameron Crowe's film *Almost Famous* into the embodiment of a sensibility uncontaminated by the sway of fashion. I then contrast *Almost Famous*'s conception of rock criticism with the use of music as a kind of affective register in Nick Hornby's novel *High Fidelity*. Finally, I will turn to the analysis of the market forces that regulate the field of popular culture, by way of the writings of Tom Frank. His work attempts to go beyond simply lambasting the sway of the "strange media effulgence," focusing instead on the institutional forces that allow that "effulgence" to shine so brightly as to leave many music fans blinded by the light.

SURRENDER TO THE BUZZ

Since its founding in 1925, *The New Yorker* has presented itself as a publication that rises above the cultural fray and attends only to those individuals and events that meet a rather refined scale of judgment. The magazine's icon, Eustace Tilley, deliberately displays the kind of hauteur to which, one imagines, many of its readers have aspired. As much an institution as a periodical, *The New Yorker* typifies the kind of elevation by virtue of the consumption of culture of which Pierre Bourdieu states, "Cultural consecration does indeed confer on the objects, perspectives, and situations it touches, a sort of ontological promotion akin to transubstantiation" (1984: 6). Longtime editor William Shawn famously insisted that the publication exists above the fray of commerce: "We have never published anything in order to sell magazines" (quoted in Seabrook 2000: 18). Shawn apparently considered commerce as something of an afterthought if he considered it at all, which is particularly ironic considering the profusion of advertising throughout the publication as well as the evident cost of much of the merchandise contained in those ads. If reading the magazine allows one to aspire to a higher cultural status in life, perusing its advertising remains for most of us a painful occasion of vicariously experiencing a way of life few of us can afford.

The elevated position of *The New Yorker* was knocked down a peg when Si Newhouse purchased the magazine for US$168 million in 1985. The publishing magnate admired the patina of authority he acquired along with his property, but his zealous business practices firmly established that, unlike Shawn, he expected to sell magazines, and assumed his editors would acquire material that enabled him to do so. Of course, *The New Yorker* was more valuable to Newhouse as a marker of cultural cachet than as a piece of journalistic merchandise: at the time of the purchase, it was losing as much as $12 million a year, and clearly was a financial sinkhole for the bottom-line-conscious executive. Newhouse expected to raise *The New Yorker*'s circulation base from 500,000 to 850,000 through energetic publicity and affordable subscription rates, much as he had done with his other properties like *Vogue, GQ,* and *Vanity Fair.* To advance the cause, Newhouse brought over British-born Tina Brown in the belief that she could find the means of making the staid periodical snap and crackle with the kind of "buzz" she had brought to *Vanity Fair.*

John Seabrook defines the notion of "buzz" as "a shapeless substance into which politics and gossip, art and pornography, virtue and money, the fame of heroes and the celebrity of murders, all bleed" (2000: 5). It is the corporate equivalent of the decimation of canonical categories that is considered one of the primary characteristics of postmodernism. William Shawn and the founding editor of *The New Yorker*, Harold Ross, saw the cultural landscape as having established boundaries, and their editorial policies amounted to a kind of set of enclosure laws. In place of those boundaries, Tina Brown established what Seabrook calls "the hierarchy of hotness" that is neither highbrow nor lowbrow but "nobrow" (2000: 28). Status in her calculus was measured not by some hierarchical standard but by virtue of the degree of fascination a subject elicits in the cultural marketplace.

One of the subjects that Tina Brown brought within the purview of *The New Yorker* was rock and roll. It had not been completely absent from the publication in the past, but never acquired the kind of hospitality granted to jazz, specifically in the work of Whitney Balliett, whose columns dedicated to the genre appeared for over 40 years. An admiration of jazz was consonant with the kind of grown-up sensibility that Ross and Shawn promoted, but rock and roll? As John Seabrook argues, rock and roll exists outside the taste hierarchy altogether, and consuming it as an adult allows him to reacquaint himself with his adolescent sensibility. There is for Seabrook something indisputably refreshing about not demanding that culture serve as a mode of moral authority, and allowing critical standards to give way to the whims of the marketplace: "In a world of relative values, the popular hit had a kind of currency that ideals about quality lacked. You could argue about what was 'good' (whose good?), but you couldn't argue with Soundscan and Amazon.com" (2000: 71).

This redetermination of the marketplace as the central locus of value leads Seabrook to his profile of Radish, a trio from Greenville, Texas led by 14-year-old Ben Kweller. In 1995, searching for the "next big thing," record executives chanced upon an actual teenager – not an adult pretending to be one – who seemed to embody the marketable angst of Kurt Cobain, the leader of Nirvana who committed suicide in 1994. Ben Kweller looked even younger than his young years. With his bottle blond hair and braces, he might be mistaken for just one more mook on the playground were it not for the fact that, once he plugged in his electric guitar, Ben seem inspired – no, possessed – by the artists he emulated. As Seabrook notes, "he seemed to know how to move like a grown-up rock star, to execute that simple opera of rock gestures that rivets your eyes to the performer" (2000: 102). Without a beat, he adopted "the slacker-slouching-around-making-a-lot-of-noise Cobain style, once in a while throwing in swooping ax chops with the guitar neck or guitar-as-extension-penis thrusts reminiscent of Slash" (ibid.).

Seabrook discovers that Ben has ADD (attention deficit disorder). His skills at spelling and computation were minimal, and his handwriting rarely advanced beyond a scrawl. Like many with ADD, however, Ben possessed a striking capacity for mimicry. The images, chords, and words that MTV transmitted to him became part of Ben's instinctive repertoire. The fact that this boy in a small

Texas town could plug into a electronic grid and connect to a body of behavior once thought of as either avant-garde or antisocial only illustrates the breakdown of established categories that typifies the age of "buzz." Want to be a rebel? Sign up for cable and learn how to fight the corporate system so effectively that you wind up with a major record-label contract.

Considering the sources of his inspiration, it comes as no surprise that Radish's repertoire failed to question the governing wisdom of the airwaves and could easily fit into the existing programming niches of college and alternative radio. The record executives who flocked to hear Radish during auditions at dingy clubs on New York's Lower East Side recognized that Ben had latched onto what was now a marketable brand. He challenged none of the assumptions about what rock and roll was supposed to be; so capable was Radish's mimicry, it was almost as if the group had done market research in order to determine how best to leap over the customary barriers to a record deal. More ironically still, the executives relished how Ben possessed what to them was that most marketable of commodities, authenticity. Here was a kid singing about what kids go through, not a geezer with a comb-over pretending to be an adolescent. By contrast to the plethora of what John Strausbaugh, in *Rock Till You Drop*, has caustically dubbed "colostomy rock" (2001: 3), here was someone just past the need for Clearasil putting on the moves.[1]

Ross Elliott, a scout for Viacom's Famous Music publishing company, said of the young man, "What's coming out of Ben is raw shit.... Ben is honest. He's so young he can afford to be honest" (quoted in Seabrook 2000: 111). Elliott's sentiments are dear to the heart of the music business, but they can cost dearly as well: Ben signed with Mercury Records for US$2.5 million on a three-record deal. He received a $750,000 signing bonus and a 13.3 royalty rate, a concession customarily given only to bands with established track records. Famous Music acquired his publishing rights for $1.2 million. The executive who engineered the record deal was Danny Goldberg, the person who signed Kurt Cobain and Nirvana to Geffen Records.

For record executives and culture-beat writers, the ease with which one might vicariously relive the dreams of one's adolescence through Ben's elevation to wealth and potential stardom was damn near irresistible. Any number of the adults with whom Ben interacted on his flirtation with fame – Seabrook included – evidenced the symptoms of admiration tinged with envy. As Seabrook puts it, "In spite of the fact that I was old enough to be the boy's father" – he is Ben's senior by 24 years – "we were both on the same side of the real generational divide in the culture, the one the culture wars were fought over" (2000: 121). For him and the band, "pop culture was *folk* culture: our culture" (2000: 122). That sense of commonality, however, does not dissuade Seabrook from acknowledging that Ben's musical skills rarely exceeded those of a journeyman. Nonetheless, Seabrook concludes that even if Radish's songs appealed to no one besides other 14-year-olds, they had fulfilled a need. In the end, "It didn't matter whether Ben was an artist; what mattered was that Ben was a kid. Kids were the artists of Nobrow" (2000: 128).

On the other hand, what did matter to the record company was that Radish failed to reach those kids, 14 or older. Their debut recording, *Restraining Bolt*, stiffed, while another group of teenage aspirants, Hanson (also signed to Mercury), sold 5 million copies of their debut record that contained the chart-topping single "MMM Bop." The next sighting of Ben Kweller was in the tiny metropolitan weekly, the *New York Observer*. Young Ben, now 20, had successfully invested his advance money in the stock-market and was embarked on a real estate venture in Brooklyn's Carroll Gardens. "Negotiating a record deal is a lot easier, because you don't do all the talking," he stated to reporter Dan Maccarone. "But here, I don't have a manager. It's just me. You feel very alone.... It's crazy" (quoted in Seabrook 2000). Danny Goldberg's comments to John Seabrook on the aftermath of Radish's nosedive from notoriety have, by contrast, a notable serenity: "In the end, it all worked out for Mercury. We got our Christmas bonuses" (2000: 130).[2]

Goldberg's curt conclusion to the enthusiastic courtship and abrupt dismissal of Radish reminds one how much of the music business and how much of the professional commentary on rock and roll is driven by a species of infatuation. Scouts and executives jockey for the attention of artists at bars and clubs much as hopeful suitors cruise for partners at the very same environments. One observes in the superlatives employed by Elliott and Goldberg a kind of calculated swooning, both men being carried away with the potential they intuit in Ben Kweller's catalog of songs. That diction of emotional investment radiates throughout much of writing of popular music critics; think, for instance, of Jon Landau's classic encomium to Bruce Springsteen that he wrote after hearing him at Joe's Place in Boston, Massachusetts, in 1974:

> Tonight, there is someone I can write of the way I used to write, without reservation of any kind. Last Thursday, at the Harvard Square theater, I saw my rock 'n' roll past flash before my eyes. And I saw something else: I saw rock and roll's future and its name is Bruce Springsteen. And on a night when I needed to feel young, he made me feel like I was hearing music for the very first time. (quoted in Goodman 1997: 227)

This declaration not only comes across as the journalistic equivalent of a mash note, but also marked the transition on Landau's part from detached writer to committed agent. He had found his man, and thereafter dedicated his life to the perpetuation of his talents.

Seabrook demonstrates a similar emotional abandon in his attraction to Ben Kweller and his bandmates. Even though he recognizes how the "mutually exploitative relationship between adults and children that colors Nobrow as a whole" (2000: 111) affects the manner in which the group is treated by the record industry, he freely admits to feeling drawn into the "enchantment" that surrounds this young man (2000: 118). Somehow being immersed in the "blaring aural superhighway of Buzz," he cannot help but feel as if the years that separate him and the performers peel away (2000: 122). The admirable empathy that results enables him, and his readers as well, to be drawn into the drama of whether or not Radish will be signed and if their CD will succeed with the public. At the same time, that empathy for the performers does not endow Seabrook with sensitivity either to the machinations of the music industry or, more importantly, to the manner in which audiences received (and refused) Radish's material.

By saying that Seabrook fails to acknowledge the full extent of the machinations of the music business, I do not mean to imply that he fails altogether to comprehend the devices that generate the "hierarchy of hotness." As much as anyone, Seabrook grasps how Nobrow's collapse of cultural hierarchies has created a more substantial audience for popular culture. He understands as well that a market-oriented rather than a status-oriented system possesses a greater capacity for the widest possible range of cultural forms. However, when it comes to the matter of how individuals compete to achieve a position on that "hierarchy of hotness," Seabrook does not account for the curious fact that the executives who court Ben Kweller conceive of the marketplace (however mistakenly) as a body of pliable consumers who can be bent whichever way they wish depending upon how they position the artists they have to sell. When Ross Elliott talks about "these kids" and the "raw shit" that indexes their honesty, we get no idea of whether he has any sense that one of these kids might define raw shit and honesty in a way that he would not understand. He and Mercury Records imagine that a body of people will be swayed as a mass and respond to music in a uniform fashion. I suggest, simply enough, that he and Goldberg position popular music to appeal to young people because, as the infamous bank robber Willie Sutton surmised, "that is where the money is."

The manner in which Seabrook depicts the record industry's marketing practices bears an uncomfortable resemblance to the notion of the "tipping point" that was promulgated by Malcolm Gladwell in a celebrated *New Yorker* essay published during the same period. Gladwell proposed the idea as the best way of explaining why, for example, an outmoded product like Hush Puppies shoes suddenly takes off and captures the public consciousness. Gladwell suggests that the transformation occurs in three stages: (1) interest in and desire for the product becomes contagious; (2) small changes in behavior lead to big effects; and (3) the desired effect takes hold all of sudden in one dramatic moment (2000: 9). The metaphor Gladwell uses to define the system in which these behaviors occur is that of an epidemic. "Ideas and products and messages and behaviors," he writes, "spread just like viruses do" (2000: 7). Those viruses spread by virtue of their "stickiness," the degree to which they are memorable to or instantaneously adopted by those who encounter them (2000: 25). The body of individuals who are most receptive to forming such attachments are few in number, but the decisions they make influence a wide number of acquaintances. Those few individuals transform a society, culturally or otherwise, by acting as "mavens," brokers of information or forms of expertise that attract the interest of other people (2000: 69). The influence of these individuals outstrips most other people because, "some of us are very good at expressing emotions and feelings, which means that we are far more emotionally contagious that the rest of us" (2000: 85). Whether deliberately or not, "mavens" induce us to take chances that we would otherwise overlook. In the realm of cultural property, their influence is obvious and quite deliberately solicited whenever possible by those who control what enters the marketplace.

The "buzz" that Seabrook celebrates is one of the most contagious of the infections Gladwell defines in *The Tipping Point*. Unfortunately, neither author analyzes the factors that drive individuals to choose one artist over another or, equally important, how individuals' purchases are employed to generate meaning in their lives. Implicit in both "buzz" and the "tipping point" is a perspective that transforms individuals' likes and desires into a kind of hydraulics of the imagination: apply the right pressure at the proper position and a generation or a subculture can be swayed to appreciate and purchase one performer or form of music rather than another. Unfortunately, what's also implicit in these perspectives is a notion of the consumer that fails to rise above a caricature. Not only does it resurrect the outmoded sense that mass culture appeals to undifferentiated individuals, but it also effaces any notion of how those people actively make choices. Both Seabrook and Gladwell seem to assume that forms of culture possess uniform meanings assigned to them by "mavens" or those forces that elaborate the "hierarchy of hotness." All decisions would, it seems, have been made for us, and we have merely to acquiesce, surrender to the hype. To make this assumption, writes Simon Frith, "to gloss over the continuous exercise of taste by the pop cultural audience is, in effect, to do their discriminating for them, while refusing to engage in the arguments which produce cultural values in the first place" (1996: 17). One does not argue with a virus or question how one caught it. But in the end, interestingly enough, it would appear that the public had been inoculated against Radish. Or maybe they just were not listening to the right "mavens."

MAKING THE SCENE WITH THE "NOISE BOYS"

Some of the principal "mavens" that serve as gatekeepers to the weekly US effusion of 700 or more recordings are also known as record critics. Once they were few in number, the outlets for their enthusiasms and abominations even fewer. Nowadays, reviewing recordings is a marketable skill. Magazines devoted to specific musical genres proliferate, as do websites. The annual "Pazz and Jop" poll of the best popular music of the year conducted by the *Village Voice* calls upon between 100 and 200 participants. Few of the individuals who voice their opinions in this venue possess anything approaching household names. Try to think of who wrote album reviews in the latest *Rolling Stone*: hard, isn't it? The commentators who have published collections of their reviews or possess some degree of cultural cachet are mostly in their forties and fifties. A number of them comprise the subjects interviewed on the fascinating website http://www.rockcritics.com. The body of questions they are asked have a certain ritual consistency, one of them being who they read of current critics. Most confess a failure to keep up with the field. If anything, the general impression one gets from this dependable resource is that contemporary critics are more knowledgeable as well as more professional than their predecessors, yet lack a distinctive voice or style that makes their commentary equal in influence to the material about which they write.

Simon Frith provides a unique perspective on the role of the music critic, for he has simultaneously inhabited the newsroom and the academy. In the former, he crafted an ample amount of critical commentary, while in the latter, he helped to formulate the emerging field of popular music studies. In *Performing Rites*, Frith argues that musical judgments do not solely address musical matters. What is really at issue in a critical response is *feeling*. Whether we like or dislike a recording becomes a matter for which we must find an appropriate language. Sometimes we need to explain familiar feelings; at other times we must find a way to give form to responses we can't easily account for. When we formulate those responses for readers, the hope is that our statements assist an audience in their own efforts to account for what they have heard. "Criticism," Frith states, "is not just producing a version of the music for the reader but also a version of the listener for the music" (1996: 68). The role of the music writer therefore is inescapably social. In the end, the critics champion a way of listening to music more than they distinguish worthwhile from disposable recordings. Their aim is to create a "knowing community," a means of orchestrating a collaboration between the makers of music and those who purchase music as a means of making sense of their lives (1996: 67).

One of the most influential groups of music writers that created a "knowing community" for a distinct body of popular music is the trio dubbed the "noise boys" by James Wolcott: Richard Meltzer, Nick Tosches, and the late Lester Bangs (1949–82).[3] These three men praised music that emitted energy and emotion and detested material that was serious and self-consciously artistic. As Bangs wrote, each record purchase potentially fulfilled "the eternal promise that this time the guitars will jell like TNT and set off galvanic sizzles in your brain 'KABLOOIE!!!' and this time at least at last blow our fucking brain sky-high" (1987: 11). Long before punk was a genre and garage bands a subculture, these three close friends and frequent collaborators drew attention to music that was untamed and pulled no punches. Anything that advocated mischief and mocked the sobriety of conventional society was Top Ten on their list. When rock and roll became respectable in the wake of the Beatles being accepted as canonical composers, Meltzer and Tosches in particular backed away from any attachment to the contemporary scene. Meltzer's fancy ran more and more to avant-garde jazz, while Tosches exclusively praised the pre-Elvis body of rhythm and blues and rockabilly before "the beast of rock 'n' roll had been tamed for the circus of the masses" (1991: vii). Bangs' taste remained more catholic, and he retained a dedication to rock 'n' roll. As much as anything, Bangs sought out whatever supported his unassailable assumption that "music is about feeling, passion, love, anger, joy, fear, hope, lust, EMOTION DELIVERED AT ITS MOST POWERFUL AND DIRECT IN WHATEVER FORM, rather than whether you hit a clinker in that third bar there" (1987: 373–4).

If the "noise boys" deliberately set themselves apart by the sphere of musical culture they preferred, they also were a stylistic community unto themselves by virtue of the fact that they composed their writing in a manner that paralleled in language what they were drawn to in sound. All three men were strongly influenced by the verbal spontaneity of the "Beats" as well as the manner in which innovative journalists like Hunter S. Thompson and Tom Wolfe injected themselves into their copy. Therefore, the "noise boys'" reviews were anything but balanced and objective. Readers were drawn to them as much by their manner as by the subjects they addressed – or addressed only indirectly, for Meltzer often never listened to the records he reviewed. Each had a unique stylistic signature. Tosches combined levels of diction with a masterful touch, oscillating between Latinate formalism and a street kid's patois. Meltzer brought a philosophical sophistication to the everyday record review along with an absurdist sense that taking popular culture seriously was a mug's game. Bangs' prose was a weather vane of his emotions and chronicled the interaction between his fanatical devotion to particular sounds and their influence upon his life. No matter how often he was disappointed and how many of his idols turned against him, Bangs remained convinced that "the best music is strong and guides and cleanses and is life itself" (1987: 13).

In 2000, Lester Bangs once again emerged upon the cultural radar by virtue of two occasions: the publication of his biography, *Let It Blurt*, by rock journalist Jim DeRogatis, and his appearance as a character in the film *Almost Famous*, directed by former music journalist Cameron Crowe. Both men had a personal investment in the perpetuation of Bangs' persona. DeRogatis had interviewed him shortly before his death and claimed Bangs as a primary influence upon his choice of profession. Crowe knew him as a fellow professional and accompanied Bangs on a number of press junkets during the 1970s when the director was a teenager working for *Rolling Stone*. At the same time, each of them wishes to eradicate the web of mythology in which Bangs' life and legacy had become entrapped: DeRogatis endeavors to fully document the pharmacological and alcoholic excesses to which Lester was prone without giving the impression that Bangs gave his life to rock and roll; Crowe presents him as the embodiment of the conviction that the music matters more than the marketing, however difficult it might be to separate the two. The unpredictable appearance of both the biography and the film in 2000 provoked many rock critics, professional and amateur, to examine what compels our affection for popular music as well as what leads us to pursue the "hierarchy of hotness" in the first place. Is it possible to be consumed by the 'buzz" and remain convinced, at the same time, that music elicits "EMOTION DELIVERED AT ITS MOST POWERFUL AND DIRECT IN WHATEVER FORM"?

Jim DeRogatis's exhaustively researched biography of Lester Bangs vividly illustrates the dilemma of virtually all biographies of rock figures, steering, as it does, between the tawdry and the transcendent. In the case of Bangs, there is ample evidence of both. Greil Marcus, the editor of Bangs' posthumous writings, estimates that his 300-plus-page collection leaves out the remaining 3 to 5 million words Bangs wrote on other occasions. So far as his various excesses are concerned, to cite just the pharmacological, he ingested most mind-altering substances and had an especial affection for alcohol and cough syrup, often consumed in combination. His untimely death may not have been overtly suicidal, but Bangs can be said to have courted the Big Reaper on and off all his life. DeRogatis attempts to attend to both the literary and the extracurricular excess, yet the jacket copy of the book clearly indicates what his publisher pursued as a sales pitch: "He lived the rock 'n' roll lifestyle, guzzling booze and Romilar like water, matching its energy in prose." Apparently, most readers will be attracted to Bangs' bad-boy "lifestyle" first and foremost. Nonetheless, the introduction to *Let It Blurt* illustrates how such a position is hopelessly ass-backwards. DeRogatis relates the memorable occasion in the summer of 1974 when Bangs appeared on stage with the J. Geils Band. He accompanied them on his electric Smith-Corona, soloing in sentences while the band wailed blues-infected riffs. As an homage to Pete Townshend and other masters of destruction, Bangs concluded his performance by knocking the typewriter to the floor and jumping up and down on it until it broke in two. Juvenile as the episode might seem, it reinforces how logocentric Bangs was from first to last. Notwithstanding his attempts to be a professional musician, the *raison d'être* of his career was the transformation of musical experiences into literary artifacts. Type on, Lester, type on.

DeRogatis argues that the timeline of Bangs' professional life coincides with the devolution of rock criticism from a venturesome pursuit by flamboyant fans to the crassest kind of journalistic careerism. The manner in which Bangs tried to create a style that depended upon chronicling the fine modulations of his nervous system increasingly collided with the corporate agenda of the music business. They wanted, and got, the focus of most mainstream music journalism to be upon the personality of their artists. In the process, the celebrity profile took precedence over the critical commentary. Record reviews became shorter and more impersonal. They engaged in a variety of cheapened forms of evaluative shorthand, like letter or numerical grades and the thumbs up–thumbs down approach.

When DeRogatis interviewed Bangs in 1982 as part of a high-school senior journalism project, the writer castigated his chosen field: "I think a lot of the music out there and a lot of the writers who are out right now, they both deserve each other. Because they both have no personality and no style of their own and no soul" (DeRogatis 1999). However, he did not insist that his own idiosyncrasies constituted the route to good writing. "I call it like Hunter Thompsonism," he told the young student; "It's when you pay more attention to your image than you do to your work. And that destroys your writing. Hunter Thompson's never gonna do anything good again as long as he lives. I don't think anyone really cares about his drug habits" (DeRogatis 1999). These comments might, of course, just as well apply to Bangs himself, or at least the images of him that have been held up by a variety of people for public regard. The unfortunate fact about *Let It Blurt*, sympathetic and carefully composed though it may be, remains that we end up knowing more about Bangs' foibles than his erratic but remarkable endeavor to stay true to the sounds that he heard and the impact they had on his soul.

If Lester Bangs' influence on musical culture itself is difficult to assess, the manner in which he has become the designated outlaw and deified casualty of the critical whirl is difficult to avoid. The number of people who are invested in the life or opinions of Bangs may be small, but they are fierce in their dedication to his memory and his modus operandi. Cameron Crowe knew Bangs as a fellow traveler, for the now-celebrated film director began his career as a teenage music scribe for *Rolling Stone*. *Almost Famous* (2000) is a cinematic *roman à clef* about his entry into this arena and the temptations – artistic, ethical, and sensual – that he faced. William Miller (Patrick Fugit), Crowe's wide-eyed surrogate, is initially led by his wayward sister to find in music a means to set himself free and become "cool," the operative behavioral paradigm in the film. He is led to find his journalistic voice by Bangs, played by Philip Seymour Hoffman. When they first meet, however, the information Bangs passes along is not literary but affective. It is an admonition not about what to say about music or how to write about it but, instead, a sense of how to position oneself relative to the material and the body of individuals who produce and market it. He tells the boy that he "CANNOT make friends with the rock stars" if he is going to be a journalist, for "These are people who want you to write sanctimonious stories about the genius of the rock stars, and they will *ruin rock and roll* and strangle everything we love about it" (Crowe 2000: 24). He adds, "I'm telling you, you're coming along at a very dangerous time for rock and troll. The war is over. They won. Ninety-nine percent of what passes for rock now...SILENCE would be much more compelling" (Crowe 2000: 24).

This spirited monologue, to which William attends dutifully, initiates Bangs' role in the film as, in Mark Olson's clever phrase, "Billy's conscience and integrity-cop" (2000: 62) (and it's worth attending to the similarities between this scene and DeRogatis's 1982 interview with the Lester Bangs who declared that the soulless music industry deserved its soulless music critics and vice versa). The two of them communicate three times during the course of the narrative. In each case, Bangs reinforces his assumption that William must retain some distance from his subject, the fictional band Stillwater, in order to write about them with any honesty or veracity. William must perceive of himself as the enemy of the successful and good-looking as well as remain hopelessly and irredeemably uncool if he is to maintain the appropriate stance for a journalist of being "honest and unmerciful" (Crowe 2000: 172).

However, the trajectory of Crowe's film remains in conflict with Bangs' conviction that "The only true currency in this bankrupt world is what we share with someone else when we're uncool" (Crowe 2000: 172). Even if the story he submits to *Rolling Stone* reveals an image that Stillwater would rather keep out of the public eye, William retains the band's friendship as well as his professional objectivity. Bangs' precautions are pretty much thrown to the wind, for the issue in the end is not William's integrity but rather his inclusion in an alternate community comprised of Stillwater, their roadies, and the flock of young, female "band aids" that accompany them on tour. Fittingly, by contrast to Bangs' career, Crowe's own work for *Rolling Stone* was rarely provocative, and promoted the image of groups from the musical mainstream. By and large, he wrote the kind of celebrity-focused journalism that Jim DeRogatis insists has corrupted the role of the music scribe. Cameron Crowe may now position Lester Bangs as the Jiminy Cricket of *Almost Famous*, but the point he espouses ultimately comes across as idiosyncratic and alienating in the face of the social bonds experienced on the road by William Miller. For all that Bangs attempts to drill into his head, Crowe's teenage surrogate remains committed to his friends far more than to any abstract sense of what music should be or how a reporter relates to the people who create it. Crowe has observed of his adolescent role as a journalist, "That was my persona, that was the role I played: the fan who had several masters to serve – one of which was *me*" (Crowe 2000: xxiv). Bangs was more single-minded; other masters violated his point of view and vitiated the very lifeblood of the music that was his reason for being.

Therefore, rapt as William might look each and every time Bangs delivers his pearls of wisdom, the narrative thrust of *Almost Famous* consistently favors the young journalist's access into the realm of the "cool" as embodied by Stillwater. Even if the film appears to valorize, even render heroic, Bangs' point of view, it contradicts and undermines his ideas time and again. In the end, *Almost Famous* is not about music so much as it is about feeling included in a body of emotionally connected individuals, whether a band or a nuclear family. Consequently, despite the fact that its protagonist is a professional commentator on popular music, the film offers very little evidence of that enterprise. Judgment of music takes a back seat to matters of social acceptance and sexual conquest. Whether the ultimate aim is to satisfy his mother or fulfill his attraction to Penny Lane (Kate Hudson), William treats music as a vehicle to the conduct of his life, not as something fundamental to his affective existence.

Compare this deliberately limited perspective on the importance of evaluating popular music to the utter centrality of critical judgment in the eminently successful 1995 novel by Nick Hornby, *High Fidelity*. Its protagonist, the lovelorn record store owner Rob Gordon – played in Stephen Frears's 2000 film version by John Cusack – is an inveterate maker of lists. He firmly believes life's inescapable chaos can be momentarily mitigated by the form of order constituted by "best-of" rankings: Best Side One Track One, Top Five Elvis Costello Songs, Top Five Favorite Films. The constant exercise of evaluative critical judgment allows Rob – along with his coworkers, the brusque and belligerent Barry and the recessive and repressed Dick – to impose their meaning on the music they consume. In the process, they enact for themselves and to one another their relative positions in the system of cultural capital. Squares who request such pop drivel as Stevie Wonder's treacly "I Just Called To Say I Love You" account for nothing. Debating the contents of a particular list establishes a creditable set of sanctions over what is worthy of consideration and what is not. Even when their tastes diverge, the three young men concur that "what really matters is what you like, not what you *are* like" (Hornby 1995: 117).

Despite the fervent manner with which Rob asserts this distinction, *High Fidelity* goes beyond a single-minded fanboy fixation with hierarchies of taste, for Hornby believes music is more significant than that. It offers a kind of affective index to life, an illustration of superior states of being and understanding that can be applied to nonmusical issues. *High Fidelity* illustrates in the end that the distinction between "what you like" and "what you *are* like" amounts to a false dichotomy, for how we feel about music accounts for one of the most crucial means by which we construct our personalities and conduct our lives. Hornby illustrates this assumption most vividly in two passages that contain Rob's observations on Bruce Springsteen and Al Green. In the first, he broods over whether or not he should call his departed girlfriend, Laura, and attempt to resolidify their bond. He says, "There are men who call, and men who don't call, and I'd much, much rather be one of the latter. They are *proper* men . . . It's a safe, solid, meaningless stereotype: the man who appears not to give a shit" (Hornby

1995: 157). This rather adolescent perspective alters when Rob recalls that in "Bobby Jean," a song on Springsteen's 1984 release *Born in the USA*, the protagonist tries to relocate a long-lost girlfriend, only to discover she left town years before. The disjunction between Rob's turbulent feelings and the dramatic closure of the song compels him to reconsider his initial impulse to choose sangfroid over simple sentiment:

> I'd like my life to be like a Bruce Springsteen song. Just one. I know I'm not born to run. I know that the Seven Sister's Road is nothing like Thunder Road, but feelings can't be so different, can they? I'd like to phone all these people up and say good luck, and good-bye, and then they'd feel good and I'd feel good. We'd all feel good. That would be good. Great, even. (1995: 158)

Rob's attachment to Springsteen's music and his judgment of it serves in this context as a means of calculating the content of his character. Seeking parallels between his experience and that depicted in "Bobby Jean" permits him to decide not how much his affection for Springsteen calibrates what it is to be "cool," but rather the manner in which the song illustrates something about what it is to be a man. Or, as Rob dubs it, just a "bloke." Sometimes, what you like can help to determine what you are like, for better rather than for worse.

The importance of the body of recordings by Al Green to Rob is that Green, unlike Rob, embraces and expresses in song the widest possible range of emotions. So raw and direct and compelling is Green's range of feelings that Rob cannot imagine someone not liking his material or, even worse, dismissing the human experience it illustrates. To do so would be to illustrate a callous lack of feeling rather than simply some failure of aesthetic discrimination. Al Green makes you recognize the necessity of living life at the pitch of emotion, and the deadness that ensues when you do not. Placing his material at the core of one's life is painful, but utterly necessary. His music provides a register whereby experience can be processed and evaluated, not taken in passively or put at a distance through the possession of a "cool" affect. Rob observes,

> It seems to me that if you place music (and books, probably, and plays, and anything that makes you *feel*) at the center of your being, then you can't afford to sort out your love life, start to think of it as a finished product. You've got to pick at it, keep it alive and in turmoil, you've got to pick at it and unravel it until it all comes apart and you're compelled to start all over again. Maybe we all live life at too high a pitch, those of us who absorb emotional things all day. And as a consequence we can never feel merely content: we have to be unhappy, or ecstatically, head-over-heels happy, and those states are difficult to achieve within a stable, solid relationship. Maybe Al Green is directly responsible for more than I ever realized. (Hornby 1995: 169)

Craving Al Green records provides Rob with access to a model for living through, rather than evading, his emotions. If he had earlier put a chasm between personality and taste, he now understands through his consumption of and judgments about music that individual identity and cultural appetites coexist, though never in a simple or easily satisfied fashion. William's pursuit of Stillwater seems, by contrast, not so much a matter of what Stillwater's music does to him as how it will permit him access to the privileged sphere of the band's inner circle. Rob hopes that his love of music will provide him with illustrations of what it is to be a "bloke": a person able to balance his personal obsessions with the needs and demands of another person. In Rob's case, this means reconciling with Laura, with whom he establishes what appears to be a lasting relationship. Rob's love of music allows him access to a kind of emotional template from which his life does not fall short. Little about that process involves being "cool," and Hornby's novel concludes with a character endowed not with cultural capital alone but also a dependable supply of emotional wealth.

ALTERNATIVE TO WHAT?

Faced with this surfeit of pop-cultural stimuli, some critics and theorists have tried to cast the act of consumption as an act of liberation. Though they may be persuasive in arguing that we are the generators of the meanings of the goods we purchase, they often don't attend to the commodity's influence on our lives, and consequently their work winds up seeming like little more than the academic equivalent of the Home Shopping Network. The more goods we own, musical or otherwise, the more potential forms of meaning our lives might possess. Perhaps – unless we just end up with more and more stuff.

Thomas Frank is one of the most forceful writers to tackle the thorny question of agency in commodity consumption, and to do so with a willingness to deflate intellectual shibboleths current in American cultural studies. For more than a decade, he has edited the influential journal *The Baffler*, which bills itself as "The Journal That Blunts The Cutting Edge." Conceived in the tradition of H. L. Mencken's *The American Mercury, The Baffler* takes a certain pride in tackling the public's addiction to "buzz," and pays particular attention to the widespread predilection for "alternative" media among cultural critics and knowing consumers. The editors chose the journal's name as a dig against what they perceived as the hopeless obfuscation of too many cultural commentators, even those with whom they sometimes agree. Central to *The Baffler*'s critique of contemporary society is the fact that the rhetoric of social liberation proposed by the cultural studies left, and that of the business community in its efforts to induce us to change our lives through commerce, are virtually one and the same. As Frank and

Matt Weiland argue in the introduction to *Commodify Your Dissent*, a collection of "salvos from *The Baffler*":

> For all the flash and cosmopolitanism of contemporary American life, we reasoned, never before has it been so directly a product of the corporate Imagination. As we waded through the unplumbed depths of management literature, our original suspicions were confirmed. When business advice literature warmly embraces chaos, celebrates the collapse of high and low, and heralds the demolition of intellectual order as a profit-maximizing opportunity, it's time to dust off those much-vilified meta-narratives. And when the partisans of corporate-sponsored transgression responded by labeling us both reactionary elites and a bunch of Reds, we knew we had hit the interpretive jackpot. Yes, postmodernism is the cultural logic of late Capitalism. (Frank & Weiland 1997: 15)

Frank skewers again and again the ways in which the academic-intellectual investment in "difference" manages, strikingly, not to differ from the corporate marketing of nonconformity. For, as Frank points out, advertising no longer celebrates the comforts of conformity: button-down shirts and two-car garages are a thing of the past, just as the urge to nest in suburban comfort no longer drives the corporate sales agenda. Rather than "Just Say No," the business world's motto would seem to be "Just Do It." Frank cites the transformation of such antinomian figures as Allen Ginsberg and William Burroughs into corporate shills as the sign of the irreversible deflation of the counterculture. When the poet appeared in ads for The Gap and the novelist on television spots for Nike, it became clear that "the Culture Trust is now our leader in the Ginsbergian search for kicks on kicks" (Frank & Weiland 1997: 34). Nowadays we howl when our mail-order catalog item does not appear on time, not when the finest minds of our generation buckle under the weight of conformity; and the corporate literature that governs the agenda of the business school and the boardroom inveighs against conventionalist thinking-inside-the-box. Think of the slogans that litter the public media: "Sometimes You Gotta Break The Rules" (Burger King); "Resist The Usual" (Young & Rubicon); and "Innovate Don't Imitate" (Hugo Boss). So pervasive is this transformation of corporate discourse into the lingua franca of our day that it is difficult for Frank to discern a truly alternative way to think and feel. Frightful as this prospect is, "It is putting itself beyond our power of imagining because it has become our imagination, it has become our power to envision, and describe, and theorize, and resist" (Frank & Weiland 1997: 274).

Frank has elaborated upon his commentaries in *The Baffler* in two challenging and provocative works, *The Conquest of Cool: Business Culture, Counterculture, and the Rise of Hip Consumerism* and *One Market Under God: Extreme Capitalism, Market Populism, and the End of Economic Democracy*. The former locates how the countercultural discourse of the 1960s is replicated in that of corporate advertising; the latter focuses its energies upon the irrepressible attraction of what Frank calls "market populism." According to Frank, market populism emerged in full force during the course of the 1990s as the country turned to venturesome entrepreneurs as our principal cultural heroes. Buoyed by the infusion of investment capital, these buccaneers of the boardroom advanced the notion that the market itself constituted a form of democracy superior to any other ideology. Frank writes:

> American leaders in the nineties came to believe that markets were a popular system, a far more democratic form of organization than (democratically elected) governments. This is the central premise of what I call "market populism": That in addition to being mediums of exchange, markets were mediums of consent. Markets expressed the popular will more articulately and more meaningfully than did mere elections. Markets conferred democratic legitimacy; markets brought down the pompous and the snooty; markets gave us what we wanted; markets looked out for our interests. (Frank 2000a: xiv)

If, in fact, markets embody and express the will of the people, then to criticize their operations is to slight the very population around us. Only an elitist who despises how individuals might reap rewards and lead a comfortable life would think of toppling such an intellectual and institutional edifice. The notion of "market populism" also puts a dent in the pervasive rift of class in this country. All of us ostensibly stand to gain from the workings of the marketplace – who is not invested in their company's 401(k) retirement plan? – and therefore what once was thought to distinguish one sector of American society from another evaporates in the face of stock options and the Dow Jones average.

Market populism's legitimation of an extremely narrow realm of behavior and ideology, in turn, sets up Frank's argument that the omnipresent turnover in cultural goods is predicated upon how the market defines what is "alternative" and what is not. Just as he is committed to demolishing the edifice that supports market populism, Frank wishes with equal ferocity to strike down the dubious commitment on the part of music mavens to their conception of "authentic" music that goes against the norms of the marketplace. The unexamined investment in antinomianism that led to Ginsberg and Burroughs being used as corporate shills occurs time and again, Frank believes, in the music business. For him, the "true culture war" is not over "family values" or "cultural elitism," but a more basic concern: "the power of each person to make his own life without the droning dictation of business interests. If we must have grand, sweeping cultural judgments, only one category seems to matter anymore: the adversarial" (Frank & Weiland 1997: 158). Frank commits himself to the "possibility of a worthy, well-screamed *no*" (Frank & Weiland 1997: 159). Should all else fail, he chooses a kind of self-designed gulag: "the secession, the internal exile, the thrashing release, the glorious never never never" (Frank & Weiland 1997: 160).

Admirable as this *cri de coeur* might be, when one examines how Frank negotiates himself amongst the cultural goods he finds in the musical arena, a less heroic image emerges. In 1998, Frank published an essay entitled "Variations On a Descending Theme" in *Harpers's Magazine*. At the core of the piece was the struggle on the part of his childhood friend, Chris Holmes, to land a deal with a major record label. Frank compares Holmes to F. Scott Fitzgerald's Great Gatsby and imagines that the musician's capacity for "unlimited possibility" parallels that of the bootlegger (1998: 42). Holmes possesses prodigious musical skills yet seems to lack the kind of militant commitment to success that will enable him to put commercialism above all other priorities. However, when his band Sabalon Glitz (named after a character on the BBC cult television series *Doctor Who*) receives attention from the Atlantic record label, things change. The record company wants to sign Holmes, but not the rest of the group, as part of their "alternative" roster. Frank distinguishes this position within the mainstream record business as follows: "Alternative adopted indie's anti-fake postures and noises as a way to capture its authenticity but simultaneously dropped indie's anti-industry bias, thus becoming something bizarre: fakeness at a second remove" (1998: 43–4). Holmes recognizes the position he has been put in and meets it with a deliberate strategy of his own. Aware of how the pop machinery will attempt to define him, he "planned to deliver authenticity not with some coarse yelpings but by holding a mirror up to the whole process" (1998: 44). He calls his new ensemble Yum Yum and conceives of them as "an ironic pop band – ironic, that is, if you understood 'pop' as the softest, most openly sold-out, most compromised, most manipulated music ever produced" (1998: 44). Knowing that whatever he does will be invariably falsified by the process to which he has committed himself, Holmes will "*fake fake itself*" (1998: 44).

While Frank's article describes in detail the eventual failure of Yum Yum and the demise of the band, what interests me more is the description of a gig they performed at "an enormous lifestyle palace" called Pierre's in Fort Wayne, Indiana (Frank 1998: 46). The venue is comprised of five separate bars, "each dedicated to the safe pursuit of whatever subcultural practice appealed to one's particular demographic" (ibid.). Frank takes on the guise of an ethnographic researcher as he moves between the various spaces, but what's alarming about his approach is the tone he adopts about the bands and the clientele. He admires how they seem uninterested in the kind of clothing that pervades the fashion of their suburban peers, but characterizes what they wear as "rural alienation garb" (ibid.). He scoffs at how the local DJ that introduces Yum Yum has an out-of-date mullet haircut and describes disdainfully how he believed his programming might help to "Make Fort Wayne hip." As he moves to another performance space, Frank is taken aback by how "people were line-dancing to the hardest-core hip hop; high school youths were rubbing their bodies against one another with desperate abandon; the DJ was shrieking about fucking" (1998: 47). Confronted with this stimuli, all Frank can observe is "how effectively their lives had been reduced to acts of pure consumption," for at Pierre's "the growling pseudo-nihilism of Alternative" was the "winner in the local authenticity sweepstakes" (ibid.).

What's dismaying about these observations is not simply Frank's almost haughty distance from the people around him, but how little he apparently found it of interest to ask any of them what they liked about this music or what purpose it served in their lives. For all we know, the young people of Fort Wayne are hungry for an alternative to "alternative," but Frank seems more convinced of the hand-me-down quality of their leisure time than intrigued by what motivates them to seek out this material and this venue in the first place. Rather than chastising the crowd for their acts of pure consumption, Frank might have asked them a few questions without deciding in advance what the answers should be. For all his pronouncements about the desirability of democracy, Frank seems less than willing to allow forms of expression that he dislikes to find an audience.

The conundrum Frank faces reminds me of the *Frontline* documentary entitled "The Merchants of Cool" that appeared on PBS in February of 2001. It surveyed the ways in which corporate America has targeted teenagers and packaged their entertainment for them to such a degree that it seems as if they have no minds of their own. In one sequence, Todd Cunningham, MTV Senior VP of Brand Strategy and Planning, visits a teenage young man in Iselin, New Jersey. With cameras running, Cunningham queries John about his clothing, tastes in music, and attitudes about social issues of the day. The taped material is cut, edited to music, and shared with the various departments at MTV as a means of sharpening their product. What does MTV learn, the show inquires, rather than a body of market data? No answer to that question is given, and, ironically, the program ends with the host, Douglas Rushkoff, making the following propositions:

> So is there anywhere the commercial machine won't go? Is there any room for kids to create a culture of their own? Do they even have anything that's theirs alone? All eyes are on our kids. They know they're being watched. But what or whom can they look to themselves? And what if they turn and fight? The battle itself is being sponsored, packaged, and sold right back to them.[4]

Telling as these questions are, they come at the end of the program and not the beginning. One wishes that we could go back to Iselin, New Jersey, and spend some more time with John or, for that matter, return to Pierre's and chat with the crowd over a beer. The truth in the end is that the question of how and why we value popular music has as many answers as there are listeners. In some ways, we would be wise to begin by making the kind of inquires I allude to in my title. For many years Dick Clark's *American Bandstand* featured a record-rating segment. Teens appraised new disks, and a common response would be how the song had a good beat and dance potential. Simple-minded as those responses might seem, they do begin to provide access to how music is an active part of people's lives as the source of movement and social intercourse. Analyzing how music is nothing more than an emanation of "buzz," or the expression of forms of emotion without which life is insupportable, or the embodiment of some kind of alternative to the status quo – all these avenues of inquiry may tell us many interesting things, but in the end we will still want to know if this is a groove that can move us.

NOTES

1   See my review of Strausbaugh 2001 at http://www.popmatters.com/books/reviews/r/rock-til-you-drop.html.
2   More recently, Kweller has released two CDs – *Sha Sha* (2002) and *On My Way* (2004) – that have met with critical approval and reasonable sales, suggesting that his solo career may, after all, turn out to be something more (and better) than a matter of surrendering to the buzz.
3   Their representative works on music include Richard Meltzer, *The Aesthetics of Rock* and *A Whore Just Like the Rest: The Music Writings of Richard Meltzer*; Nick Tosches, *Country: The Twisted Roots of Rock 'n' Roll* and *Where Dead Voices Gather*. My review of *Where Dead Voices Gather*, "Memorializing Emmett Miller," is published online at http://www.popmatters.com/books/reviews/w/where-dead-voices-gather.html.
4   Douglas Rushkoff's copious writings on young people are replete with questionable or unexamined assumptions. My analysis of them appears in Sanjek 1998.

REFERENCES

Bangs, Lester. 1987. *Psychotic Reactions and Carburetor Dung*, ed. Greil Marcus. New York: Vintage.
Bourdieu, Pierre. 1984. *Distinction: A Social Critique of the Judgment of Taste*, tr. Richard Nice. Cambridge, MA: Harvard University Press.
Christman, Ed. 2001. "Album Sales Increase By Only 4% in 2000." *Billboard*, Jan. 13: 1, 88.
Crowe, Cameron. 2000. *Almost Famous*. (Screenplay.) New York: Farrar, Straus and Giroux.
DeRogatis, Jim. 1999. "A Final Chat with Lester Bangs." *Perfect Sound Forever*, Nov. Online at http://www.furious.com/perfect/lesterbangs.html.

——. 2000. *Let It Blurt: The Life & Times of Lester Bangs, America's Greatest Rock Critic*. New York: Bantam Doubleday Dell.

Frank, Thomas. 1997. *The Conquest Of Cool: Business Culture, Counterculture, and the Rise of Hip Consumerism*. Chicago: University of Chicago Press.

——. 1998. "Variations on a Descending Theme." *Harper's Magazine*, March.

——. 2000a. *One Market Under God: Extreme Capitalism, Market Populism, and the End of Economic Democracy*. New York: Doubleday.

——. 2000b. "The Rise of Market Populism: America's New Secular Religion." *The Nation*, Oct. 30.

—— and Scott Weiland. 1997. *Commodify Your Dissent: Salvos from The Baffler*. New York: Norton.

Frith, Simon. 1996. *Performing Rites: On the Value of Popular Music*. Cambridge, MA: Harvard University Press.

Frontline. 2001. "The Merchants of Cool." Program no. 191, Feb. 27. Barak Goodman and Rachel Dretzin, prod. Barak Goodman, dir. Written by Rachel Dretzin. Douglas Rushkoff, Correspondent and Consulting Producer. Transcript available online at http://www.pbs.org/wgbh/pages/frontline/shows/cool/etc/script.html.

Gladwell, Malcolm. 2000. *The Tipping Point: How Little Things Can Make a Big Difference*. New York: Little, Brown.

Goodman, Fred. 1997. *The Mansion on the Hill: Dylan, Young, Geffen, Springsteen, and the Head-On Collision of Rock and Commerce*. New York: Vintage.

Hornby, Nick. 1995. *High Fidelity*. New York: Putnam.

Meltzer, Richard. 1988. *The Aesthetics of Rock*. New York: Da Capo.

——. 2000. *A Whore Just Like The Rest: The Music Writings of Richard Meltzer*. New York: Da Capo.

Olson, Mark. 2000. "Uncool." *Film Comment* 36(5) (Sept./Oct.).

Sanjek, David. 1998. "'I Ain't Afraid of No Kids!': Douglas Rushkoff and the Ascendence of the Digital Sublime." *The Review of Education/Pedagogy/Cultural Studies* 20(2): 173–97.

Seabrook, John. 2000. *Nobrow: The Culture of Marketing, the Marketing of Culture*. New York: Knopf.

Strausbaugh, John. 2001. *Rock Till You Drop: The Decline from Rebellion to Nostalgia*. London: Verso.

Strauss, Neil. 1998. "Restless Music Fans Hungry for the New." *New York Times*, Jan. 28: E8.

Tosches, Nick. 1991. *Unsung Heroes of Rock 'n' Roll*, rev. ed. New York: Da Capo.

——. 1996. *Country: The Twisted Roots of Rock 'n' Roll*. New York: Da Capo.

——. 2001. *Where Dead Voices Gather*. New York: Little, Brown.

7

Cultural Studies and the New Populism

BARRY FAULK

Most of the readers of this book are likely to assent to the claim that cultural studies is a dominant force in English departments. However, even scholars who think of themselves as working within cultural studies would admit that the field has a problematic and troubled hegemony. For one, it is not clear what texts, contexts, methods, or interpretive models the label "cultural studies" designates for many, beyond a concern with popular culture and a partisanship for the cultural lowbrow. Moreover, cultural studies commonly meets with resistance from advocates of what I'll call a "new populism," who charge cultural studies theorists with an insensitivity to the discreet charms of form and structure in literature and a callous disregard for standards of excellence in the arts. In what follows, I'll suggest that what most unsettles cultural studies' new populist critics is the supposed presumption of the field's practitioners – the people who look like those proverbial folk who know too much, folk about whom we have been duly warned. On my reading, cultural studies gets a lot of bad press for having scholars who know *that they know*, and for the means by which they display their knowledge.

But if this is the case, then the complaint renders visible a kind of cultural fault-line, a cultural divide over how to display cultural capital. Educated taste in the arts, artistic savvy, is often accompanied by the performance of knowledge. In a culture saturated with information, a culture which respects (and literally pays for) the specialized knowledge of experts and their mastery of abstract concepts, knowledge counts. As long as knowledge counts, "knowing" attitudes seem inevitable; they serve as coin in the cultural realm, the fungible counters of symbolic capital. If knowledge counts, then knowingness pays, and commands deference. Thus, a culture that respects specialization, training, and credentials is inevitably bound to generate a public for art that seeks knowingness as a means by which people distinguish themselves, as a token of social respect. Yet critics of cultural studies' knowingness are both fascinated and alarmed at the theatrics of savvy and hip that seem to accompany the encounter between performer and theorist in cultural studies, as if the performance of knowingness were somehow *exclusive* to cultural studies.

I want to address the (real and imaginary) relations between knowledge and knowingness in cultural studies, and in the new populist backlash, not because the backlash threatens the good name of cultural studies, but because construing cultural studies as a discourse that illegitimately aspires to lord it over art (and construing its practitioners as more-knowing-than-thou dilettantes) renders academic professional work at a considerable disadvantage. I want to defend cultural studies not only because of my enormous debt to scholarly work within this tradition, but because its founding texts provide a more honest account of the position in which I find myself located as a research scholar within the humanities than I find in comparable work by the new populists, who so far have provided no account of the conditions under which they labor within the academy. I work in a state-funded research university, and it's nice work once you get it, if you can get it. There is nothing magic about the conditions under which I work. Academic professionals, like all professionals, pride themselves on their autonomy, and like to believe that their work is more than "mere" labor. Debates about work in English thus often take the form of a quarrel within the profession about what its larger public desires, in an attempt to fix the meaning of the services we believe we provide. Whatever one's dissatisfaction with this state of affairs, there is no way to transform English from within without an attempt to see clearly one's location within its division of intellectual labor. A fundamental problem with the new populism, by these lights, is that it functions within English as a new brand of antiprofessionalism that operates in willful ignorance of its working conditions. To put this another way, the desire to speak for Beauty places academic professionals in an unproductive double bind in regard to their own labor.

I can begin to bear out this claim by reminding readers of some remarks about the attractions of antiprofessionalism for professional academics, set out by Stanley Fish nearly 20 years ago. "At least in its literary form," Fish counseled, antiprofessionalism "urges impossible goals (the breaking free or bypassing of the professional network) and therefore has the consequence of making people ashamed of what they are doing" (1985: 211). Antiprofessionalism functions, despite its intent, as a mode of professional discourse; inevitably it shakes the foundations of its advocates' own arguments. And insofar as new populism promotes the conclusion that art is best left in the hands of impassioned amateurs (lest it be defiled or degraded by the critical impulse), it counsels, as Fish suggested with regard to antiprofessionalism in general, "a shamefaced relationship with the machinery that underlies their labors." What intrigues me about the new populists' complaints, coming as they do from a variety of cultural professionals, is that they add up to much more than a call for the return to the formal apparatus of aesthetics in the mode of Elaine Scarry. Rather, they function quite deliberately as a mode of political populism: and like most versions of "the people," the "popular" is primarily an intellectual fabrication. Strange as it may sound, the new populism stands for – or wants to stand for – a new intellectual bloc unified against the perceived excesses of academic professionals. Like any emergent discourse, it hails people from various locations, both inside and outside the university. It includes professional journalists like Ron Rosenbaum and independent cultural critics like Thomas Frank as well as academics like Richard Rorty and Andrew Delbanco. These figures offer their readers a new version of a story with considerable history, a story which has played a sizable role in national discourse: in this story, the public rises up and displaces the self-appointed and presumably self-serving expert. Yet Delbanco and other new populists, while arguing for the autonomy of beauty, transform the term, putting it to work in the service of a specific configuration of the profession of English. "Beauty," apparently, will not save English all by itself; it requires the public demonstration of one's love. The saving confession works, in new populist accounts, to contradictory effect: testifying to art's redemptive power both serves to take back lost ground for the profession and marks the critic's saving distance from the heartless expertise of careerist professionals.

I don't mean to suggest that cultural studies in the Anglophone academy deserves no blame for the public relations problem it currently faces. The practice of cultural studies in the United States, I believe, bears some responsibility for perpetuating this image of scholars so supremely and expertly within the game that they are also somehow above the game, or at least operating at a safe remove from the objects they scrutinize. If cultural studies is portrayed in new populists' arguments as the domain of hyperprofessional specialists immune to the blandishments of the culture they inhabit, at least some of the portrayal arises from the self-presentation of cultural studies theorists as culture aficionados and experts of cool. In other words, some of us who work in cultural studies made some strategic errors: while spinning our elaborate and sweeping critiques of aesthetics, we failed to make our interest in – and passion for – art and judgment known to the public outside the academy. Theorizing representations of all kinds, we neglected to see to attend to how theorists of representation were represented.

Still, our troubles aren't entirely our fault. My peers and colleagues who appreciate cultural studies work of the Birmingham School do not go to museum exhibits merely to mock the complicity of representation or realism with oppressive social orders, or to feel smugly superior to the expressive endeavor embodied in a Jackson Pollack drip painting. They might appreciate the *Exile on Main Street* CD you lent them and are as likely as any to forget to return it to you. In most respects, cultural studies scholars are not any more tone deaf to the music of the spheres than anyone else. To paraphrase Raymond Williams, cultural studies theorists are ordinary.

Indeed, while one strand of new populism criticizes cultural studies for being too aloof and smug, another strand criticizes cultural studies for being insufficiently discriminating – even (of all things) a form of intellectual populism. In Thomas Frank's *One Market Under God*, for instance, cultural studies is cast as "a populist celebration of the power and 'agency' of audiences and fans" (2000: 282). What Frank refuses to acknowledge, however, is that most of the texts he criticizes as exemplars of academic anti-elitism were among the most ambitious, compelling, and exciting books of cultural studies, the kind of scholarship that attracted and attracts bright graduate students regardless of whether it fostered the creation of new consumer organizations or counterhegemonic political blocs. Frank characterizes Lawrence Levine's 1988 book *Highbrow/Lowbrow* as an exercise in populist self-congratulation: "by parading before readers a series of vignettes in which repulsive, upper-class Yankee snobs – each of them coupled carefully with their racist and otherwise offensive remarks – looked to high culture for a refuge from democracy, Levine sought to prove that hierarchies of taste were analogous to social hierarchy generally and to racism specifically" (2000: 281). But Levine did much more than confirm readers in their virtuous distance from racist nineteenth-century Yankee cultural elites; he also showed that the putatively free judgment of taste was often blind to its own links to local circumstance, to self-interest, and to anxieties related to identity and status. Levine presented compelling evidence – in the pronouncements of theatergoers and their insistent complaints regarding unruly public demonstrations in the public space of the theatre – that most nineteenth-century middle-class culture mavens often *did* confuse cultural hierarchy with social hierarchy, and Frank, with a Ph.D. in American history from the University of Chicago, surely knows this. Likewise, Frank singles out Andrew Ross's *No Respect* as an exemplar of preening academic populism, claiming that Ross finds "in virtually any iteration of highbrow taste a tacit expression of contempt for democracy" (2000: 281). Yet only 14 pages later, Frank writes that "Andrew Ross, for example, brilliantly dissected the power of intellectuals to 'designate what is legitimate' in his 1989 book *No Respect*" (2000: 305). It is an odd passage, and it speaks to a larger problem in Frank's attack on cultural studies. To wit: Frank has good fun mocking academic populism in the nineties and cultural studies' obsessions with consumer "agency." But most of the theorists who serve as Frank's targets were articulating a more complex and ultimately more convincing argument about culture and distinction: namely, that social and cultural hierarchy were clearly linked in most historical circumstances, and that it requires historical knowledge to grasp the relation between aesthetic concepts and the mechanisms of social exclusion. Judging by the fact that Frank practically takes back his critique of the aims of Ross's book, I suspect that Frank himself knows better than he lets on in his more polemical moments, and that he has no real desire to undo cultural studies' attempts to theorize the formation and maintenance of hierarchies.

Stuart Hall has famously remarked that cultural studies emerged out of the nagging sense that Marxism missed the boat on culture. The dogmatic Marxist insistence that culture was but one superstructural epiphenomenon among many was, no question, a reductive misreading of the work art did within the world, and a noticeable omission for a theory that proclaimed itself to be indispensable for an understanding of historical change. Cultural studies was thus born from the sense that old-school Marxism overlooked other kinds of "real" conditions: namely, the power of symbols, signs, texts, and culture.[1] Nevertheless, while cultural studies was founded on the recognition of the power of the symbolic, it's true that cultural studies has viewed aesthetics – but, crucially, not art – with suspicion. Cultural studies theorists have indeed, as Frank suggests, focused on the history of complicity between aesthetic discrimination and social or class-based discrimination. The essential texts of this critique include Raymond Williams's *Keywords* (1976), which provides a history of usage for keywords of aesthetic discourse such as "Art," "Taste," and "Sensibility," and in which Williams underscores how these words were used to sanction the particular and interested views of an emergent bourgeoisie under the shield of universal values and disinterested judgment. Pierre Bourdieu's *Distinction* (1984) elaborates upon a statistical study of different social strata in postwar France to establish that class affiliation and conflict saturate aesthetic discourse, and that aesthetic distinctions serve to justify social distinctions. Barbara Herrnstein Smith's *Contingencies of Value* (1988) brings the lessons of deconstruction to aesthetics, demonstrating the contingency of supposedly axiomatic distinctions between aesthetic values and other value schemes. Terry Eagleton's *The Ideology of the Aesthetic* (1990) spins out a crucial aspect of Pierre Bourdieu's critique, the privileging of mind over body constitutive of "high" aesthetic discourse, and traces the career of this binary in Continental philosophy. Whether formulated by Lord Shaftesbury, universalized by Kant, or given a dialectical spin by Adorno, aesthetics, Eagleton argues, privileges cognitive over tactile pleasures.

The reason for cultural studies' suspicion of aesthetics is straightforward: aesthetic codes developed in a world where art was believed to allow virtue to trickle down throughout the social order, and thus historically did little more than sugarcoat invidious class distinctions. The persistence of aesthetic ideology, according to the cultural studies critique, sustains the neofeudal habits of the bad old days in a new social order in which advancement depends more on professional expertise than on accidents of birth. In the culture of professionalism, by contrast, middle-class hegemony no longer depends on maintaining a superior and disdainful attitude toward vernacular culture, and so social discrimination need not be validated by the demonstration of aesthetic refinement.[2] No one believes that CEOs and senators rule over us by virtue of their finer sensitivity to the rhythms of dactyllic hexameter or their ability to distinguish Bach from Haydn. Now, it may be that the genial aesthetic pluralism currently demonstrated by the professional-managerial class towards popular culture represents a considerable advance from the scornful exclusion of the popular maintained by elites a century ago. Maybe not. But undeniably, vernacular talk about art and culture in terms of comparative, contingent value creates greater common ground – a more demotic and democratic means of evaluation than the discipline of aesthetics can allow for.

Cultural studies should therefore do more than insist that it likes art just as much as any new populist. While it's true that cultural studies scholars are capable of liking beautiful things, and that we habitually concern ourselves with the aesthetic forms of social life, we also have a compelling case against aestheticism that we should not downplay, but elaborate. Displacing aesthetic codes in cultural studies is not mere play; it is a necessary prelude to building schemes of evaluation more in keeping with democratic norms on the ground it clears. Cultural studies should eschew traditional aesthetics, and its history of correlating artistic and social discrimination, in favor of the homely, ordinary practice of evaluating. Responding to art means making judgments, value calls, and choices, and a savvy cultural studies would do so not (for instance) by ranking the genre of epic as more elevated than the genre of lyric, but by speaking in the vernacular language of Top Ten lists, Picks & Pans, thumbs up/thumbs down, and Cheers and Jeers.

I have argued that cultural studies, far from quarreling with art, was founded on the recognition that art resolutely refuses to be ignored. And I would assert moreover that one way in which cultural studies honors art is by making a place for it in a democracy, by valorizing ordinary acts of evaluation. Yet cultural studies practitioners have regrettably done their part to mystify their position on art and aesthetics, and make their antagonism to the latter seem like a dismissal of the former. At a crucial juncture early in the nineties, when the field attracted adherents in the American academy, it failed to make its deeply democratic trust in the act of evaluation tangible to those in the academy or outside it. The cultural studies critique of aesthetics was, disastrously, taken for a statement about the ultimate powerlessness of art before the social world. Accordingly, the mode of dismissive knowingness has come to seem to be cultural studies' stock-in-trade.

There is a good deal of history behind the association. Cultural studies, insofar as it draws on the work of Antonio Gramsci, is committed for political reasons to name and scrutinize the popular. Gramsci's notion of a national popular, in Bruce Robbins's formulation, constitutes "an imperfect and historically determined version of common sense, perhaps only emerging but significant enough to be worth tracking, that links the thoughts and feelings of ordinary people to the fate of others in a larger collectivity" (1993: 86). In this conception, the national popular bridges the culture of cultural and academic professionals with nonprofessionals. For both ethical and political reasons, therefore, cultural studies needs to make common cause with the popular, and – most interestingly, for my purposes – "knowingness," far from being the preserve of a hip cultural elite, is inevitably a modality of the popular, with a specific history. Knowingness in popular culture seems to have emerged with the growth of mass leisure from vernacular forms. Peter Bailey argues that the central trope of performance organizing nineteenth-century popular theater, like the English music-hall, was a performer and spectator linked by their "inside" knowledge of urban life. "Knowingness" was a social structure, a byproduct of audience collusion and participation with comic singers and performers. It was both inclusive (offered up to a paying public) and exclusive, meant to foster in discerning elites a sense of their superiority to the crowd.[3] Knowingness was founded on the shared perception that, indeed, there was sex in the city (of London), despite the censorship of public authorities and media. Performers gestured toward the fact, and audiences, complicit in mischief, prided themselves that they, too, were in on the "joke."

Knowingness, then and now, does not necessarily mean being cool or hip, but it can be, and too often is, taken this way – and over the past decade and a half, cultural studies theorists themselves helped to confuse the issue. Sometime around 1990, the very demeanor of the academic conference-goer changed. How could you tell the players from the sideliners? Verily, ye knew them, not by their works, but by their wardrobe. The sartorial signs of the CS academic – the blazon of dark leather, dyed hair, or skinhead chic, subculture cool – signified achieved acumen. In order to combat cultural elitism and outright snobbery in the academy, cultural studies scholars performed a valuable cultural good, by resisting ranking cultural artifacts according to their place on the register of high and low. At the same time, some scholars trumpeted their primary allegiance to bohemian and underground traditions, and accordingly, they accrued the kinds of charisma that clings to those who invest their cultural capital wisely.

Similarly, championing Madonna in the early 1990s seemed to be, and sometimes was packaged as, a shock tactic, a lapse in taste maintained in the face of high-but narrow-minded academics. But cultural studies' enthusiasm for Madonna put itself in a unfortunate position when it positioned itself as resistance to orthodoxy, or as a kind of academic-subversive heresy. The argument, in retrospect, should have been made on different terms: Madonna was worth thinking about on formal grounds, as well as for the response she evoked, as well as for the organizing intelligence she exhibited with regard to her public persona. There are stylistic reasons to appreciate Madonna, and to acclaim her as the canny cultural carpetbagger she was and is. Popular culture, in other words, is worth studying and thinking about not because it is consumed in ways that demonstrate an always resistant army of canny consumers, in perpetual and sophisticated struggle with advertisers and marketers, but because popular artifacts in some regard demonstrate interesting form and/or appealing structure, just as they evidence or gesture toward the controlling, regulating intelligence and craft of a maker/auteur. As people in the know would know, many artifacts of popular culture display all the characteristics that we associate with – you guessed it – art.

Neil Nehring sounded the alarm almost a decade ago. Three years after the publication of the landmark *Cultural Studies* anthology, Nehring noted that cultural studies theorists risked having their commitment to mass culture signify a careless relativism toward the notion of value rather than a principled judgment call. "The relativist refusal to make positive and negative discrimination in evaluating popular culture, ironically, makes the utilitarian critic useless to the world outside academia," Nehring wrote, adding that "if cultural studies exists to suggest particular political directions to the culture at large, it needs to offer forthright illustrations of practices it considers exemplary" (1993: 77–8). Over the course of the 1990s, cultural studies work too often failed to elaborate on the rationale behind the critique of aesthetics, a rationale made explicit by Andrew Ross (and, as we have seen, acknowledged even by Thomas Frank): namely, that the boundary between high and low culture was a construct of experts with a considerable interest in maintaining the boundary in order to obtain and legitimatize their symbolic capital as taste arbiters. The critique of aesthetics should have been explicitly linked to an affirmation of demotic practices and ordinary value judgments exercised by various publics in relation to the arts. Instead, many outsiders came to regard cultural studies as not much more than the display of a confident demeanor and supercilious charm amid a world of consumer options.[4] It would have been far better if cultural studies theorists in America had learned to speak in the language of their 1990s contemporaries, Beavis and Butthead: this is cool, and that sucks. Of course, I don't believe that pleasure exists outside of history, since there are social structures that produce the competence that produces our pleasure in the face of art; and what's more, I think academic professionals are honor bound to reflect on the conditions that produce their pleasure.[5] However, in purging affect and partisanship from evaluation while seeming to stand above the ordinary act of evaluation, cultural studies began to look like a superior knowingness – paradoxically, as if the critic were speaking for a universal knowledge, the kind offered by the universal truths of aesthetics rather than by the partial truths of the popular. And who knows? Perhaps a cultural studies that appropriated the Beavis and Butthead methodology for video criticism, offering the spectacle of intellectuals relinquishing some cultural capital while at the same time asserting their right to choose and judge objects, might even have headed off the new populist backlash – or at least that wing of it that complains about cultural studies' lamentable lack of discrimination.

For apparently it was the alleged composure of cultural studies critics before art that spurred Richard Rorty's conflicted account of what he perceived as a paradigm shift in English departments. In Rorty's diagnosis, the rise of cultural studies has resulted in the ascent of the "knowingness" pose, practiced to ensure critical immunity to "romantic enthusiasm" toward art (1998: 126). Rorty also articulates what would become a common presupposition in new populist polemic, namely, that cultural studies constitutes less a methodology than a pose conducive to professional advancement. Cultural studies provides its practitioners with a prophylactic against the "inspirational value in a text" by allowing them to believe that art is simply "the product of a mechanism of cultural production" (1998: 133). Protected from the shock of an encounter with art, the scholar becomes uniquely poised to achieve a privileged place within the discipline; what you lose in affect you recoup with career gains. As Rorty has it, "the natural tendency of professionalization and academicization is to favor a talent for analysis and problem-solving over imagination, to replace enthusiasm with dry, sardonic knowingness" (1998: 135). His deliberately contrarian essay, "The Inspirational Value of Great Works of Literature," therefore argues for the legitimacy of the "connoisseurs of charisma" whose mode of learning and teaching is "different from the kind that produces knowingness, or technique, or professionalism" (1998: 134).

I admit I'd prefer to think of myself as one of Rorty's self-effacing literary "charismatics" than as one of the smug experts: who wants to be on the wrong side of *that* divide? But there's something very wrong with this picture, and you'll see it the moment you ask yourself, with Harold Bloom in mind, whether you esteem the believers and ecstatics that you know for their humility in the face of great art. So while I'm intrigued by – and partly in agreement with – Rorty's criticism of the politics of smugness, I am less convinced by Rorty's equation of "knowing" cultural studies scholars with the culture of professionalism that he views with such suspicion. If cultural studies practitioners really suffer from excess pride in their methodological acuity, why couldn't this excess be a problem raised and resolved within routine institutional practice? Rorty seems to argue that professional conduct, once established, can only change if practitioners step aside from their vocational interests, or somehow escape their institutional location: the "natural tendency of professionalization and academicization" will apparently defeat any attempt to change the profession from within. But professions change from within all the time, and in order to advocate for changes in professional practice it is not necessary to invoke a higher ground outside rules and norms, where the heart reigns and our souls are redeemed. (You wouldn't think that a pragmatist would need to be reminded of this – or of the pitfalls of speaking about the "natural tendencies" of cultural phenomena.) "Knowingness" as a mode of doing business might be "redressed" in the same way that indie rock-band Radiohead rejected and transcended the surrounding irony-heavy music culture of Britpop circa 1995. "The Britpop movement was wrong for us because it was so awash with this knowing irony," Radiohead guitarist Jonny Greenwood remarks, before delivering this helpful diagnosis: "In some ways, it wasn't about ... being serious about being in a band." (See the Radiohead fan site, www.followmearound.com.) Along similar lines, cultural studies' knowingness might be understood not as a malady of heart and soul besetting cultural professionals, but as a failure of seriousness, focus, and aspiration within professional protocols. Such attitudes could be addressed by more worldly means.

Rorty shares with new populists the desire to restore heart to the arts; and if the new populists brought with them the recognition that people find art valuable because art changes lives, and we judge – that is, seek to organize our response to – art because art challenges us, I would cheer them on against the aloof cultural studies crew. Unfortunately, the new populist critique is full of bad faith; and whereas it takes the form of antiprofessionalism from within the profession, it takes the form of *faux* populism when advanced by cultural journalists in the general media. Thus, for instance, when Shakespeare scholar Linda Charnes proclaims that academics have failed to win hearts and minds with their "critiques of [the world's] epistemology," and declares that "post-humanism may exist in the academy but it won't be found in the hearts and minds of the book-buying public," she wins space in the *New York Times Review of Books* and the hearty praise of cultural critic Ron Rosenbaum. Charnes speaks almost in the tones of a convert or a penitent, repudiating the arid domain of cultural studies to which she once claimed allegiance in favor of the Harold Bloomian world of literature and passion which contains, in her words, a "humor" and "poignancy" predicated on Bloom's "openly avowed love of art" – a love that, in speaking its name, also wins public support (quoted in Rosenbaum 2000: 12).

Significantly, it is not enough for Charnes to forswear "the institutionalized debunking of the bourgeois autonomous or essentialist humanist self" (Rosenbaum 2000: 12). It doesn't suffice to love literature; your ardor must be "openly avowed," in Charnes' words: that is, confessed, literalized, and, above all, made public and ceremonial. Charnes' revelatory embrace of Bloom manages to partake of both kinds of bad faith: adopting an antiprofessionalist rhetoric, it actually constitutes a routine professional procedure in English studies, namely, recalibrating one's professional aims with an eye toward a "public" that is imagined as excluded from and hostile to the deliberations of professionals.[6] In other words, where Rorty suggested that the cultural studies theorist adopts a stance of sardonic knowingness in order to advance her academic career, it could be suggested in response that Charnes adopts a stance of renouncing sardonic knowingness in order to advance *her* career as a newly reformed advocate of ardor. I am not proposing that we read Charnes as an ex-careerist attacking other careerists; but I am speculating that this is precisely how Rosenbaum wants his praise of Charnes to function. For if you look at the context in which Rosenbaum's citation of Charnes appears, it becomes altogether obvious that Rosenbaum sees in Charnes (and Charnes presents herself as) something like a saving remnant. Rosenbaum writes, with Charnes as Exhibit A, "that there are indications – hints, clues, suggestions – that the flood tide of theory in the academy has begun to ebb and that questions of value and aesthetics have begun to creep back in" (2000: 12). Celebrations of passion, love, ardor, and antiprofessionalist amateurism – all presented here as (maybe, just maybe) the profession's New Wave.

Thus, in Andrew Delbanco's less mystified polemic for the new populist cause, the love of the beautiful explicitly emerges with a demonstrable use value: critical ardor can revivify and justify the profession of English studies. Delbanco has emerged as perhaps the most thoughtful spokesperson for grounding the profession in a passionate relation between its adherents and their subject matter; indeed, as I'll note in more detail below, Delbanco even desires to make an ardor for literature count as part of the Ph.D. credentialing process in graduate programs. In his 1999 *New York Review of Books* essay, "The Decline and Fall of Literature," Delbanco is as dour as Charnes on the failure of cutting-edge departments to win public support and recruit students to literary and humanistic study. "Outside the university," he states plainly, and impatiently, "one hears a growing outcry of Enough!" (1999: 32). Enough of jargon, critiques of the subject, and the pretense to know more than "mere" literature: scholars must attune themselves to the formal qualities of texts, take stock of their expressive means, and most of all, learn (and profess) to love what they teach.

Delbanco admits that cultural studies is responsible for expanding the subject matter of English studies, but this admission quickly becomes a lament, since the expansion of the discipline has not been accompanied by a rise in critical discernment. On the contrary, those who practice "cultural studies" (Delbanco's scare quotes) seem to be presumptuous neophytes insistent on their inside knowledge of popular culture and little else of substance. Such scholars move "with callow confidence into the interpretation of visual, legal, and even scientific *texts*" (1999: 33), thus replacing the image of the professional-as-expert with the image of the professional-as-mountebank.

While debunking cultural studies pretenders, exposing them as scholars living far beyond their intellectual and spiritual means, Delbanco attests to the frightening prevalence of cultural studies' pretensions within the profession – frightening because the new field draws enough graduate students from the dwindling numbers of students entering the field to constitute a new dominant, and to convince administrators to shut down English departments, or divert literary study into interdisciplinary centers. Somehow, cultural studies is blamed for driving students away from the humanities and for bringing the wrong kind of students in.[7] In response to the "callow" show of intellectual pomp in cultural studies, Delbanco provides a brief counterhistory of English that serves to legitimate his claim to have divined the special mission of the profession. For

Delbanco, the critic begins and ends with a love for literature that passes show; literary scholars, like the melancholy Dane, "know not seems." They are as they appear, and must declare it, professing a love of literature that can be conveyed to others through a demonstration of fervor. English academics, if they wish to survive, are enjoined to become "professor[s] in the religious sense of that word – ardent, exemplary, even fanatic" (1999: 34). Thus the contemporary English professor, working from the inspiration derived from inspirational works of great literature, is no mere professional; he is an adept who transcends knowing and knowingness, achieving true *gnosis*. Delbanco writes, "Students who turn with real engagement to English do so almost always because they have had the mysterious and irreducibly private experience of receiving from a work of literature 'an untranslatable order of impressions' that has led to 'consummate moments'" (1999: 34). The source of Delbanco's ecstatic language is of course Walter Pater, whom Delbanco reclaims as the real father of academic literary study. Insofar as the discipline was originally constituted as a replacement for revealed religion, Delbanco, recovering Pater's Orphic intent and the faith of the Founder, underwrites his claim to know what's best for the profession.

No one I know wants to be insensitive to "consummate moments," whether we find these in Pater's *The Renaissance* or in that *Exile on Main Street* CD. Yet I think we should be properly skeptical – though not sardonic or smug! – about Delbanco's relentless emphasis on the private aspects of the individual encounter with literature, and the attempt to ground the profession in a realm of miracle and transcendence that resists full articulation or rational justification. Not only does this emphasis seem to be an overreaction to the perception of presumption in the precincts of cultural studies, it seems to be a serious mistake: rather than challenging cultural studies scholars in the academy to declare their allegiances, Delbanco chooses to pit untrained readers (that is, those who "turn with real engagement to English") against their more accredited and professionalized counterparts in order to suggest the greater purity and authority of the former. The response of the passionate amateur is thus more authentic *because* more emotive than that of the professor. We are no doubt familiar with the populist rhetoric which insists that certain jobs, like those of the state legislator or public school teacher, are best handled by earnest amateurs rather than trained experts. Delbanco's polemic adds literary criticism to this dubious list.

In a subsequent *PMLA* forum on the future of graduate training in English, Delbanco goes even further to propose revisions to doctoral programs in order to make room for more evangelical commitments to literature. Delbanco suggests that graduate students be compelled, in oral examination, to provide an account as to why the single author they have chosen to study is worth defending and preserving, against the imaginary detractors that this figure might have. This, he hopes, will leaven expertise with enthusiasm:

> We want, I think, to find ways to reinject into the Ph.D. something of the amateur passion that brought us to literature in the first place. We want to produce professors in the religious sense of the word – which has always been hard to do, because there is something fundamentally at odds between the zeal of the amateur and the professionalism of institutional imperatives. (2000: 1208)

Of course, the qualifying clause here tends to win one's affection for the writer; it admits the tentative, exploratory quality of Delbanco's proposal. To create the hybrid of expert and devotee that he desires, Delbanco proposes a return in literary studies to currently unfashionable studies in "major authors." While conceding, no doubt with an eye toward the canon wars of the last decade, that "the choice of author can be left up to the student," he insists all newly minted Ph.D.s "ought to be able to make a convincing case for why a given author is worth reading" (2000: 1208).

While I admire the frank statement of purpose, I wonder at the severity of the crisis that Delbanco perceives as the impetus for this curriculum revision. Humanists seem to exist in a perennial crisis over their public image; yet the cure here sounds fully as dire as the crisis. Must we reorganize English study so as to enable graduate students to serve as defense attorneys capable of persuading the public that their authors are worthy of attention – and that literature is a therefore a realm of transcendent value, worthy, on those terms, of public support? If so, we legitimate our labor by presiding over a permanent, institutionalized crisis over the value ascribed to our field, and oblige ourselves to perpetuate the emergency with every oral exam, all in order to create a sense of disciplinary mission. Sympathetic as I am to the idea that critics should be able to advance and justify their evaluative frameworks, I find it hard to believe that literary studies will be saved by requiring thousands of graduate students to tell their examination committees why Austen, Melville, Hurston, and Shakespeare are worth the time and effort. In fact, I can imagine no surer prescription for the annual production of thousands of rote recitations of professions of amateur zeal.

I believe the real question at stake here is whether a profession compatible with theory can reproduce itself as a going concern. I've argued that cultural studies has underplayed its rationale for pursuing humanistic study, and misplayed its expertise in the popular, failing to see expertise as *itself* a popular mode of engaging the popular. But I think the new populist critique of cultural studies professionalism is just hopelessly confused about its own condition of possibility. In order to convince the public and the profession of the cogency of their claims, new populists must persuade readers that their arguments come from outside the academy and represent popular sentiment (in the public square where the people cry "enough!"); thus, in a curious reversal, aesthetics returns not as an apologia for social hierarchies but as a neopopulist creed. The uncanny revival also has the effect of ceding professional identity to cultural studies, thus making professionalism precisely the thing that has to be overcome if we are to save the profession.

Professionals of all sorts, including cultural studies academics, can stand a good deflating now and then. Yet the real losers of the new populism, paradoxically, would be the public outside the academy, the very public the new populists like to imagine clamoring at the university walls and demanding that professors stop "interrogating" innocent works of literature. For when we think of expertise as an encumbrance, and our identities within the profession as a matter of passion rather than knowledge and know-how, training and credentialing, the result isn't so much the dissolution of professional structures as the dissemination of the bad faith argument that training isn't necessary with the humanities, and that anyone can do it, or already does it. It is as if our true desire (and the public's) is to have Frank Kermode throw up his hands and proclaim, "I give up – I don't know what social codes or histories lurk behind the desire for narrative closure. I don't actually have a sense of the sense of an ending: I just like stories." This would then be followed by an oral examination in which Kermode persuades his interlocutors that Wallace Stevens is worth studying. But I don't believe anyone really wants a Kermode who merely emotes in the presence of the text; we do the public a considerable disservice by assuming that they want critics to abdicate their skills and insights. Credentialing passion is tantamount to confusing criticism with soul making. Such conceptual blurring might seem to empower the public but in fact serves to discourage laypersons from understanding both the history of literature and the project of criticism, and perhaps from enlisting in the field and becoming a specialist. And insofar as such a critique of the profession – often, but not exclusively, produced from within academic precincts – dissuades the external public from wanting to be trained in the field, it thereby reinforces the exclusive power of tastemaking elites, who mystify their power and status even as they presume to speak for the public. The odd but incontrovertible fact is that both cultural professionals and amateurs alike require – indeed, demand – the production of critical stances and critical knowledge.

It would be unfortunate, to say the least, if new populists' efforts to convince academics to treat art with more reverence wound up not merely promoting the critical virtues of emotion and affect but also, more dangerously, discounting the virtues of critical reason – and the virtues of those annoying, carping critical reasoners who think they know so much. One does not have to strain to imagine new-populist antiprofessionalism making common cause with the more insidious forms of anti-intellectualism that often accompany conservative populism. But even if the new populism is more benign than this, scholars in cultural studies should respond rigorously to it nonetheless, making it clear to the nonacademic public that our critiques of aesthetics are launched in the service of a more ordinary, demotic practice of evaluation applicable to any and every form of cultural practice. For ultimately, it will be the public that loses if professional critics choose to genuflect before art rather than exercise – and inspire their students and readers to exercise – the powers of reason and critique.

NOTES

1 Maya Jaggi, "Prophet at the Margins." *The Guardian*, July 8, 2000.
2 John Seabrook's *Nobrow* (2000) offers one account of how class identity became disassociated from the consumption of art with high cultural capital. More dubiously, Seabrook sometimes assumes that class has been superseded simply because there is broader-based patronage of the popular by elites.
3 See Peter Bailey's *Popular Culture and Performance in the Victorian City* (1998), in particular "Conspiracies of Knowing." T. J. Clark makes similar claims about the connoisseurs of the popular attending the Parisian café-chantant in his study of the social contexts of Impressionist art, *The Painting of Modern Life* (1999).
4 Zoe Heller (2000) assumes Marjorie Garber's book *Sex and Real Estate* can be categorized as a cultural studies project largely because its author blithely disregards checkpoints across the cultural divide: "Like the kosher product of the cultural-studies mill that it is, *Sex and Real Estate* brims with multidisciplinary references – wacky juxtapositions of high culture and low culture – designed to demonstrate the democratic breadth of the author's interests." In other words, Garber gets annexed to cultural studies in large part because Heller feels she's a show-off.
5 This is not to say that cultural studies criticized the aesthetic enterprise because it wanted to end up with a crude version of impressionism. A crucial component of the history of cultural studies consists of its struggle with, and admiration for, antihumanist thought: for Claude Lévi-Strauss's structuralism and Louis Althusser's structuralist Marxism. When the smoke cleared, cultural studies theorists such as Stuart Hall relinquished the academic dream of providing the most elaborate account of ideology, largely because such accounts would require an extraordinarily synoptic vision of the social totality. Still, the structuralist project is hardwired within the field of cultural studies, and a significant part of its history. This intellectual transaction precludes any simple, pre-ideological return to the subject of pleasure. See Brantlinger 1990: 68–108.
6 Bruce Robbins elaborates on the porous nature of the expert/public divide through a historical account of academic criticism in *Secular Vocations* (1993). Particularly apposite here is Robbins's observation that as part of their normal routines of professional self-scrutiny, "critics impersonate and ventriloquize outsiders – and not any outsiders, but precisely those who are most critical of professions and their pretensions to self-sufficiency" (1993: 74).
7 Delbanco's argument relies on numbers provided by Lynn Hunt's "Tradition Confronts Change: The Place of the Humanities in the University" (1998).

REFERENCES

Bailey, Peter. 1994. "Conspiracies of Meaning: Music Hall and the Knowingness of Popular Culture." *Past and Present* 144: 138–170.

———. 1998. *Popular Culture and Performance in the Victorian City.* Cambridge: Cambridge University Press.

Bourdieu, Pierre. 1984. *Distinction.* Cambridge, MA: Harvard University Press.

Brantlinger, Patrick. 1990. *Crusoe's Footprints: Cultural Studies in Britain and America.* New York: Macmillan.

Clark, T. J. 1999. *The Painting of Modern Life.* New Haven: Yale University Press.

Delbanco, Andrew. 1999. "The Decline and Fall of Literature." *New York Review of Books* 46(17) (Nov. 4): 32–8.

———. 2000. "What Should Ph.D. Mean?" *PMLA* 115(5) (Oct.): 1205–9.

Eagleton, Terry. 1990. *The Ideology of the Aesthetic.* Oxford: Blackwell.

Fish, Stanley. 1985. "Anti-professionalism." *New Literary History* 17(1): 89–127.

Frank, Thomas. 2000. *One Market Under God: Extreme Capitalism, Market Populism, and the End of Economic Democracy.* New York: Doubleday.

Heller, Zoe. 2000. "House Arrest." Review of *Sex and Real Estate: Why We Love Houses,* by Marjorie Garber. *The New Republic,* July 3: 27–9.

Hoskyns, Barney. 2000. "Karma Police." *Gentleman's Quarterly,* Oct.: 157–64.

Hunt, Lynn. 1998. "Tradition Confronts Change: The Place of the Humanities in the University." *The Humanist on Campus: Continuity and Change.* American Council of Learned Societies: Occasional Paper no. 44: 8.

Jaggi, Maya. 2000. "Prophet at the Margins: The *Guardian* Profile of Stuart Hall." *The Guardian* (UK), July 8: 8.

Levine, Lawrence. 1988. *Highbrow/Lowbrow: The Emergence of Cultural Hierarchy in America.* Cambridge, MA: Harvard University Press.

Nehring, Neil. 1993. *Flowers in the Dustbin: Culture, Anarchy, and Postwar England.* Ann Arbor: University of Michigan Press.

Robbins, Bruce. 1993. *Secular Vocations: Intellectuals, Professionalism, Culture.* New York: Verso.

———. 2002. "The Sweatshop Sublime." *PMLA* 117(1): 84–97.

Rorty, Richard. 1998. *Achieving Our Country: Leftist Thought in Twentieth-Century America.* Cambridge, MA: Harvard University Press.

Rosenbaum, Ron. 2000. "The Play's the Thing, Again." *New York Times Book Review,* Aug. 6: 12.

Ross, Andrew. 1989. *No Respect: Intellectuals and Popular Culture.* New York: Routledge.

Seabrook, John. 2000. *Nobrow: The Culture of Marketing, the Marketing of Culture.* New York: Knopf.

Smith, Barbara Herrnstein. 1988. *Contingencies of Value: Alternative Perspectives for Critical Theory.* Cambridge, MA: Harvard University Press.

Williams, Raymond. *Keywords.* 1976. Oxford: Oxford University Press. Rev. ed. 1983.

8

Beauty on My Mind: Reading Literature in an Age of Cultural Studies

IRENE KACANDES

When I first read Elaine Scarry's book, *On Beauty and Being Just*, shortly after it appeared in 1999, I immediately wondered against whom or what she thought she was defending beauty. For though the book is rather beautifully written, it also engages in a practice I can't abide: setting up bogey adversaries by not naming anyone specific. When Scarry writes that "The banishing of beauty from the humanities in the last two decades has been carried out by a set of political complaints against it . . . I do not mean that beautiful things have themselves been banished . . . I mean something much more modest: that conversation about the beauty of these things has been banished" (1999: 57), it's not only her repetitive passives that obscure the "guilty" party, it's also the lack of footnotes. Despite her objectionable tactics, my second reflection was: there *is* a problem with "beauty" and contemporary academic study of cultural production, but her "conversation" isn't going to help us get to it.

By now there are plenty of cultural critics who have fingered Scarry's "culprit" and others who have defended it: cultural studies is to blame; cultural studies is innocent. Since my first point, however, is that it is an intellectual disservice to set up scapegoats or bogeymen so that the author and her argument can look good, I will offer my own version of evidence that "beauty" and aesthetics have not been banished by cultural studies – not by the founding fathers, and not in recent work. I will do so briefly, though, for it seems to me that the more productive and urgent contribution I can make here is to review what I think is the real problem with regard to cultural studies, aesthetics, and literature, and to start some new conversations, specifically by showing how cultural studies can foreground formal, aesthetic considerations in order to generate productive ways of reading. I take my case studies from German cultural studies on purpose, for it seems to me that one of the charges that legitimately *can* be leveled against cultural studies, especially as it has been practiced in the United States, is that it is overwhelmingly Anglocentric.

Let's assume that if Scarry had documented her accusations, she would have cited cultural studies' interest in power or popular culture or Raymond Williams's proclamation that "culture is ordinary." Reading even a little into the history of cultural studies, however, one realizes that there is actually much evidence to support the opposite thesis: that "all of cultural studies has ultimately been a debate with aesthetics" (Davies 1995: 67; see also Hunter 1992: 347). From the German roots of cultural studies one doesn't have to belabor the obviousness of Lukács's and Adorno's interest in aesthetics and ideology. But even those cultural studies theoreticians who have been held to be most "political" – say, Antonio Gramsci and Raymond Williams – certainly did not disavow the exist- ence of the aesthetic dimension of cultural products or banish it from "conversa- tion." Gramsci insisted, for example, that it was possible to appreciate the aesthetic merits of a literary work even while repudiating the ideology that informs it (letters from prison to his wife, June 1, 1931 and September 5, 1932). Although Gramsci never drafted a full-fledged aesthetics of his own, when he set out to articulate an approach to literature that is consistent with his philosophy of praxis, his "Marxism," he was particularly anxious not to have ideological tendentiousness interfere with and occlude aesthetic judgment (Buttigieg 1998). He addressed this question most directly in the opening paragraph of a relatively long note entitled "Art and the Struggle for a New Civilization":

> Two writers may represent the same socio-historical moment, but one might be an artist and the other [a mere scribbler]. If the treatment of the question amounts to nothing more than a description of what the writers represent or express socially – that is, a more or less reliable summary of the characteristics of a specific socio-historical moment – it means that the question of art has not even been broached. All this can be useful and necessary, indeed it certainly is but in a different field: in the field of political criticism, in the criticism of customs, in the struggle to destroy and overcome certain currents of feeling and belief, certain attitudes toward life and the world. This is not criticism and history of art, nor can it be presented as such – not without causing confusion and regression or the stagnation of scientific concepts; in other words, not without the failure precisely to pursue the intrinsic aims of the cultural struggle.

(Notebook 23ss3; quoted in and trans. by Buttigieg 1998; also in Gramsci 1985: 93)

The "question of art," then, surely existed for Gramsci. True, he also believed that to study literature is to study the history of literature, and that "literary history is a part and an aspect of a much larger history of culture" (*Prison Notebooks*, Italian edition, p. 1740, as quoted in Buttigieg 1982–3: 27). Gramsci's extensive critique of Croce and his concomitant championing of De Sanctis, which I won't take the space to review here, provide further evidence of Gramsci's engagement with aesthetic issues. His interest isn't negated or diminished, in my view, by the fact that he insists specifically on the value of situating the literary work and the critic in history.

Likewise, Raymond Williams's engagement with aesthetics requires a cultural and historical situating of the artistic work rather than the banishment of "beauty." In his chapter on "Aesthetic and Other Situations" in *Marxism and Literature*, for instance, Williams extends the ideas of Lukács and Mukarovsky in order to situate the aesthetic and the arts in "the full social material process itself" (1977: 155). Williams proposes that to do this is not really that difficult:

> Anyone who is in contact with the real multiplicity of writing, and with the no less real multiplicity of those forms of writing that have been specialized as literature, is already aware of the range of intentions and responses which are continually and variably manifest and latent. The honest muddle that so often arises is a consequence of pressure from both ends of a range of received and incompatible theories. If we are asked to believe that all literature is "ideology" in the crude sense that its dominant intention (and then our only response) is the communication or imposition of "social" or "political" meanings and values, we can only, in the end, turn away. If we are asked to believe that all literature is "aesthetic," in the crude sense that its dominant intention (and then our only response) is the beauty of language or form, we may stay a little longer but will still in the end turn away. Some people will lurch from one position to the other. More, in practice, will retreat to an indifferent acknowledgement of complexity, or assert the autonomy of their own (usually consensual) response. But it is really much simpler to face the facts of the range of intentions and effects, and to face it *as a range*. (1977: 155)

What Williams rejects, as did Gramsci before him, is the idea of the aesthetic as a separate, abstract, independent function (Williams 1977: 156; for Gramsci's rejection, see Buttigieg 1982–3: 29); but this does not mean that Williams denies the real experience to which that abstraction has been used to point. To the contrary, Williams takes pains to stress corporeal markers of the "aesthetic" when he states that, "The true effects of many kinds of writing are indeed quite physical: specific alternations of physical rhythms, physical organization: experiences of quickening and slowing, of expansion and of intensification" (1977: 156). Furthermore, in arguing for a history of art that is part of a larger history of culture, he pointedly mentions that "to enter any part of this history, in an active way, we have to learn to understand the specific elements – conventions and notations – which are the material keys to intention and response, and more generally, the specific elements which socially and historically determine and signify aesthetic and other situations" (1977: 157). In other words, as I see it, Williams is even arguing for the special training needed to understand the aesthetic dimension of the artwork in question. What Williams might have been wrong about is the difficulty of describing and assessing aesthetic effect ("it is really much simpler to face the facts of the range . . ."), for an enormous amount of work today seems to stick to the crude senses he describes at the poles.

Still, some recent scholarship in cultural studies has honored the preoccupations of the field's foundational thinkers by asking questions like: What are the qualities of this literary work, piece of architecture, painting, musical composition, philosophical text, etc. admired by readers, viewers, listeners in a particular epoch in a particular culture, and cited by them as expressions of "beauty," "truth," "goodness," "sublimity"? That is to say, a cultural studies approach need not – indeed, must not – ignore the aesthetic dimension of cultural production. However, it also must not assert that the text, building, painting simply "is" beautiful, truthful, good, sublime. Rather it must ask when, how, and why the object was granted such status and by whom. To answer these questions, it is of course necessary to investigate what was meant by the categories of "beauty," "truth," "goodness," "sublimity" for a specific culture and at a specific time. What work did these categories do for that culture?

One of the best examples I know of this kind of study is on a German topic: cultural historian Celia Applegate's analysis of Felix Mendelssohn Bartholdy's revival of Johann Sebastian Bach's *St. Matthew Passion* in Berlin in 1829 (1997: 139–62). Bach's *St. Matthew Passion* was originally performed in Leipzig in 1729 and then not again until exactly 100 years later on March 11, 1829, in the new Schinkel building of the Singakademie in Berlin with the 18-year-old prodigy Felix Mendelssohn Bartholdy conducting, with approximately 200 members of the Singakademie singing in the choir, with soloists from the Royal Opera, and with orchestra members about equally divided between amateurs and members of the Philharmonic Society (Philharmonische Gesellschaft). For the March 11 performance, the building was filled to overflowing with about a thousand people; more than a thousand would-be listeners were turned away. Among those in the audience were the Prussian king and such luminaries and luminaries-to-be as Schleiermacher, Hegel, Droysen, the young Heine, and Rahel Varnhagen von Ense (Geck 1967: 34–5). There was a second, similarly successful performance in Berlin, followed by performances in Frankfurt am Main (1829); Breslau (1830); Stettin (1831); Königsberg (1832); Kassel (1832); and Dresden (1833).

Applegate's concern touches directly, but not exclusively, on the aesthetic: Why did Mendelssohn and his contemporaries put so much stock in their aesthetic experience of the *St. Matthew Passion*? Her study is particularly helpful for my purposes because it illustrates how this question exceeds the reach of a purely formal musical analysis. In other words, Applegate remarks on an historical aesthetic fact and realizes that to understand it, she must try to place it in the "full social material process itself," in Williams's phrase. What factors allowed the same piece of music to be transformed for the very same listeners/performers from something that was "difficult [schwierig]"; "old [alt]"; "strange [selten]" to something that produced "a true enthusiasm [eine wahre Begeisterung]" (contemporary Julius Schubring as quoted in Geck 1967: 34; my trans.)? In Mendelssohn's own account:

> In the beginning, no one wanted to approach it, they thought that it was too confused and outrageously difficult. However, already after a few rehearsals all that changed, and they sang with a reverence [Andacht] as if they were in church. Then the first two performances also went magnificently. It shows once again, that the public is always good [gut] when one gives it the Good [das Gute]. (as quoted in Geck 1967: 42; my trans.)

Applegate explores the institutional resources necessary to stage a work as complex as the *St. Matthew Passion*, but even more importantly, how the very mustering of those resources depended on numerous types of people deciding that the work to be performed was not only good, but the Good. Or, to put it more precisely in terms of the actual process, that before people would commit to the project, they had to decide that what at first seemed difficult was also superior aesthetically and morally ("das Gute"). In the course of her analysis Applegate touches on transformations in the role of music itself that led to large numbers of individuals wanting to create or attend such a performance, where the music "was no longer taken for granted as an accompaniment to royal grandeur or an act of homage to God but rather treated as something to be understood on its own terms and imbued with intrinsic significance" (1997: 147); on the development of voluntary music-making generally and specifically of the Singakademie (whose singers and material resources were eventually put at Mendelssohn's disposal); on the cultivation of music within the family sphere (which nourished Mendelssohn himself and his interest in Bach); on the development of a musical press (which fostered interest in the piece of music and the upcoming performance as well as reviews of it afterward, keeping the performance in the public "ear" long after the actual event). Most relevantly for our discussion here,

Applegate also tries to explain this success by looking at "what 'implicitly defined functions' this particular piece of music served, or to put it otherwise, at why this music seemed suddenly just right to people, a more-than-adequate expression of values they already held and were in the process of constructing" (1997: 152).

I'd like to end this section by quoting the long paragraph in which Applegate reflects on her methodology, since it echoes with the statements of Gramsci and Williams quoted above and with my contention that aesthetics is very much a concern of contemporary cultural studies analyses:

> by focusing on "implicit functions" of the piece and the performance, I do not mean to rule out the possibility that people simply found the music beautiful, hence played it and listened to it and valued it. This was certainly the case, at one level, and much has already been written about why, precisely, the *St. Matthew Passion* is so beautiful, what about its harmonies and melodic gestures strikes the ear with such pathos, what about its combination of chorus, chorale, recitative, and aria creates such drama, what in its musical tonality so moves us. Formal analysis takes one deep into the music but perhaps not so far into the culture that played the music. Implicit functions might, at the other extreme from aesthetic formalism, indicate a reduction of the music to an instrumental plane of action, in which it serves only to reinforce certain social norms, like bourgeois self control (hence, perhaps, the silence in the concert hall?), or certain relationships, like monarch to subject (hence, perhaps, the presence of the Prussian king?). But I do not wish to pursue such interpretive strategies either, for they are rarely able to account for the aesthetic force of the music in question nor the complexities of its craft. Avoiding both instrumental reductionism and aesthetic formalism, I hope to speak...of music's general representational or ideational function, its capacity, in Clifford Geertz's words, to "materialize a way of experiencing, bring a particular case of mind out into the world of objects, where men [*sic*] can look at it." (1997: 152–3)

Applegate concludes this reflection by admitting that "explaining all this is a tall order," complicated in her example "by the triangular relationship between the artist whose work is being revived, the artists who conceived and carried out the revival, and the public" (1997: 153). Nevertheless, I think she acquits herself admirably, discussing the growing consensus that music could be deeply serious (1997: 154); the identification its audience made between Bach, Protestant Christianity, and being German (1997: 155); the centrality of a sense of "participation [Teilnahme]" on the part of the chorus and the audience. In other words, with beauty on her mind, Applegate shows how this particular piece of music had the capacity "to make both audible and visible the idea of a German community" (1997: 153). Contemporaries called this capacity "beautiful [schön]" and "great [großartig]." Applegate's demonstration brings in analysis of the music itself; contemporary ideas about music and composers;

contemporary social relations and institutions; history and philosophy. Her analysis extends a longstanding cultural studies tradition of asking certain kinds of questions through/with aesthetic considerations, and can also serve as a model for the way many different disciplines must be mobilized to understand aesthetic judgment and function in any given period, culture, or event.

For I take it as a given that the particular development of cultural studies, at least in North America, has forever transformed our very notions of "literature" and "literary studies." From my perspective, no credible departments of literary studies can "go back" to teaching exclusively "high literature" in New Critical fashion. What the heat of the cultural wars and specifically of the spurious "aesthetics vs. cultural studies" debates has distracted us from is a serious consideration of what course literary studies should take from here. I'm not particularly troubled by current or future transformations in institutional forms of the teaching of literature, like whether foreign-language departments merge or whether cultural studies is considered the province of the English department or vice versa. But I am perturbed by the gimmicky calls for preservation or restoration of "beauty" or "the canon" that distract us from answering the more urgent question of what is at stake in the production and consumption of literature.

To begin to answer this question I have found Walter Ong's idea of "secondary orality" (1982) key to understanding why interest in writing may have shifted and yet why writing and the ability to read it do still matter. In what follows, then, I will recapitulate some of Ong's ideas on the hybrid communicative quality of our age, then engage several commentators on basic literacy and the teaching of literature. Finally, I'm going to move to a presentation of some approaches to a specific literary text, Gerturd Kolmar's *A Jewish Mother* (originally written in 1930–1, published posthumously in 1965), to illustrate how a cultural studies analysis of texts (which necessarily includes aesthetic elements, as I've argued above) can revitalize the literature classroom.

To be sure, oral speech has always been the dominant method of communicating in terms of numbers of people and numbers of minutes per day in which it is used. The term secondary orality is meant to reference (among other things) the proliferation of modes for the conduct of oral speech, as well as the replacement through those modes of written or printed communication, for instance the diminution of personal letter-writing through use of the telephone. (The surge in the use of email and in the use of oral conversations through the internet illustrates just how quickly technology facilitates shifts between oral and written forms.) The idea of secondary orality derives from diachronic approaches to the study of human communication, in which societies are assumed to progress from an exclusively oral mode of communication ("primary oral") to one based on writing (and therefore "literate," "textual," or "chirographic"). A subsequent ("second") oral age, which privileges speech, serves as an addendum to this model (see Ong 1982). Simply put, we hear more speech during our waking hours than our parents, grandparents, and great-grandparents presumably did. How does this inundation of speech affect us? And why do we need to know how to read, much less read literature, if we are "oral" once again?

The short answer to this second question is that we are not "oral" once again, we are "secondary oral" for the first time, only very recently having "woken up to the presence of orality as a contemporary fact in our midst" (Havelock 1986: 118). Within a diachronic oral-literate schema, the designation "secondary" refers not only to its chronological sense of coming after something else (i.e., secondary orality comes after a primary oral and literate stage[1]), but also to the idea of being "auxiliary" or "subordinate." That is to say, secondary orality could not come into being without the written word, both because the technologies which facilitate the resurgence of the spoken word rely on written language for development and operation, and also because the changes in mentality associated with literacy endure in this communicative age, for example, a privileging of individualism and self-consciousness, and a sense of communication as transfer of information. On this score, the expression "secondary orality" is opaque, only indirectly signaling the *literate* components of the phenomenon. Though Ong coined the term "secondary orality" and though he has written persuasively about the mentalities of primary oral and literate cultures (1982, esp. 31–77 on primary orality and 78–116 on literacy), he doesn't say much about how the hybrid forms of secondary orality shape individuals and human interaction. Books like Mitchell Stephens's *The Rise of the Image, The Fall of the Word* (1998) and my *Talk Fiction: Literature and the Talk Explosion* (2001) explore some dimensions of our secondary oral world, but clearly this is one area cultural studies could be working on if we weren't so preoccupied with defending our field.

In the meantime, plenty of social critics who don't seem particularly aware of secondary orality are screaming their heads off about illiteracy. Despite their apocalyptic rhetoric and the revanchist politics that often go along with it, there is a point in there that we shouldn't miss. Given that ours is a *hybrid* age, at once oral and literate, there *is* reason to be concerned about growing numbers of people who can't function as readers. Though I find the tone and particularly the attitude toward new technologies of authors like Sven Birkerts (e.g., *The Gutenberg Elegies*, 1994) and Barry Sanders (e.g., *A is for Ox*, 1994) unhelpful, I do believe these commentators describe real phenomena about which we all should be concerned. Coining the term "post-illiterates," Sanders, for instance, points out that many youngsters today never experience enough oral contact with their parents, or with other real human interlocutors, to develop a delight in the playfulness of language that is a prerequisite for the hard work necessary to learn to read and write. "Once a person faces literacy as an enemy, it is hard to ever give its other side, its ability to empower, a real chance" (Sanders 1994: 223). Furthermore, without having experienced reading and writing's power "to imagine the lives of others," it is easier for such individuals to engage in acts of violence or despair that "can be carried out best without feeling" (Sanders 1994: 179, 177). Unfortunately, I have personal experience that verifies this conclusion. I volunteer at a "Homework Club" in the local homeless shelter. One of the patterns I see there is that of children who can't understand something in the assignment immediately taking out their frustrations by trying to hurt (or at least distract) a child sitting near by. The directness of the connection is uncanny. The response of us helpers has been to emphasize basic reading skills, offer as much individual attention as possible, and in the meantime to strictly enforce our one hard rule: no violence of any kind. As the children's reading skills have improved, so have their social skills. Those of us privileged enough to work at the post-secondary level may have much more mediated experiences with incomplete literacy and violence, but my experience in the shelter has led me to lose patience with in-house faculty fighting about disciplinary protocols and scholarly rivalries in the humanities: it simply seems so much more important to help those students who do come into our purview become more literate/secondary-oral.

At Dartmouth College, where remedial reading and writing programs are taken seriously, my attention has been occupied with the more specific question of reading literature. (I'm using the phrase "reading literature" to stand in for close reading and viewing of any kind of fictional text, written or visual. I myself work most of the time with written texts.) Each year, my students arrive at university having read fewer and fewer literary texts of any kind, "high" or "low." My administration and even my presumed allies in German cultural studies seem to demand justification for the teaching of literature: what is literature good for and why should students want to learn about it? Insofar as these are genuine questions, I find the answer that "literature is beautiful" to be woefully insufficient. With the analyses of Ong and Sanders in mind, I suggest that questioning the value of being literate might be related to the opacity of the role of literacy in a secondary oral epoch more generally, and questioning the value of literature may be a kind of defensive cover for those whose literacy skills are simply not strong enough to get pleasure from written work.

For more than 10 years now, I've been obsessed with a particular text, Gertrud Kolmar's *A Jewish Mother* [*Eine jüdische Mutter*]. Drafted toward the end of the Weimar Republic in 1930–1, but only published in 1965, long after Kolmar's deportation and presumed extermination in Auschwitz in 1943, it makes a particularly good case study for an examination of literary valuation and cultural context, since it essentially had no reception during the author's lifetime, and has been instrumentalized – as has its author – in various ways depending on the historical moment (including this one) in which it's been read.[2] I find *A Jewish Mother* fascinating, and yet parts of it are embarrassingly bathetic. Does this mean that it's a bad novel and that I am weird or at least idiosyncratic for wanting to study it? Or can my own aesthetic response point me to work the novel has done or could do? I want to answer no to the first question and yes to the second, sharing the fact that I have used my emotional reactions to and aesthetic judgments of the novel to develop some reading strategies that I hope can become a model for reading other novels of the Weimar Republic and beyond to contribute to a more vital role for literature in the curriculum. As I discuss the novel in the pages that follow, I'm not trying to offer an adequate reading of it, but rather to offer just enough details to demonstrate how one can use aesthetic concerns to get at cultural contexts and vice versa.

Kolmar's novel may appear least artistic and most melodramatic when introduced through its plot. *A Jewish Mother* is set in the cosmopolitan Berlin of the Weimar Republic, the late 1920s to be more precise. Its protagonist, Martha Wolg, née Jadassohn, is an outsider, literally, as a Jew born in an eastern province, and figuratively, as a loner in the urban culture of the German metropolis in which she marries, bears a child, is abandoned by her gentile husband Friedrich, and struggles to make a living for herself and her daughter, Ursula (Ursa, for short). When her 5-year-old child does not return home one evening at the accustomed time, Martha sets off in search of her; Martha's initially casual walk turns into a mother's nightmare. Although she finds Ursula's playmates at a river bank, her daughter is not among them. Ursa went off, the children report, with a man who said her mother was looking for her. After a frantic evening of questioning the neighbors, a sleepless night, and an agonizing morning, Martha discovers her daughter's limp body in an abandoned shed in an outlying garden district, which locals refer to as the "Colony Refuse-Disposal [Siedlung Müllabfuhr]" (1997: 35; 1981: 38).[3] The child is still breathing, but her torso is bloodsoaked. Martha, with the assistance of some alarmed local women, manages to get the unconscious child to the nearest hospital. Several days later, the ravaged child is helped to her presumably inevitable death through sleeping powder administered by her mother. Martha swears revenge against the murderer of her child, whom she assumes to be lurking somewhere in Greater Berlin. Two-thirds of the book concern Martha's life after the child's death, following her as she is rebuffed or ignored by those whose aid she seeks – especially a lawyer, Albert Renkens, who had known Friedrich in America after Friedrich had abandoned Martha and Ursa, and whom Martha takes as a lover. Martha's attempt years later to terminate her search for the perpetrator – and, thus, to cease to define herself as a mother – also proves impossible. Rejected by Renkens, she plunges into the River Spree, ending her life with the sense of expiating a crime *she* perpetrated.

Child abduction, rape, revenge, sleeping powder, suicide: the plot certainly contains sensationalistic elements. More minor scenes which border on kitsch include Martha's memory of herself as a child being exposed to a flasher, and an unintended visit of the bereaved mother to a gay bar. One could further build a case against the artistic merit of the novel (if one wanted to do that) by citing rhetorical excesses in the language of numerous characters. For example, after an initial, accidental meeting with Renkens, Martha hatches the idea of making him into her instrument of revenge against the perpetrator of Ursula's rape. Having invited Albert for tea, Martha waits:

> She was ready. She knew exactly what she wanted. She did not delude herself. She did not think of the beginning of a love affair, of ardent glances and tender words, of the first searching kiss. She thought in brutal terms: tonight or right now this afternoon he will be in my bed. He shall cover me, I am hot. I don't love him. But he shall carry out my will, and I shall have to pay for it. I don't know any other way. And I have been fasting for a long time and we shall extract all the lust from us we are capable of. (1997: 106)[4]

Martha herself is certainly revealed in this passage, as in others, as a radically different kind of woman from the completely virtuous young lady of stereotypical Victorian (or Hollywood) melodrama. (In fact her sexual appetite and behaviors are a major subject of the book.) But I would suggest that her interior language often partakes of the "stupidity of received ideas," to cite one aspect of kitsch (Kundera 1988: 163). Interestingly, some of the most stereotypical phrases in this example, as in others, actually occur in the "no man's land" of free indirect discourse or narrated monologue, where technically the discourse retains the (third) person of the narrator, but to express thoughts that are more likely correctly attributed to the character (see Cohn on narrated monologue): "ardent glances [heiße Blicke]"; "tender words [zarte Worte]"; "first searching kiss [erster suchender Kuß]." Kolmar's extensive use of narrated monologue makes it hard to determine what position the text itself is taking in relation to the events and characters. I have come to believe that this was completely intentional on Kolmar's part: this kind of language ultimately led me to decide that there were numerous aesthetic clues – teasers, on some level – that could draw one in to take a closer look at the novel and what kind of cultural work it might be doing. As with Applegate's object of study, this novel poses aesthetic problems for which the analysis of "beauty," and the question of whether it is good or bad art, is completely insufficient. In other words, the question of aesthetic value opens onto what I consider to be the more important and interesting questions of how and by whom aesthetic value is assigned – and what that attribution of value might tell us about the society in which the artwork was created.

So, let me turn now to closer interrogation of textual features that caught my eye because they appeared melodramatic, kitsch, stereotypical, etc. The plot of the novel contains numerous genuinely traumatic events and situations: Ursula's abduction and rape, her poisoning, and her mother Martha's suicide. Even more critical, for the kind of approaches I ultimately have taken to the novel, is the backdrop for these events: the abandonment of Ursula and Martha by Friedrich Wolg; Martha's experience of her child's rape and others' unwillingness to help her find the perpetrator; Martha's profound sense of loss and isolation once the child is dead; and Martha's inability to create long-term intimacy with another human being. The novel suggests, partly through the plot itself and partly through techniques like free indirect discourse, which complicate readers' attempts to attribute specific discourses to specific characters (including the narrator), that all of these negative experiences are somehow connected. In short, I propose that the events and their reporting create a sinister portrait of the Berlin society in which they occur. Furthermore, a close reading reveals a striking pattern of blaming the victim: it is as if Martha deserves to be abandoned by her husband because she is too Jewish and loves her child too much; as if she deserves to have her child abducted because she is a working mother and an outsider; as if she deserves to lose her lover because she behaves too passionately both toward him and toward her dead child.

My prior analyses of the novel (Kacandes 1999 and 2001) have therefore proceeded along two lines. In the first approach, I investigate the novel as a text not only about trauma but also as one which itself enacts trauma. That is to say, literary texts can be about trauma, in the sense that they can depict perpetrations of violence against characters who are traumatized and then successfully or unsuccessfully witness (within the story) to their trauma. But texts can also "perform" trauma, in the sense that they can "fail" to tell the story by eliding, repeating, and fragmenting components of it. A reader's activity of serving as witness to such a performance constitutes a response that essentially creates a new narrative about the text of/as trauma. In the second approach, I trace how various debates within the Weimar Republic, especially those about gender roles, sexuality, and racial hygiene, worked together to create a society that was ripe for the conception of targeting groups for marginalization, persecution, and even extermination. Kolmar's novel shows how Martha comes to be regarded as someone who cannot be assimilated into mainstream Berlin culture. Perhaps even more frighteningly, it shows how Martha herself comes to believe this: "I am different [Ich bin anders]" (1997: 49; 1981: 52), she explains to her employer. Thus the story sets up Martha's suicide as a kind of logical conclusion, at least within the context of Berlin society's misogyny, sexual intolerance, and antisemitism. I emphasize my qualifiers, the "as ifs" above and the "at least" just now, because our inability to be sure about how to evaluate Martha or any other character – which is compounded by the fact that the novel never identifies Ursa's murderer – contributes to my idea of "Berlin" and the larger society as the problem. These claims can sound grandiose, so I'd like to ground them in two of many possible examples.

My first point comes from a mode of cultural studies analysis in which I use Kolmar's novel to understand how three debates in early twentieth-century Germany were converging: one on gender roles, and specifically on the "New Woman" (Martha, the protagonist, is a single, working professional, a talented

167

photographer); one on sexuality (Martha is depicted repeatedly as a passionate woman with a great sexual appetite); and one on racial hygiene (Martha is clearly identified as a Jewess, and as such as an outsider, a stranger). To offer one specific illustration: Though the gentile Friedrich Wolg seems to fall in love with the Jewess Martha Jadassohn at least partly because she is "different" from other women he knows, her difference quickly becomes displeasing to him. In a small amount of textual space presumably corresponding to a short amount of chronological time, the narrator describes a distinct series of changes in Friedrich's attitude toward his wife. First he considers whether her behavior is not a sign of her superiority to other women but a sign of her essential otherness: "Maybe it was because she was of different blood, a Jewess" (1997: 13; "Dies vielleicht, daß sie aus anderem Blut, daß sie Jüdin war," 1981: 17). He entertains this thought despite the fact that Martha does not observe the Jewish sabbath nor go to the synagogue. (Framing her difference in terms of "Blut" draws directly on the racialist discourses dominant in the early decades of the century.) As if having the thought makes the fact true, the text then narrates an incident in which religious difference plays a role. The future parents go shopping and see a pretty dress in a shop window. When Friedrich comments that it would make an appropriate baptismal dress if they have a girl, Martha answers in amazement: " 'But our children will not be baptized' " (1997: 13). And what begins as a calm exchange about religious upbringing quickly escalates into an unspecified threat: " 'consider,' she said softly, 'that our child is still inside of me, in my womb and that you, once it is born, cannot take it with you to the factory, and if you take it from me, I will find it no matter where' " (1997: 14).[5] In conveying the argument to his parents Friedrich adds with great distress: " 'I beg of you just one thing, don't fight with her, let her be. You don't know her. She is capable of killing the child; she is a Medea!' " (1997: 14).[6] First wondering about his wife's unorthodox social and sexual patterns, Friedrich suddenly believes she could commit murder. In a parallel fashion, Martha goes from stating that their offspring will not be baptized to assuming that Friedrich would try to abduct the children.

The rhetorical and emotional leaps that each spouse makes here contribute to the melodramatic feel of the novel and may cause readers to make an aesthetic judgment: the novel is bad, the novel is kitsch. However, I suggest that we mustn't stop here. In addition to leading us to make a judgment about the aesthetic merits of the text, such leaps provide ways of detecting the unspoken dogmas of Weimar Germany – in this case, the idea that Jews are hysterical, possessive, and ultimately dangerous.[7] Clearly Friedrich and his parents must be labeled antisemitic – there are numerous plot elements and snatches of conversation that support this judgment – but Martha herself displays some stereotypical traits attributed to Jews by Gentiles in her society: we might say that she has internalized others' view of her. What is Kolmar doing? Through these and many more examples, I conclude that by 1930 Kolmar had sensed how some people were being marginalized by being seen as dangerous others, and this sense compelled her to write a story of such a marginalization. Accordingly, I emphasize (a) the *literary* fact that Kolmar made this portrayal so morally ambiguous, and (b) the *historical* fact that she did not try to publish it, as indications of her desire to portray what she was seeing around her and yet not to contribute to the acceleration of the social processes she had discerned. One really needs to acknowledge both things to draw such a conclusion, the first garnered from close reading and the second garnered from historical/biographical research.

My second illustration comes from my lengthy analysis of *A Jewish Mother* as a text of and as trauma. One clue to the possibility that the text is performing trauma, in my view, has to do with the quality of its prose. Kolmar's language strikes the German ear strangely. Kemp calls it a late-Expressionist style (as quoted in Woltmann 1995: 157). Smith makes a more specifically aesthetic judgment, saying it lacks confidence and is inconsistent (1975: 30). I suggest, however, that its inconsistency is another one of these "aesthetic flags." By calling attention to itself as awkward – decidedly not elegant or "artistic" – it invites further analysis. Its hesitancy, I argue, is one sign of the text's performance of trauma. Since a convincing demonstration of this would involve working closely with the original German, I'd like to offer an example of the text's enactment of trauma that does not rely so heavily on close reading. I observe that, consistent with the novel's general indirectness, the closest we readers come to the central trauma, Ursula's abduction and rape, is through seeing its effect on others. Even in those instances in which characters react to what has happened to Ursula, readers are shut out in a way that textually mimics one aspect of the experience of being traumatized. The most poignant instance of this mimicry occurs when the mother Martha finally discovers the body of her child. She enters an abandoned shed:

> There was a sleeping bag, seagrass stuffing welled from the slit in a red pillow. And there...She stared, a second only, and did not believe it. She did not believe it. Then she fell screaming to the ground. [Martha groans over the child, finally picks it up and goes outside.]
>
> It was still breathing. Suddenly she pulled back the hand that had supported it by the bottom. It was wet. It was full of blood. And suddenly she knew that her hand had felt the child's naked thigh, not its undergarments, its panties. She drew back the little skirt. Mercy!...
>
> She fell on her knees. She was blind with tears, deaf from moaning. (1997: 36–7: modifications by me to reflect original).[8]

Twice in this crucial sequence the text withholds what Martha sees. When we assume the role of sympathetic fellow witness to the textual testimony in this passage, we "see" with Martha the scene in the shack, the old mattress, the slit pillow, the stuffing, but when her eye reaches the child, the text offers ellipses: "And there ... [Und da ...]." Similarly, we "feel" with Martha the moisture, the bare legs, but when the skirt is raised, we "hear" Martha's cry for mercy, and then we get "silences," the ellipses again. I suggest that these ellipses serve to evoke the context of the production of the text: the experience of being traumatized itself. That is to say, in encountering Kolmar's ellipses, the reader encounters the inability to register what is before Martha's eyes but what she does not actually see because she cannot fathom it. The text imposes gaps on its narratee, and by extension on its readers the way that the shock of "seeing" her violated child inflicts blindness on Martha. For Martha, the sight of Ursa triggers trauma that blocks her vision. For readers to respond as fellow witnesses they must recognize Kolmar's ellipses as the textual equivalent of that psychological experience. The ellipses mark the space to which, as trauma theory puts it, "willed access is denied" (Caruth 1995: 152). While these textual gaps might be considered quite conventional adherence to the decorum of the period, an additional and not incompatible interpretation would be that the text, too, is blinded by the shock – traumatized – and therefore neither witnesses nor transmits to the narratee and readers the site of the transgression. Readers should not "fill in" these gaps. Rather, as fellow witnesses, they should notice the lacunae and register them as "raising the matter" of trauma.

In both approaches, I instrumentalize the question of aesthetics in order to foreground *A Jewish Mother* as a cultural product that does certain work in a certain society. But what work is that? If Kolmar never published the text – and, as it appears, didn't even show it to anyone except the beloved sister who preserved the typescript and eventually allowed it to be published after the end of the Nazi dictatorship – can *A Jewish Mother* tell us anything at all about the Weimar Republic? I would answer that it can. But we'll have to be precise about what that is. Certainly it tells us about how at least one person, Gertrud Kolmar, an educated, assimilated, upper-middle-class Jewish-German, used literature in the terms William Paulson has recently set out in *Literary Culture in a World Transformed*, where he describes cultural work as "among the means by which people respond to the state of the world and attempt to act on it" (Paulson 2001: 119). In this case it is relevant that the attempt was not completed. Following Walter Benjamin's observations in the opening of "The Storyteller," I conclude that the whole fabric of Weimar society was very much affected by the trauma of the Great War (see Benjamin 1969: 84 and Kacandes 2001: 89–90). In a traumatized society, as Shoshana Felman and Dori Laub have suggested, "literature [may] become a witness, and perhaps the only witness, to the crisis within history which precisely cannot be articulated, witnessed in the given categories of history itself" (1992: xviii). I have therefore proposed that it becomes the role of those at a geographical or chronological remove to serve as witnesses to that society in crisis, terming this "transhistorical, transcultural witnessing." This is what I have tried to do with my close readings of *A Jewish Mother*, though I grant that to be convinced by my arguments one needs to read more supporting evidence for them (see Kacandes 2001, esp. 119–40; 2003: 99–116).

I also want to suggest that what I've called two approaches should really be considered part of a single multilayered one that involves very different intentions and responses from those at the poles of the range Raymond Williams describes as purely ideological or purely aesthetic. To return briefly to the issue of the ellipses, I have argued that they are mimicking or performing the blinding that can occur with the infliction of trauma on humans. And I have acknowledged that they could reflect (merely) the decorum of the period with regard to the depiction of certain kinds of violence. Moving more deeply into literary and aesthetic history, we could read them as a sign in the language of banality, of emotion that doesn't need to be spoken within the genre of the romance novel or kitsch.[9] We could and should say even more about them to embed them in Williams's "full social material process" – but how much more? Again, I propose that this is an issue that is not reducible to the question of beauty.

In my teaching, I have tried to emphasize not the mechanical formulas into which we can pour a text and evaluate it, deciding that it is beautiful or ugly, good or bad art, but rather the ways in which we, as readers, are witnesses who have a moral obligation to try to understand how, through literature and other forms of cultural production, individuals have tried to "respond to the state of the world and attempt to act on it," in Paulson's (2001) phrase. In class I explain terms like "narrated monologue" when my students and I read a critical passage together, the better to make a case for the cultural work that this formal feature might be doing in a text like *A Jewish Mother*. For to achieve such an understanding of literary techniques and literary works, we need close readings of specific texts *and* broad knowledge about the societies in which those texts were produced. If this kind of attention to textual and historical detail seems basic to cultural studies, that's fine with me; indeed, it's what drew me to cultural studies in the first place. But in the future, I think we could stand to say a great deal more about what first drew us to cultural studies, and about what should be basic to cultural studies analyses of literature.

NOTES

1   Although it is not directly relevant to this discussion, the global dissemination of communication technologies allows some cultures and subcultures to jump from a primary to a secondary orality without themselves passing through a fully literate phase. Also, some commentators are beginning to speak of a "new literacy" or of a "post-textual literacy," by which they mean the way digital processing has

proliferated the circulation of images and (nonverbal) sound that future educated classes will need to be familiar with as well (Markoff 1994).

2 For the instrumentalization of Kolmar, see Kacandes 2001, esp. 136–7.

3 Since I incorporate so many of the quotations from the novel into my own English prose, I have used the English translation and then provided the German original whenever there are multiple meanings or discrepancies that might be of interest; otherwise the German is to be found in the notes. The first reference, then, cites Brigitte Goldstein's competent 1997 translation, and the second, the (German) Ullstein Taschenbuch edition of 1981.

4 "Sie war bereit. Sie wußte gut, was sie wollte. Sie spielte sich selbst nichts vor. Sie dachte nicht an Liebesbeginn, an heiße Blicke und zarte Worte, an den ersten suchenden Kuß. Sie dachte brutal: Heut abend oder gleich jetzt nachmittags soll er in meinem Bette sein. Er soll mich decken. Ich bin heiß. Ich liebe ihn nicht. Aber er soll meinen Willen tun, und ich muß dafür zahlen. Ich weiß nichts Besseres. Und ich habe lange gefastet, und wir werden die Lust aus uns pressen, deren wir fähig sind" (1981: 107).

5 " 'Aber bedenke', sagte sie leise, 'daß unser Kind noch in mir ist, in meinem Schoß und daß du es, wenn es geboren ist, nicht mitschleppen kannst in deine Fabrik und daß ich es, wenn du es mir auch nimmst, überall finden werde' " (1981: 17–18).

6 " 'Ich bitt euch um eins, zankt bloß nicht mit ihr, laßt sie in Frieden. Ihr kennt sie nicht. Sie ist imstande und tötet das Kind; das ist eine Medea!' " (1981: 18).

7 For more on the idea of the unspoken dogmas of a culture, see Primo Levi 1961, esp. 5–6; and Kacandes 2003.

8 "Da lag ein Bettsack, ein rotes Kissen, aufgeschlitzt, draus das Seegras quoll. Und da... Sie starrte, eine Sekunde nur, und glaubte es nicht. Sie glaubte es nicht. Dann glitt sie schreiend zu Boden. [Martha groans over the child, finally picks it up and goes outside.] Es atmete doch. Sie zog auf einmal die Hand zurück, die unterm Gesäß es stützte. Die war feucht. Die war voll Blut. Und plötzlich wußte sie, daß ihre Hand des Kindes nackte Schenkel gefühlt, nicht seine Wäsche, sein Höschen. Sie schlug das Röckchen empor. Erbarmen... Sie brach in die Knie. Sie war vor Tränen blind, sie war taub von ihrem eigenen Schluchzen" (1981: 39, 40).

9 My great thanks to Leslie Morris for this point.

REFERENCES

Applegate, Celia. 1997. "Bach Revival, Public Culture, and National Identity: The *St. Matthew Passion* in 1829." In *A User's Guide to German Cultural Studies*, eds. Scott Denham, Irene Kacandes, and Jonathan Petropoulos. Ann Arbor: University Michigan Press, pp. 139–62.

Benjamin, Walter. 1969. "The Storyteller: Reflections on the Works of Nikolai Leskov." In *Illuminations: Essays and Reflections,* ed. and intro. Hannah Arendt and tr. Harry Zohn. New York: Schocken, pp. 83–109.

Birkerts, Sven. 1994. *The Gutenberg Elegies: The Fate of Reading in an Electronic Age.* New York: Fawcett Columbine.

Buttigieg, Joseph A. 1982–3. "The Exemplary Worldliness of Antonio Gramsci's Literary Criticism." *boundary 2*: 21–39.

——. 1998. "Gramsci." *Oxford Encyclopedia of Aesthetics.* Oxford: Oxford University Press.

Caruth, C., ed. 1995. *Trauma: Explorations in Memory.* Baltimore: Johns Hopkins University Press.

Cohn, Dorrit. 1978. *Transparent Minds: Narrative Modes for Presenting Consciousness in Fiction.* Princeton: Princeton University Press.

Davies, Ioan. 1995. *Cultural Studies and Beyond: Fragments of Empire.* London: Routledge.

During, Simon, ed. 1993. *The Cultural Studies Reader.* London: Routledge.

Felman, Shoshana and Dori Laub. 1992. *Testimony: Crises of Witnessing in Literature, Psychoanalysis, and History.* New York: Routledge.

Geck, Martin. 1967. *Die Wiederentdeckung der Matthäuspassion im 19. Jahrhundert: die zeitgenössischen Dokumente und ihre ideengeschichtliche Deutung.* Regensburg: Bosse.

Gramsci, Antonio. 1985. *Selections from the Cultural Writings*, tr. David Forgacs and Geoffrey Nowell Smith. Cambridge, MA: Harvard University Press.

Grossberg, Lawrence, Cary Nelson, and Paula Treichler, eds. 1992. *Cultural Studies.* New York and London: Routledge.

Havelock, Eric A. 1986. *The Muse Learns to Write: Reflections on Orality and Literacy from Antiquity to the Present.* New Haven: Yale University Press.

Hunter, Ian. 1992. "Aesthetics and Cultural Studies." In Grossberg et al. 1992: 347–67.

Kacandes, Irene. 1999. "Narrative Witnessing as Memory Work: Reading Gertrud Kolmar's *A Jewish Mother*." In *Acts of Memory: Cultural Recall in the Present*, eds. Mieke Bal, Jonathan Crewe, and Leo Spitzer. Hanover: University Press of New England, pp. 55–71.

——. 2001. *Talk Fiction: Literature and the Talk Explosion.* Lincoln: University Nebraska Press.

——. 2003. "Feminizing, Sexualizing, and Racializing 'Others' in late Weimar and early Third Reich Germany: The Case of Gertrud Kolmar's *Eine jüdische Mutter*." *Women In German Yearbook* 19: 99–116.

Kolmar, Gertrud. 1981. *Eine jüdische Mutter.* Frankfurt am Main: Ullstein Taschenbuch Verlag.

——. 1997. *A Jewish Mother from Berlin. Susanna*, tr. Brigitte M. Goldstein. New York and London: Holmes and Meier.

Kundera, Milan. 1988. *The Art of the Novel*, tr. Linda Asher. New York: Grove Press.

Levi, Primo. 1961. *Survival in Auschwitz. The Nazi Assault on Humanity*, tr. Stuart Woolf. New York: Collier Books.

Markoff, John. 1994. "The Rise and Swift Fall of Cyber Literacy." *New York Times*, Mar. 13, p. A1.

Nelson, Cary, Paula A. Treichler, and Lawrence Grossberg. 1992. "Cultural Studies: An Introduction." In Grossberg et al. 1992: 1–22.

Ong, Walter. 1982. *Orality and Literacy: The Technologizing of the Word.* London: Methuen.

Paulson, William. 2001. *Literary Culture in a World Transformed: A Future for the Humanities.* Ithaca, NY: Cornell University Press.

Sanders, Barry. 1994. *A is for Ox: The Collapse of Literacy and the Rise of Violence in an Electronic Age.* New York: Vintage.

Scarry, Elaine. 1999. *On Beauty and Being Just.* Princeton: Princeton University Press.

Smith, Henry A. 1975. "Gertrud Kolmar's Life and Works." In *Dark Soliloquy: The Selected Poems of Gertrud Kolmar,* tr. Henry A. Smith. New York: Continuum, pp. 3–52.

Stephens, Mitchell. 1998. *The Rise of the Image, The Fall of the Word.* New York: Oxford University Press.

Williams, Raymond. 1977. *Marxism and Literature.* Oxford: Oxford University Press.

Woltmann, Johanna. 1995. *Gertrud Kolmar: Leben und Werk.* Göttingen: Wallstein Verlag.

9

Inventing Culture (Behind the Garage Door)

STEVEN RUBIO

Bearer of the flag, from the beginning.
Now who would have believed, this riot grrrl's a cynic?
— Sleater-Kinney, "#1 Must Have"

For only the second time in our lives, my wife and I are traveling together outside the USA to Europe, and one rainy evening we find ourselves with an English friend and her family at a "Proms in the Park" concert in Bournemouth, England, in the summer of 2000. The concept of the "Proms" is a bit foreign to us; it appears to be similar to the "Pops" style of symphony concert in the States, where an orchestra plays a blend of well-known popular classics and a dollop of less familiar but equally amenable tunes. The Proms are apparently quite popular in England, featured annually on the BBC, where the best symphonies are presented, and in various smaller venues across the country, including Bournemouth, where we caught up with the event.

In this case, we were lucky enough to experience the "Last Night" at the Proms, one particular aspect of which (we were warned about in advance by our friend) was the overwhelmingly nostalgic patriotism that permeated the atmosphere. Our friend was quite disturbed by the expected mass displays of chauvinism (although it must be said that her family didn't even mention it in advance, not finding this point to be particularly noteworthy). I assured her that there was no need for embarrassment; I'd feel the same way if we were at a similar function in the States, but since I was vacationing, I'd be taking in English patriotism as just another foreign treat to be enjoyed and later examined.

And so it was with a combination of distanced irony and fun-seeking that I huddled under a "brollie" and took in my first Proms in the Park. There were the expected "popular" tunes from the likes of Tchaikovsky, along with several pieces that, while clearly "popular," based on the response of the crowd, were beyond my limited knowledge of classical music.

And then, suddenly, my wife and I found ourselves enthralled, for the orchestra was playing what the conductor claimed was a selection from *Barber of Seville*. Our excitement had little or nothing to do with Rossini, and everything to do with our own, American, brand of nostalgia. For as the notes from Rossini cascaded down from the bandstand, both my wife and I were transported to the days of our childhood, to the Bugs Bunny cartoon, "Rabbit of Seville."

THE RABBIT OF SEVILLE

> I wonder how many men, hiding their youngness, rise as I do, Saturday mornings, filled with the hope that Bugs Bunny, Yosemite Sam and Daffy Duck will be there waiting as our one true always and forever salvation?
> – Ray Bradbury, "Why Cartoons Are Forever"

As this Chuck Jones cartoon, made for Warner Brothers in 1949, begins, an audience files into a large outdoor amphitheater while an orchestra warms up. On tap for the evening is Rossini's *Barber of Seville*. The audience in the cartoon waits expectantly for the opera to begin; the audience for the cartoon waits expectantly, as well, for the comedy to begin. Suddenly we hear shotgun blasts in the distance, and Bugs Bunny, the target for the shots, rushes through a backstage door, followed quickly by his nemesis, the hunter Elmer Fudd. Elmer's search for the rabbit takes him unwittingly to the amphitheater stage. Using his trademark carrot, Bugs hits a switch marked "CURTAIN," the curtain rises, revealing Elmer to the audience in the cartoon, and with a puzzled shrug and a look at his wrist watch, the conductor begins to lead the orchestra in the opera.

What follows is a brief (the cartoon lasts a mere 7 minutes) translation of the Rossini opera into the Bugs Bunny universe. It must be noted here that my understanding of the "faithfulness" of the adaptation of Rossini is limited by my lack of exposure to the original; when people like my wife and myself hear the melodies, we think, not "ah, Rossini!" but rather "hey, it's Bugs Bunny!" (And this is, in fact, what we do at the Proms.) The cartoon version assumes a rather literal interpretation of the opera's title, and so, regardless of what the "real" plot of the opera might be, Jones's cartoon is about a barber in Seville, with the lead actor, Bugs Bunny, in the title role. Dressed in barber garb, Bugs begins to sing:

Welcome to my shop
Let me cut your mop
Let me shave your crop
Dain - ti - ly! Dain - ti -ly!

Bugs performs atrocities to Elmer's head, face, feet, and everything else he can get his hands and barber's tools on, all the while singing to Rossini's melodies. When Elmer finally gets a word in edgewise ("Ohhhhh, where do I get that wab - bit?"), Bugs performs a variety of costume changes (Spanish señorita, Eastern fakir, whatever works) and takes turns tormenting Elmer and escaping from his shotgun. Finally, after a series of exchanges in which Elmer and Bugs threaten each other with increasingly large weapons, Bugs wins Elmer's heart with flowers, candy, and a ring. Elmer dons a wedding gown, the two are married, and Bugs dumps Elmer into a huge cake with the inscription "Marriage of Figaro." And all of this happens to the accompaniment of Rossini.

And this is what my wife and I are thinking about when we hear the music at the Proms.

BUGS BUNNY, AMERICAN

"And now, that Oscar-winning rabbit, Bugs Bunny."

It would be easy to assume at this point that Bugs represented a pop-culture uprising against the classical music of Rossini's opera. But such an assumption would be wrong. Not only was the Proms itself something of a pop-culture version of classical music to begin with, but also "Rabbit of Seville"'s relationship to Rossini is too complicated for easy assumptions. While at first glance, it appears Bugs and Elmer are interrupting the classical program as they rush into the amphitheater, the opera does not come to a halt upon their arrival. On the contrary, the opera begins when Bugs raises the curtain on Elmer and his shotgun. And while what follows isn't exactly Rossini, Bugs must force himself into the world of Seville at least as much as that world must make room for Bugs. "Rabbit of Seville" is not merely a pop-cult commentary on high art, nor is the purpose only to bring high art to its knees. The purpose is to blend the two, bringing opera to Looney Tunes and rascally wabbits to the opera. Their mutual association enhances both opera and cartoon.

The pleasure my wife and I enjoyed at the moment when the strains of Rossini first drifted over the crowd at the Proms was not, in the beginning, the pleasure of the unwashed in the presence of the haughty. Instead, it was the pleasure of recognition, even nostalgia. We were taken back to the mornings of our endless childhood, when getting ready for school was accompanied by the soundtrack of a thousand cartoons playing on the television set. I, at least, was glad to finally hear a song I knew; it validated the underlying concept of the Proms in bringing "popular classics" to the audience, because for me, nothing could be more popular or more classic than Bugs Bunny. On some basic aesthetic level, Bugs Bunny, Rossini, and the symphony orchestra all made perfect sense.

Until one remembered the proud chauvinism of the Proms. We weren't just celebrating classical music; we were also celebrating England. As the second half of the program moved inexorably into songs clearly understood by the English audience to represent the glories of the empire, Bugs began to take on, not the mantle of popular culture (for what we were experiencing in Bournemouth was itself popular culture), but the mantle of America. The songs sent patriotic messages obviously not lost on the English, and at times even their American guests understood. "Rule, Britannia" was obvious enough even for a Yank, but who knew that "Pomp and Circumstance," in America a sure sign that someone was graduating, was known in England as "Land of Hope and Glory," with lyrics so familiar that virtually everyone, no matter how drunk, could sing along:

> Land of Hope and Glory,
> Mother of the Free,
> How shall we extol thee,
> Who are born of thee?
> Wider still and wider
> Shall thy bounds be set;
> God, who made thee mighty,
> Make thee mightier yet.

And "Jerusalem," straight out of William Blake:

> I will not cease from mental fight,
> Nor shall my sword sleep in my hand,
> Till we have built Jerusalem,
> In England's green and pleasant land.

As these songs were played, the audience not only sang heartily along, but they also waved what seemed like thousands of Union Jacks of all sizes. Rain was pouring down, but nothing could dampen the spirits of the patriotic crowd.

The outsider, the Yank, felt a bit different at this point, as if I were surrounded by a delusional mob. Pride in country is one thing, I thought, but the sun has been setting on the British Empire for a long time now. Who did these people think they were kidding? I was outnumbered, of course, but that didn't stop my puzzlement. And then I remembered my friend, my AMERICAN friend, the one character who knew how to put a stop to this kind of nonsense. It was the duty of

Americans to insert the wisecrack that could deflate the delusion, and for more than 50 years, one figure had been a representative of the great American wiseacre. And so I imagined that Bugs Bunny might reappear into the Proms, hopping madly atop the heads of the flag-waving, anthem-singing crowd, chomping carrots and asking "What's up, doc?" I wanted Bugs to be the hero, not of the masses against high art, but of Americans against the English, as if the Revolutionary War needed to be refought, Bugs vs. Elgar in a battle to the death.

Bugs Bunny's cockiness in the face of danger was as usefully appropriate to Americans in the Second World War era as "Land of Hope and Glory" likely was for the English in earlier times. The irony for a lonely American at the Proms lay in my desire to call upon the Bugs icon to trounce the seeming delusions of the English crowd, when in fact, in the summer of 2000, Bugs's cockiness was, for Americans, surely becoming as misplaced as the nostalgia of the English for the empire of days long past.

And this is what I (if perhaps no longer my wife) am thinking about when I hear the music at the Proms.

LIBERATION AND ITS DISCONTENTS

My night at the Proms demonstrates the messy fashion in which we encounter works of art. Any attempt to extract a "pure" aesthetic experience from the concert is doomed, not only because of the less-than-explicit aesthetics of the Proms, with the appeals to the "popular," the quite explicit patriotism, and the massive fireworks display with which the program concluded. Any "pure" representation of the Proms would already be tangled in these threads. But my subjective response, a subjectivity not only personal but paradoxically connected to my membership in the group called "Americans," is necessarily more than just an aesthetic response. However, it would be equally foolish to assume that aesthetics was absent from my experience; what was happening can't be described by narrowly utilizing the symphony's music as a text through which I construct a "pure" cultural experience. And this is true even though my interaction with the aesthetics of the music was inextricably muddled by my prior encounters with the melodies in many different situations.

Instead, "my" Proms allowed for more aesthetic appreciation than might be expected, while the liberatory function of my use of the art, whereby I create new meanings from found objects and in the process build potentially antihegemonic spaces, is never clearly liberatory in a global sense, is always tied to my own selfish and none-too-trustworthy needs. The aesthetic beauty of the music never completely overwhelmed me; when I was most responsive, the intensity of my response was closely related to my cultural memories. But those memories were not only "cultural"; they were also aesthetic. I heard Rossini, I thought of Bugs Bunny, but my rabbit musings were also reconsiderations of Rossini through prior aesthetic responses to the Merrie Melodies. That is, when I first encountered Rossini, as a child watching "Rabbit of Seville," I was experiencing an aesthetic response to both the cartoon and the music, and so my memories as I attended the Proms were a tangled blend of aesthetics and nostalgia, as I simultaneously interacted with the music and confronted my past.

As for the liberatory possibilities, they certainly existed, but what did I ultimately make of them? I felt a bond, via Bugs Bunny via Rossini, to my fellow Americans as I traveled in a foreign land, but my recreation of Rossini amounted to little more than a mirror image of the very chauvinism I was finding so bothersome. England has "Jerusalem" and they've stolen "Pomp and Circumstance," they pretend there's still an empire (and that the empire was worthy), but "we" have Bugs Bunny and we ARE still an empire (and think that the empire is worthy). What kind of liberation am I achieving? I'm using Bugs Bunny to construct a new space, but it's hardly antihegemonic. In critiquing the patriotism of the English, I'm falling back on the patriotism of the USA, in the process guaranteeing that if I'm still alive in 50 years, I'll surely be singing "God Bless America" and waving the Stars and Stripes.

GUERNICA

> "We must live an uneasy cerebral relation to the bric-à-brac of life."
> – Dick Hebdige, *Subculture*

The relationship between nationalistic feelings and works of art goes much farther than the dilettantish vacation sagas of middle-class Americans. Nowhere was this more apparent to us than on a later stop at the Centro de Arte Reina Sofia in Madrid, where Picasso's masterwork *Guernica* is housed. *Guernica*, of course, spent several decades residing outside of Spain, at the artist's request, Picasso famously stating that as long as Franco and the Fascists were in power, his painting (and Picasso himself) would remain in exile. The return of the painting to Spain after Franco's death was a great triumph for the new Spanish republic. *Guernica* had been used for political purposes since its creation, although the more didactic proponents of the painting's political power might have preferred a less-abstract presentation of the horrors of war. Its reappearance in Madrid marks not only the culmination of Picasso's own wishes that the work eventually reside in Spain, but also the separation of the Republic from the Fascist past, thus making room both for aesthetic enjoyment and governmental/nationalistic appropriation. Since my own paternal roots are in Spain (I am, in fact, half-Spanish), and since much of our vacation had been spent in the country where my grandparents had lived, I imagined that at least a small part of *Guernica*'s "aura" would touch whatever remnants of Spain lived in my heart.

And, indeed, *Guernica* seemed to impart an aura, but it was nothing like what Walter Benjamin might have imagined. When I first realized our hotel in Madrid was only a few blocks from the museum housing the famous Picasso painting, I knew at once that I had to see it. As we walked down the city streets to the Reina Sofia, my eyes filled with tears of joyous excitement. The work had brought me to tears before I'd even seen it! The "aura" seemed to have escaped from the painting itself and wafted its way onto the streets, where it compelled me with an insistent uniqueness. "Yes," it said, "you've seen reproductions of me before, but now you're going to see the real me, and it will astound you!" I scarcely made it into the museum, such was my anticipation. Or rather, I assumed it was anticipation. As it turned out, the Guernican aura on the street was itself what I'd been waiting for; to be in the presence of great art mattered more than the art itself. The aura had taken over from its source.

And so, when finally I stood in the room with Picasso's *Guernica*, my first thoughts ran to the sacrilegious. The painting was not as big as I expected, although by the time I saw it, my expectations would have been dashed by anything smaller than a drive-in movie screen. Oh, it had power. It was certainly a "great" work of art. But I was probably incapable at that point of truly appreciating the greatness. My aesthetic sensibilities had been sidetracked; getting there, it seemed, was more than half the fun. What had brought me to tears on the streets (the possibility of being in the presence of greatness) had little to do with aesthetics, and much to do with the cultural "meaning" of art-as-commodity. All of the reproductions I'd seen of *Guernica*, all of the stories I'd read about its travails, convinced me of its importance before I'd ever "really" seen it, leaving little for the actual painting to offer. It wasn't that I couldn't be moved (my tears on the street proved that). It was that my most powerful reactions were to matters extraneous to the painting itself. It was impossible for me to experience *Guernica* in anything approaching a "pure" state, which is not to say that the entire experience was less than powerful.

And as I stood in the museum, taking in the Picasso, I did not feel like an American, nor did I feel like a Spaniard. I just felt like another member of the sad human race. But I did wonder if, when *Guernica* finally returned to Spain in 1981, the Spaniards felt something like I did on that summer afternoon in Madrid. I wondered if the waiting for *Guernica* took on an importance of its own, if even this greatest of paintings might have been a little disappointing once the aura of expectations had been replaced by the concrete reality of the abstract painting. As a symbol of a new republic, and as a reminder of past atrocities, *Guernica* retained its power. But did this power come at the expense of an unsullied aesthetic appreciation of the work itself? Or was the entire notion of "unsullied" just another case of nostalgia for something that never existed in the first place?

THE GARAGE DOOR

> "Culture is the locus of the search for lost unity."
> – Guy Debord, *The Society of the Spectacle*

Some years ago, though, I had experienced a different *Guernica*, an artifact that came upon me too suddenly for any auras to appear. Pittsburg, California, is a smallish town, barely 30 miles from San Francisco as the crow flies but in another cultural land from the big city nonetheless. This is true in the twenty-first century; it was much truer in the mid-1970s, when I happened upon a remarkable thing. Driving down a side street in Pittsburg, we discovered a garage door onto which had been painted a replica of *Guernica*. We were as startled as we might have been if Bugs Bunny had actually showed up at the Proms. In the midst of a cultural landscape out of which had come such artistic landmarks as the Mitchell Brothers' porn movie classic *Behind the Green Door*, in an area where the only Spanish presence I had ever noticed before was a small section in the adjacent town of Antioch where a few Spanish expatriates lived, here was *Guernica*! Not the original, of course, although, like the original at that time, it was living in exile from its Spanish homeland, waiting for Franco to die. In my memory, this version isn't the right shape; forced into the geometric confines of a garage door, it looked like a Cinerama movie on television in the days before letterboxing. It didn't make me weep; it didn't make me feel "Spanish." It simply startled me: that someone in Pittsburg, California, not only knew *Guernica* in the first place, but knew it well enough to reproduce it, loved it so much they splashed it across their garage door.

I imagine the owners of that house . . . they must have tired of waiting for Franco to die. Perhaps, like my own grandmother (who came to America from Spain before 1920 and never returned home despite living another 70 years), they tired of waiting to return to their homeland. They decided to bring their homeland to Pittsburg instead. It was a running joke of the times that Franco was never going to die; even Picasso, who lived into his nineties, couldn't outlast the Generalissimo. And so this anonymous American decided to give *Guernica* a home where Franco couldn't touch it. Surely a garage door was a bit prosaic for such a masterpiece? But what better place for an American homage, than the building that houses our favorite possession, the automobile? In painting *Guernica* on their garage door, one family had made Picasso's work their own. *Guernica* guarded their cars, no, *Guernica* guarded their home itself, from the inevitable invasions of American daily life. It was their nostalgic reminder of an unrecoverable past, it was an attempt to impose their own histories on the world. It was their Bugs Bunny at the Proms.

BEHIND THE GARAGE DOOR

> Culture is what we make it, yes it is. Now is the time, now is the time, now is the time, to invent, invent, invent, invent, invent, invent.
>
> — Sleater-Kinney, "#1 Must Have"

On occasion, something will remind us of our summer adventure, and we'll wish we were once again on a vacation, free of work, allowed to seek out the new without fears of tomorrow. But one lesson of our travels is that escape is exceedingly difficult. America has long arms; they reach across the waters, the appendages of an empire, ubiquitous if already in decline.

Ultimately, though, we didn't want a total escape, whatever we might have imagined before we began our trip. Part of being on vacation is building up experiences that will help us see our ordinary lives in different ways once we return from vacation. Even while we travel we think about home. And certainly vacations can be full of searches for what seems exotic to our eyes, but we often remember best what reminds us most of home. We hear Rossini, we think of Bugs, we see Picasso, we think of garage doors.

And nostalgia is a terrible thing, it pulls at us, it demands that we place everything in the context of the past. Nostalgia gnaws at our attempts at liberation; we try to use the found objects of our culture for their liberatory potential, and always there is nostalgia, making our thoughts hazy with memory.

If there must be a hero in our story, then, let it be the owners of the garage door. While there were likely large dollops of nostalgia inspiring them to recreate *Guernica* on that garage, while one can imagine them thinking back to the homeland of their past, there was also a need to make culture, a passion to invent. It wasn't enough to let *Guernica* sit in their memories. It wasn't merely about the past: NOW was the time to invent, to splash *Guernica* across the front of their house, to announce to the world that the people of that house had something they wanted, needed, to say. And they said it. The aura of that garage door floats across decades to the pages of this essay. And the creators of that garage door join Rossini, and Chuck Jones, and Picasso, and Elgar, artists who provide us with the culture that, when we resist nostalgia, allows us to invent our own liberations.

REFERENCES

Bradbury, Ray. 1989. "Why Cartoons Are Forever." *Los Angeles Times*, Dec. 3. Available at http://raybradburyonline.com/quotations.htm.

Debord, Guy. 1995. *The Society of the Spectacle*, tr. Donald Nicholson-Smith. New York: Zone Books.

Hebdige, Dick. 1979. *Subculture: The Meaning of Style.* London: Routledge.

"The Rabbit of Seville." Dir. Chuck Jones. In *Elmer Fudd's Comedy Capers.* Warner Home Video, 1986.

Sleater-Kinney. 2000. "#1 Must Have." *All Hands on the Bad One.* Kill Rock Stars records.

10

The Cringe Factor

LAURA KIPNIS

Until this moment, I have rarely availed myself of the services of the academic first person, a mode of writing sometimes termed "autobiographical criticism," or "confessional criticism," or "autocritography," and an increasingly frequent feature of cultural studies prose over the last decade. I confess that this has not been just a simple matter of benign neglect or circumstances beyond my control, but that I am probably guilty of having actively discriminated against it. Actually, if I were being truly honest I would be forced to admit to secretly disdaining it as a linguistic form. This despite the fact that some of my best friends write in the academic first person, and despite the fact that I do *want* to believe that all linguistic person forms are inherently equal, were created equal – but you can't really control all those socially instilled "messages" that go through your head, can you? As we know, the protocols of academic research and credentialing procedures have long enforced the hegemony of the third person and the concomitant denigration of the first, assigning cultural capital and other unearned forms of status and privilege to the third person as its putative birthright while the first has had to struggle for even the most basic forms of dignity and respect, but clearly these are historically – perhaps even politically – determined value judgments, not anything inherent or "natural." (The second person – favored mostly by self-help writers and coked-up 1980s novelists – is clearly even worse off, though perhaps its academic moment too will one day arrive.[1])

But isn't it finally time to come out and acknowledge that the third person always purchased its textual dominance at the expense of the first by actively subjugating it: mocking it with epithets like "Durham Bull" (a low gibe about its supposed origins at Duke) or pulling disciplinary rank with jeers like "self-indulgence" or "not a contribution to knowledge"? Not to mention all those systemic and institutionalized forms of discrimination such as tenure reviews and other types of academic redlining, since aside from a few academically tenuous fields like creative writing, omniscient agentless prose has long been taken for granted as the normative academic person form. But if the uptight lexicons of abstraction and theory are privileged over those of experience and self, wouldn't this intensify the profound and unsettling effects that marginalized person forms will always pose, simply by virtue of their existence, to the very dominant conceptions and norms that have worked so hard to marginalize them?

A glance back over the last decade's academic press backlists or through one's own bookcase will indicate that challenges to third-person hegemony were already well underway by the early nineties, as our more adventuresome professors began turning to autobiographical criticism, or even, in some cases, to autobiography itself, to explore ethnic identities, or professional identities, or gendered identities (yes, it was shaping up as an identitarian decade), or to protest the forced separation of intellectual labor and personal life that academia was said to demand of the professoriat. Sometimes this was a move cast in gendered terms, notably by Jane Tompkins in her 1987 essay "Me and My Shadow" – frequently cited as one of the formative moments of the academic confessional – which argued that the public–private hierarchy is "a founding condition of female oppression," and that academic intellectuals have waged a "police action" against feeling, women, and the personal. Writing in the first person was, for Tompkins, a declaration of intellectual independence. Soon to come was a second wave of first-person prose ushered in by the academic ascendancy of American cultural studies, which, with its ties to both ethnography and left politics, consolidated those early first-person impulses by giving them a theoretical grounding and, arguably, an air of political urgency. It quickly became imperative for researchers to "locate" or "position" themselves in relation to their research; those who didn't were subject to charges of universalism or worse. And with the rise of queer studies and sexuality studies and disability studies came yet a third wave, its practitioners pushing the first-person envelope even further into the shame-ridden and thrilling terrain of bodies, sex acts, and desires.

Academic work was becoming more and more "personal" – you never knew *what* you were going to find out when you attended an academic talk. From Birmingham to Oprah as traditional academics and even the old-guard left might complain, but needless to say the form has its many defenders too, for example H. Aram Veeser, who in the introduction to his 1996 collection, *Confessions of the Critics*, offered a more or less blanket congratulation to confessional criticism for its "radically democratic, risk-taking honesty." With tributes such as these, the first person was attaining academic status and fast becoming an academic style-norm while simultaneously retaining its street cred. It even managed to suggest a defiant and courageous act, perhaps even a politically counterhegemonic act, that is if you thought – as many did – that foregrounding the personal disrupted those operations of power dependent on veiling the location or subjectivity of the writer. In short, one of the most decisive effects of cultural studies on the academy has been its effect on the aesthetics of academic prose: promoting and indeed institutionalizing the use of the first person across the humanistic disciplines, subtly stigmatizing the third (*so* old-fashioned) just as it was once stigmatized itself.

So why, despite the first person's array of newly-won testimonials and credentials as the eternally radical new thing, does this act of consorting with it myself still fill me with ambivalence, even an edge of irrational dread? Certainly it's not my old-left orthodoxy, nor my high regard for traditional academic prose. Is it something more "personal" then? My social conditioning – one of those brute family lessons, some long-ago parental message (probably never openly articulated, probably more subtle and invidious than that) that talking too much about yourself was bad form, and "people like us" didn't? (Or is that itself a convenient fiction, a screen memory blocking access to what really happened? Monological parents, or some other early trauma in the linguistic register?) What could possibly account for the squeamish feeling I decidedly in the presence of the first person, or why, even in my slightly tentative – and protectively ironic – embrace of it now, I somehow feel that I have sunk (even further than usual) in my own esteem, and certainly in my reader's as well? (Confession being the lingua franca of the first person, I trust you to treat mine with due sensitivity.) Or is the issue really a shameful conflicted desire to write in the first person myself, to publicize *my* inner life for all to savor, a desire thus far resisted, but now erupting symptomatically in the guise of feigned ambivalence, into this essay? (As we all know only too well by now, prohibition and desire are never far removed from one another.)

And what sort of personal and professional risks would I be courting if I yielded to what may or may not be this highly conflicted desire? There's the risk of exposure and its unforeseen consequences, of course, but obviously you always choose what you do and don't expose (if not its reception), even when appearing "frank." Obviously no one really expects all confessional acts to achieve Veeser's "risk-taking honesty" either, since such confessions are often just gestures, or interludes, or heuristic devices. Take the ever-growing prevalence of the opening-paragraph first-person anecdote in conference papers, frequently in the self-deprecating or personal foible mode, intended to disarm and charm an audience – this is far more insurance against risk than the taking of one. Or those meant-to-be-amusingly-revealing accounts of where the author happened to be when a particular thought occurred, for example, in a steamy bathtub at a Marriott hotel alongside a boyfriend – according to an unpublished manuscript by a (female) fourth-wave academic confessor that happens to be sitting on my desk at the moment (which is where I happened to be sitting when this thought occurred). A risky confession? The author attests that it is, but also clearly means to be committing an "intervention" – as we like to say in cultural studies – by admitting what academics presumably aren't meant to, which is that they have bodies and do things in bathtubs with boys that might or might not have some complicated relationship to what they do in their scholarship, should you care to know.

The bathtub intervention means to confront what the author feels is the shamed status of heterosexuality within feminist criticism, though in form the gesture closely duplicates Jane Tompkins's celebrated revelation in "Me and My Shadow" that she's thinking about going to the bathroom in the midst of writing the essay. Between toilets and tubs, the bathroom apparently remains, even 15 years later, a privileged locale for academic confessions, and visiting it in print presumably a bold tactic for overcoming those forms of splitting or self-alienation that academia requires of its adherents. Of course, writing about one's body in academic contexts would really only be admirably risky if the academy is indeed what impedes academics from the embodied writing we're capable of, and from overcoming that mind–body split once and for all and traversing the public–private dichotomy at will, freed of our intellectual shackles. (And, of course, if writing about one's own body actually results in interesting writing.)

If cultural studies has made a range of different objects available for potential study – low cultural objects, noncanonical archives, disreputable nondisciplinary things, the marginalia of cultural life in our times – one of those newly visible objects is also, clearly, oneself. But new and different objects also produce new and different object relations to negotiate on the part of cultural studies' audiences, who are suddenly faced with a writing subject not veiled behind the ordinary academic protocols (although perhaps veiled behind others); a subject intent on self-exposure, or on speaking to us from the bathroom, or on working through some form of injury or painful experience that others among us probably have unmastered or excitable or shame-ridden relations to as well. In reconfiguring the traditional distance–proximity ratio, personal writing does make more extensive intersubjective demands on an audience, and distance–proximity issues are rocky shoals in any relationship: one partner needs space, the other needs attention; one wants to go to sleep, the other wants to cuddle. And no less in this one, with the academic writer newly emergent as, simultaneously, a scholarly object, a damaged subject, and a spectacle: since nakedness is inherently spectacular in a clothed culture. (Academia has been, traditionally speaking, a psychically clothed culture, though unfortunately, the clothes are still all too frequently accessorized by Birkenstocks. With socks.)

Prickly questions abound. Does this subject really make an adequate or convincing object? (Is there something to be learned? Is there a new thought to be had?) Is the scholar up to the intellectual demands the object presents (an object who is also the writing subject?) Answering such questions will in itself demand more differentiated modes of criticism than those we traditionally rely on. For instance, what *is* the appropriate critical response when what's at issue isn't just the intellectual merit of a work, but the occasionally complicated nature of our personal responses to the autobiographical content in the work? What if the critical judgments are in response not to one's assessment of faulty scholarship, but to one's assessment of the scholar's faulty self-understanding?

Of course different varieties of autobiography (with their various shifts in register) also make different intersubjective demands: not all first-person writing is confessional, not all first-person writing is autobiographical, not all autobiographical writing is personal, and the motives (stated and unstated) for public self-exploration vary. Or to complicate the subject further, perhaps not all autobiography is even intentional or written in the first person. (A completely hypothetical illustration: say you can't help but notice a degree of unacknowledged *ressentiment* seeping into a critique of the academic star system, and find yourself involuntarily assessing its argument against your own knowledge of the author's vitae.) The critical distinctions required to wend our way through these intersubjective thickets are not always readily at hand.

Michael Gorra, writing a mid-decade roundup review of the first wave of academic autobiographies in the journal *Transition*, took a few heroically failed stabs at outlining both the perimeters of that particular genre and his own intersubjective problems with it. (Note in advance that he admitted his failure upfront.) First he tried to differentiate autobiographies by those over 40 from those under, characterizing the older set's message as "This is what I did," and the younger set's as "This is how I got started" – but unfortunately that distinction isn't really absolute, he admits. Then he tries distinguishing memoir from autobiography: autobiography looks in, fashioning an "I"; memoir looks out. Memoir is modest, autobiography isn't. But once again he's forced to admit failure: "In practice, the two forms are almost always mixed, the distinction between them a matter of nuance and emphasis." Why bother making failed distinctions? Or to put it another way: What's the problem they're meant to solve? I suspect it's that Gorra is trying to speak about the intersubjective dilemmas of the genre: for him, a puzzled sense of being let down; raised hopes, failed returns. When he remarks of academic autobiographies by Henry Louis Gates and Clifford Geertz that the writing in both seems oddly disengaged, what he's saying is that *he's* disengaged. Something is lacking, and it's not entirely clear what, nor is it clear that it's confined to these two examples. As Gorra puts it, "But really, one wants something more." What, though, is the nature of that "more"?

But what are you supposed to say, in public critical responses, when an autobiographical gesture intends to hail you as a fellow-traveler to some particular state of fellow-feeling and instead you fail to be enlisted, or respond "incorrectly," with detachment or voyeurism? Or worse, can't resist the easy opportunities for mockery the confessional sometimes presents, intellectual sadism not being an unknown phenomenon in the academic profession. (Such responses seem particularly available when the quantity of personal information revealed seems in excess of the intellectual payoff.) The strategic first-person writer may attempt to evade this fate by soliciting audience to states of fellow-feeling in relation to a social issue – "awareness," indignation, or activist outrage – but this technique may backfire too, producing resistance among the rectitude-averse. (I find myself, guiltily, often in this group.) Though as we know, such resistant responses are not infrequently a behind-the-scenes – in Goffman's sense – topic of debate and discussion, and when not expressed openly will often be posed informally through the jokes and snide asides we make about each other's work. (Perhaps when forms of scholarly engagement abrogate the customary protocols and distance, so do critical responses to them.)

But let me break this code of silence and confess that while there may be occasional examples of academic first-person writing that I can admire, like Gorra, I more often find myself oddly disengaged by it: skimming, a little bored. I say "oddly" because I don't entirely understand my response – ordinarily I'm as big a fan of gossip, confession, and the first person as you will find; spend endless hours with friends happily dissecting their lives or mine; willingly sit through lengthy accounts of other people's relationship problems or family psychodramas or career anxieties with unfeigned interest. So if the problem isn't just some constitutional indifference to people and their stories, what's the problem with first-person writing? Could it be something about...the writing?

Asking such questions certainly poses the danger (or the temptation) of typifying from the weakest examples. Nevertheless, a few generalizations. If the turn toward autobiographical modes of writing was, to some extent, a rebellion against the decentered subject and impersonal abstruseness of 1980s academic high theory, perhaps autobiographical writing defaults toward hyperclarity instead, toward a rather alarming degree of self-coherence.[2] This may be a salutary thing in premise, but on the page it means writing that is expository and literal-minded, perhaps a little dogged. Maybe the requirements of explaining something as complicated as a self to the world leave too little energy for textual flourishes. Maybe the gift of a naked, splayed self is meant to be reward enough and only the most churlish reader would expect pleasurable prose too. But if imagination is a fundamental feature of the self, the available modes of rendering its existence textually do seem to encounter some as-yet-unknown impediment in the academic autobiographical mode.

But let's be frank. In addition to the dissatisfaction issue that Gorra circles around, there's a certain behind-the-scenes topic he doesn't address, though not surprisingly as it's the dirty little secret of aesthetic response to the academic personal tense. I'm speaking, of course, of the cringe. Those moments when that confession turns out to be just a *little* more than you wanted to know, or when the writer means to be risky and daring and instead you feel a little appalled, or what's intended as knowing and self-aware somehow comes off as anything but. (And how could it not be so – self-knowledge isn't exactly handed out along with a terminal degree, nor is intersubjective acumen.)

In such cases, is it the work that has failed? Or has the audience failed the work? If the latter, then I am that failed audience, because let me just come out and admit it: I have had these responses. I've not just been dissatisfied, I've cringed. I'm not especially proud of it, actually I'm discomfited, and puzzled. Much as I'd like to count myself a partisan of aesthetic risks, even failed ones, and as someone on the side of revising uptight academic prose protocols, in such cases, like Gorra, my distinctions fail. My viscera become confused. Is it that cringe-making work takes too many aesthetic risks, or too few? Or is it just me: am I somehow not up to the intersubjective demands of the genre? Is the genre dangling intersubjective lures that it finally doesn't sustain? Or should we say that the opportunity to have complicated and visceral intersubjective effects that one doesn't entirely comprehend is actually one of the more interesting features of the genre, and working them through, in print (and in the first person!) is a serious response to the aesthetic challenges being posed?

In raising questions such as these, however, I fear that I have inadvertently brought myself face-to-face with one of those "risks" we keep hearing about, not only because I suspect that aesthetic judgments about the qualities of academic confessional as "writing" violates something of the spirit of the enterprise, but more to the point, how am I going to write about my own aesthetic responses to literary self-display without writing about the particular selves on display? More to the point, as I review the table of contents of Veeser's *Confessions of the Critics*, which might have provided a convenient set of examples against which to test out these awkward aesthetic responses, I quickly realize that, academia being the small world that it is (and cultural studies a tiny, bustling market town within that tiny province), at least half the contributors are people I have variously met, socialized with, or encounter on an ongoing basis; they include friends and they include the editor of the volume you are presently reading. I, as much as anyone, want to be liked, and thus my ambitions to explore this question further are currently warring with my ambitions to prevent any future tense encounters or wounded emails. Therefore, frankly, risk-taking honesty is not something likely to be achieved here by me, on this subject. (If I wanted to be pedagogical I suppose could turn my failure of courageous honesty into an emblem of one problematic aspect of confessional genres: the guise of frankness under actual conditions of self-censorship and professional *politesse*, but let's just say that's a given.)

"One dislikes the thought of abandoning observation for barren theoretical discussions, but all the same we must not shirk an attempt at explanation." So remarks Freud in his paper, "On Narcissism: An Introduction," in a sprightly defense of speculative theory. Not surprisingly, speculative theory is the direction in which I will now gratefully turn, rescued in the nick of time from the impending peril of venturing into the specifics of anyone's content. Instead, let me pose a more general question: are adverse reactions to confessional writing content-determined, or is it rather something about the form itself that produce the adverse responses? In other words, perhaps the true venue of risk in the academic first person isn't actually the bathroom, or the sexual and bodily reportage, or anything in the narrative content at all, because the real risk – and this will not be an entirely unfamiliar point – is simply that of narcissism? But if so, why does this dilemma seem to hover more problematically over academic first-person writing than it does over its nonacademic confessional counterparts?

Perhaps it's the case that despite some family resemblances, the academic first person is a fundamentally different mode of writing than mainstream autobiography, or memoir, or the first-person essay. This isn't to say that some academics don't break out of the academic first person and write "crossover" books or articles that more closely resemble their nonacademic cousins, meaning those that get published by trade presses, or appear in magazines like *Harper's*. (Michael Bérubé's *Life as We Know It* is one of the examples that comes to mind.) But most academics fail in such crossover efforts, and the reason isn't entirely due to differing levels of writerly *élan* (although that's not nothing): the reason is professional formation. Academics are people who have been trained in modes of writing whose goal is to produce knowledge, and to produce knowledge about an external object. In the not so distant past, that tended to mean a disciplinary object – a subject, a theory, a period. In our interdisciplinary, posteverything times, it can now mean just about anything. Nevertheless, the academic first person invariably retains that disciplinary unconscious: it means to produce knowledge – because that's what academics do – while, in its autobiographical or confessional forms, substituting the self for the prior external object. And this is, in the most precise sense, the definition of narcissism: not simply a matter of turning attention inward, or self-reflection, but one of withdrawing cathexes from the outer world, with the self or the subject's own body replacing an external object-choice. For the academic writer, the object abandoned and replaced is also of course one with a significant degree of magnitude and personal history: a specialization. This displaced object, even if only temporarily abandoned, was the underpinning of a professional formation, invested with every sort of aspiration and attachment. You wrestle with it; it frustrates and rewards. It's a proving ground, it's turf, you sign your name to it, are aggrieved at trespassers (an injury the protocols of citation are meant to alleviate, though hardly ever do).

But something else differentiates the academic first person from its nonacademic cousins. The particular theory Freud happens to be speculating about in the passage quoted above proposes one of the basic tenets of a psychoanalytic theory of the instincts: that there is a fundamentally different quality to the kinds of energy available for self-attention than to that directed toward external objects. The ego-instincts, which have their origins in self-preservation and are turned inward, are nonsexual, as distinct from what Freud calls object-libido, whose origin is in the sexual instincts, and are aimed outward. (And distinct from auto-eroticism also, which precedes the development of the ego.) Everyone is capable of operating in both modes, and capable of both types of object-choice: we're not talking about raging narcissists versus everyone else, since primary narcissism is, at least in the Freudian developmental narrative, a universal feature of infancy. And a state to which we all yearn to return (and often do, in times of crisis or injury): the perfect love. Even if narcissism does ultimately become superseded by object love, we all live a double existence, with the self-preservative qualities of the ego-instincts serving our own individual ends, and object-libido what connects us to others, making us quest for sexual pleasure with them, and making us links in a larger chain. (A procreationist view maybe, but also indisputable.) If, according to this premise, object-libido is sexual in a way that the ego-instincts aren't, it also seems likely that the different qualities of libido available for self-objects versus those available for external objects would produce qualitatively different forms of *writing* about self-objects than about external objects. Or it would if we subscribe to the view that writing is a fundamentally libidinal activity – or at least that it should be.

If ego-instincts are nonsexual in origin, and if the ego-instincts are drawn on when it comes to writing about the self, we might indeed expect to find a certain flatness, perhaps a detached quality to these narratives of the academic self, even by those writers capable of sumptuous prose on other – external – matters. The origins of the ego-instincts aren't in pleasure after all, but in self-preservation. If we try to imagine the aesthetic qualities likely be associated with self-preservation, we would probably expect its written forms to take a more literal path: to want to hit you over the head rather than seduce you, to veer toward workman-like efficiency rather than the playfully polymorphous imaginative leaps that expressive prose achieves – including academic prose, in moments of intellectual daring and free play. Even when the content of first-person prose trots out all sorts of sexual details, the writing itself can still lack juice. (What we call "dry" prose.) In other words, it lacks the libidinal component, and even the most confessional content won't successfully supplement delibidinalized prose: the "something's missing" effect still registers. What's missing is probably what Freud calls "forepleasure," or playing around – recommended in both sexual and creative endeavors. To fully think through these questions would entail either citing examples, or a long excursus on the psychical origins of creative energy (according to Freud, of the same origin as perversions, but available for sublimation into cultural enterprises), so instead let's just leave it here, for the moment.

But why would academic self-display be a more cringe-making form – at least for this cowering aesthetic subject – than other forms of the first person?[3] While the ego-instinct/object-libido distinction may address the "something's missing" quality that Gorra notes, it still doesn't entirely account for the uncomfortably visceral quality of my own aesthetic dilemmas, for the cringe factor, which seems, at least for me, more associated with the academic confessional than mainstream autobiography or memoir, which I manage to read with an unclenched posture.

Of course, one thing that separates academic from nonacademic autobiography is that the nonacademic first-person writer has no comparable prior knowledge-object to replace. The academic first person has the far more tangled backstory, shadowed by former loves abandoned and replaced, perhaps in grievance or disappointment. How could this not produce a more complicated set of aesthetic and intersubjective effects in its audiences – especially in academic audiences? The aesthetic barometer is a finely honed instrument, even if it registers its readings viscerally, without always fully knowing what it's responding to. And possibly it's those academics with more complicated relations to the profession who will turn to the first person. Jane Gallop's *Feminist Accused of Sexual Harassment* comes to mind, the archetypal saga of such complications, and one whose prose is also far less pleasurable than what Gallop achieves on other occasions. But as a memoir explicitly written as a defense, it is the best example possible of the prose of self-preservation, and one in which the subject may be sex, but the writing itself is anything but libidinal. On other subjects Gallop is our foremost prose seductress; here she hits you over the head with the necessity to set an injurious story straight, to have her say.

But if grievance toward the profession and the mission to rectify its wrongs colors even far less aggrieved instances of the academic first person – and no doubt even the least professionally aggrieved amongst us have accumulated our share of grievances – we academic audiences and readers are ourselves also implicated in those wrongs, temporarily solicited as their stand-ins and repre-sentatives. Do I want to represent a stultified profession and its assorted indefens-ible practices to those with complicated and perhaps distressed relations to it? Not particularly, although of course that's what it means to be part of the first-person audience: it means being abstracted and made interchangeable with a battalion of internalized critics and institutional authority figures, whose desig-nated role is to be vanquished. The cringe would actually be a reasonable response, a way of countering the combination of defense and aggression mobil-ized in such enterprises. Cringing is a form of bodily outlet or release, but it's also typically a self-protective gesture – an automatic response to perceived aggression or its threat.

Freud offers some additional remarks on the dilemmas of narcissism that seem particularly applicable to the variety of defenses and aggressions mobilized in the academic first person, and the complicated responses it can elicit. The repression of primary narcissism – our first love – is a fundamental part of development, and the agency that oversees that repression is the conscience. The conscience is, in the first instance, an embodiment of parental criticism, and subsequently, of society's standards, securing acquiescence in both spheres. The conscience is also, fundamentally, self-consciousness: the sense of being watched and criticized. One of its earliest roles is censorship of the narcissistic self-relation. The activity of this critically watching faculty can come to various fates. Critical self-observation can become heightened into paranoia, and we can learn much about the self-criticism of conscience from the paranoiac's laments, Freud notes. For the present argu-ment, two other outcomes are of special interest. Critical self-regard can – and normally does – lead to the formation of what Freud calls an ego-ideal, toward which the old narcissistic self-love is redirected under the behest of conscience. The ego-ideal, a self-idealization to which the subject attempts to conform, is something of a compromise between prohibition and self-love. It's the reason we love our consciences (when we do), since the new ego-ideal contains the vestiges of that lost first love – our perfect selves. Or there's another possibility: conscience can also be redirected toward other purposes, translated into creative endeavors like philosophy or intellectual inquiry, or other fields in which critical observa-tion is harnessed and transformed through sublimation.

Sublimation is one of the more underdeveloped Freudian concepts, and its relationship to narcissism is particularly entangled. The distinction between the ego-ideal and the superego is equally shifty, treated differently by different writers, and inconsistently by Freud himself. (The usual distinction is that the superego operates through fear and guilt, while the ego-ideal offers a positive model, fueled by the desire to recapture a lost omnipotent perfection.) On both matters, technical debates continue to be waged in the literature. What is clear, though, is that for Freud there's a clear distinction between repression and sublimation: sublimation offers "a way out" of repression, a way around the censorship and punishments of conscience. Later followers expanded the concept of sublimation in interesting directions: Melanie Klein suggested that sublim-ation is reparative; so does Joel Whitebook, a contemporary psychoanalyst, who follows analyst Hans Loewald in proposing that the salutary result of authentic sublimation is nothing less than "the nonrepressive reorganization of the ego." For Whitebook, the open-ended transformations involved in sublimation – in contrast to the rigidity of defenses and conscience – supply a model for trans-formations both in the sphere of knowledge, and for transformed relations between subjects and the external world, by promoting a reintegration of ego and id. Sublimation offers a way of forming active associations with those materials from other portions of the psyche, instead of splitting them off or disassociating ourselves from the prohibited contents of repression.

The choice between conscience and sublimation hovers over the aesthetics of the academic first person. Is creative sublimation available for the self as object-of-knowledge? Or would this be, rather, the one object most prone to the strictures of conscience? Given how close this mode of self-regard is to the basic conditions of narcissism, given its subsequent imbrication in the imperious reign of conscience, what are the opportunities for creativity and aesthetic pleasure? Or, alternatively, if the creative transformations of sublimation aren't available to the self as object-of-knowledge, what qualities of aesthetic expression are likely to emerge under the reign of conscience? Can these genres of self-regard really hope to evade the clutches of conscience – its formative role in the constitution of the adult psyche – by beating it at its own game, by substituting one version of self-regard for another? And if some of us find ourselves cringing in the vicinity of the first person, perhaps it's also an involuntary recoil from the reprimands of our own consciences, kicked into gear by the spectacle of narcissistic transgression, policing potential narcissistic propensities of our own. Clearly, keeping your intersubjectivity distinct from your intrasubjectivity is a precarious enterprise at best, on both the production and reception side: the failure rate is staggering.

Certainly these issues extend beyond deliberately autobiographical work too: the relation of the academic writer to chosen subject-matter *is* one of the murkier aspects of academic life. The rise of the first person and the ascendancy of identitarianism may have made various professional-formation chronicles more publicly available, or explicated the logic behind research-object-choices. And of course frequently nowadays the author is in some obvious identity-relation with her research question or soon announces the connection when one isn't immediately visible. But does this entirely exhaust the question? There is a public domain of cultural objects, traditionally divvied up between the different disciplines, but on what basis do these different disciplines or methodologies or objects attract their adherents? The Freudian term "overdetermined" no doubt applies, and Freud himself had provocative things to say about research content and methods, for example on the relation of paranoia to system-building, or about criticism generally as a sublimated form of the overdeveloped conscience. Joel Whitebook likens the domain of cultural objects to the role the day's residues play in dreams: more opportunities for hallucinatory wish fulfillment. Or such is their potential, at least for those able to transform disciplinary rules and norms into more supple, less determinate forms.

Changes in research methods also position the researcher in different relationships to knowledge, as do paradigm shifts. Thus would different character types emerge as exemplary within different research paradigms? The narcissist for cultural studies, the obsessive for archival history, and so on – or are research objects themselves malleable enough to suit any necessity? (This is one of those interstitial topics whose investigative difficulties prevent it from being construed as a meaningful object-of-knowledge – at least outside the domain of the academic novel.

If the assumption is that academic work isn't "personal" when it enters the world clothed in the third person, this starts to seem a bit parochial, or perhaps overly invested in the "I": the forms of fascination and erotics that fuel academic inquiry, subject-matter, and formal choices, are so evidently driven by the messy collisions of knowledge and obliviousness that underpin all object relations. In these kinds of intersubjective encounters, outcomes can be unpredictable; both subjects and objects are mutually penetrated, at risk, potentially transformable. Who hasn't felt the thrill of witnessing intellectual labor or academic inquiry change the very nature of its object, making us unable to look at that thing the same way again? Confession itself is one of the best examples: once Foucault got his hands on it, it was never quite the same.

If even non-overtly autobiographical work has its autobiographical dimensions, these elements are also often played out at the level of form or style – though once again, the relation of stylistics to compensatory logics beyond the purely intellectual tends to be an issue raised informally, "behind the scenes." Possibly because such elements often register their presence viscerally more than "intellectually," often in the felt sense of something being askew, or too intense, or a problem not entirely namable – thus becoming the topics of jokes we all make about each others' work. An example. At a recent academic talk on race and citizenship I attended, when the speaker – who had been delivering his talk in the conventional academic manner – quoted from various nineteenth-century racist texts, he did so by suddenly launching into a highly theatrical mode of speech, playing out, indeed reanimating, the venom of his long-dead sources. Something about this registered as very odd, indeed was quite uncomfortable. (I think I may have cringed.) I looked down the aisle to see how others were responding and watched two acquaintances from another department roll their eyes at each other. They happened to look toward me, and as our eyes met, we were all forced to quickly look away because we were in danger of bursting out laughing – although nothing about this was precisely funny. It was rather that some excess on the part of the speaker had registered itself on us viscerally, and this excess needed an outlet, which laughter and eye-rolling provided – if minimally, since of course we were all well-schooled in academic politeness and its attendant behavioral codes and stifled ourselves before things got too out of hand.

The point isn't to aim a charge of unconscious racism at the speaker, who acquitted himself of a perfectly adequate, perfectly liberal, well-meaning talk. (Animating the positions of one's targets is actually a frequent performative mode in the academic talk; usually it accomplishes sarcasm, or intends to, though in this particular case, the effect of sarcasm somehow wasn't fully achieved.[4]) But at the very least, this intersubjective dynamic indicates something about how emotionally complicated the research object-relation can become, even disturbingly so. And isn't this part of the erotics of research; aren't those unknowns what makes doing it and watching others do it, compelling? But those unknowns also register on readers and audiences in ways that are difficult to track. The visceral responses of those of us who cringed and laughed at that talk were to something beyond the official content of the research – though not entirely unrelated to it either. These are hardly unknown responses to academic work, but what languages are adequate, or even available, to explore these aspects of academic intersubjectivity?

To whatever degree the disciplines have loosened their grip on the profession – "cultural studies" or "interdisciplinarity" would be a few of the names this shift goes by – it has meant altered relations to knowledge and writing in the humanities, compelled by a wider variety of logics and necessities. If in its earlier incarnations, "cultural studies" tended to be code for the politicization of research, in late cultural studies, the "personal" has often seemed like the more pressing agenda. But if not all autobiographical work is intentionally so, or is even composed in the first person, perhaps the personal/impersonal or private/intel-lectual distinctions aren't descriptive enough, and more subtle distinctions are needed – though what are the relevant criteria for making them?

In her early first-person foray, Jane Tompkins defined the private as the person who "talks on the telephone a lot to her friends, has seen psychiatrists, likes cappuccino, worries about the state of her soul. Her father is ill right now, and she has a friend who recently committed suicide." She confessed to a certain amount of anger against men, she admitted to intellectual competition with an unnamed (if not unnamable) husband, and closed with the declaration, "This one time I've taken off the straitjacket, and it feels so good." Despite the fact that these are experiences that are easy to relate to and even empathize with, I feel compelled to admit that, for me, something about reading this *doesn't* feel good, though once again I'm not quite able to say why.

But perhaps the feeling is not entirely unlike the discomfort I felt witnessing the performance of the speaker on race? Though admittedly, nothing about these two instances seems in any other way similar. In the race talk, the speaker seemed to be personifying the conflicts of his chosen object: the white liberal conscience struggling against the elements of fascination and identification embedded in the modern racial dynamic. This was someone whose relation to his subject-matter seemed complicated in ways beyond his conscious knowledge or control or good intentions. To the extent that there was a confessional element to this work, it was clearly not intended, though evident nevertheless, registered viscerally by the audience in suppressed laughter and felt embarrassment. Tompkins, on the other hand, is nothing if not self-conscious in respect to her confessions and struggles; she at least seems to be in control of her intentions.

But are these two examples – one in the first person, one in the third – more related than they first appear, beyond the fact of producing discomfort in one aesthetic subject? Both suggest personal struggles waged with conscience, with academic research as the chosen venue for ego-ideals to do their public dances:

the feminist ego-ideal in one, the liberal ego-ideal in the other (just two of the many flavors available). But despite Tompkins's closing victory cry, maybe it's not the case that feeling good is what knowledge actually gains for us. Maybe feeling good is about something else altogether – meaning that if pursuing knowledge were really going to be the risky thing that proponents of the personal would like it to be, we should probably avoid any premature celebrations about shedding those straitjackets. Clearly multiple forms of censorship and operations of conscience are always lingering around our keyboards, with inner versions of obedience securing external forms of compliance, and congratulating us on jobs well done. If conscience says "You must behave like this" the ego-ideal answers, "I *should* behave like this." Thus we become the heroes of our own self-exonerating narratives ("This is how I behaved") – whether redacted for public consumption or fulsome on the subject of foibles (being disarmingly "honest" about shortcomings may be some particular ego's ideal). How could the critical self-regard of autobiography or well-meaning liberalism really detach themselves from the critical self-regard of conscience when they're sprung from the same origin? Of course it feels good: our own lost perfection is in sight!

But risk? Transformation? The wager of self-representation – of both the knowing and unknowing varieties – seems to go like this: if we successfully manage to win an audience's approval or empathy for the self on display, it's because we've achieved sufficient self-idealization to promote our audience's unproblematic identification, and not challenged their own consciences too severely. Yet this must be achieved without making self-idealization *too* evident (the failure of seeming a bit too pleased with oneself, or too evidently narcissistic). When the wager fails, when the thing isn't achieved seamlessly enough to prevent those twinges of discomfort about the whole messy enterprise of being a self wracked by incoherences, wrong desires, or embarrassing conflicts and excesses, audiences succumb to laughter and cringing: this is *too much* knowledge, and dangerous knowledge. It overwhelms, registering as an uncomfortable, even visceral excess, and requiring release. (Should you find yourself thus overwhelmed, don't panic, just make a joke, the typical outlet.)

Is there any way of representing the ego that doesn't play to the back-benches of conscience, critic, and virtue? Maybe successful sublimation is the trickster figure: *here* I am; no *that's* not me; not here, *there*. When it comes to sidestepping the straitjacket brigades, the trickster probably has the better odds. The independent external object capable of retaining a sufficient quantity of projections and fantasies and libidinal investments may be better suited to the creative "way out" that sublimation offers *vis-à-vis* repression. Of course, there are no guarantees here either: external objects don't always prove capacious or flexible enough to hold everything we may want to project onto them or sublate them into. The object difficulties involved, as with other forms of marriage, are legion and need not be rehearsed here. We're all familiar with boring academic work, which, as in boring marriages, indicates that libido has been withdrawn from the object, or was never able to maintain its attention span in the first place, or some other tale of disappointment and decathexis.

Given the often eccentric nature of the cultural studies object-choice, plus the leeway for free-wheeling stylistics, perhaps the space for reconfiguring the academic object-of-knowledge is indeed enlarged here. Though when it comes to straitjackets on writing and the first person's declaration of independence from them, was it ever really academia playing the Nurse Ratched role? Or does that cede too much authority to the wrong censorious institution? Academic protocols actually turn out to be rather easily reshaped. It's those forms of internalized authority that are far more obdurate, and wear many pretty costumes – celebrations of one's own political rectitude being one of the most attractive on the rack.

In other words, isn't self-presentation always – and whatever person-form it takes – by definition a form of political engagement? It is to the extent that the self is constantly in confrontation with the limitations on its own mobility: with its rigidities, with the ever-present restrictions on transformation, or risk, or self-contradiction. We all play dual roles in the social theater of self-presentation: presenters at one moment, witnesses the next; causing cringes in one instance, cringing away in another. The discomfiture occasionally registered in these backstage responses and perturbations is one indication of just what deeply intersubjective creatures we are. Witnessing the difficult work of self-negotiation can be a painful, unaesthetically pleasing thing when the seams are showing. But if those cracks and fissures reveal the places where business-as-usual runs slightly off-course, or where social personality, intellectual investments, and institutional protocols can become disarrayed and unsettle each other as they negotiate the object world, wouldn't this be where we in the critical aesthetics business would want to focus our aesthetic attention?

If the personal is political, it's not in cultural studies anthologies alone, or in necessarily feel-good ways. Conscience and superego house the recruiting offices where they meet up, where adherence is secured and compliance solicited for whatever master plan is in ascendancy at the moment. And do the scholarly forms we engage in collaborate with or contest those plans? Of course, it goes without saying that the only *bona fide* cultural studies procedure for answering such a question would be to upend the usual hierarchies of aesthetic response, making all the marginal and ephemeral data that comes our way – embarrassment, discomfort, twitches, and cringes – central to the investigation. Adorno once remarked that "the most important taboo in art is the one that prohibits an animal-like attitude toward the object, say, a desire to devour it or otherwise subjugate it to one's body," adding that the strength of such a taboo is only matched by the strength of the repressed urge to do just that. The cringe of conscience may be more of an oversocialized response than an animal-like one, but it too is more bodily than cerebral, more improper to the occasion than appropriate. Thus it must shortly become canonical in the cultural studies handbook – however unable we would be to comprehend such responses to our own work, so full of rectitude and good intentions are we all.

NOTES

1 Sometimes favored by this writer as well. See Kipnis, "Adultery" (*Critical Inquiry*, Winter 1998) and *Against Love: A Polemic* (New York: Pantheon, 2003).
2 A similar point had been made about the recent flood of memoirs in commercial publishing as a response to postmodern literary fiction's abandonment of character in favor of formal experimentation.
3 Since all distinctions in this realm are bound to fail, the academic/nonacademic binary itself isn't really adequate to cover all forms of first-person writing: we'd need at least one more slot for avant-garde or experimental first-person writing which is neither mainstream nor academic but circulates on the margins of both worlds; often produced by writers who have an occasional relationship to academic life (often to the art world as well), and published in literary magazines, zines, or by alternative presses. Chris Kraus's *I Love Dick* is a good example of those crossovers: written by an occasionally teaching writer-filmmaker about her relationships with well-known academic men (and to academic discourses), self-reflexively *about* self-exposure, and published by a small grant-supported press, Semiotext(e), with a Columbia University mailing address. In terms of aesthetic response, these forms of writing are often in a performative vein, and often seem intended to evoke the cringe factor, with confession an updated tactic in the *épater la bourgeoisie* arsenal.
4 Freud also makes the point – as have others – that one of the tendencies of the modern writer is to split his ego into many component-egos or characters as a means of personifying conflicting trends in his own mental life.

REFERENCES

Adorno, Theodor. 1984. *Aesthetic Theory*, tr. C. Lenhardt. London: Routledge & Kegan Paul.

Bérubé, Michael. 1998. *Life As We Know It: A Father, a Family, and an Exceptional Child*. New York: Vintage.

Freud, Sigmund. 1908. "Creative Writers and Daydreaming." In *The Standard Edition of the Complete Psychological Works*, ed. James Strachey, vol. 9.

——. 1910. *Leonardo da Vinci and a Memory of His Childhood*. In *The Standard Edition of the Complete Psychological Works*, ed. James Strachey, vol. 11.

———. 1914. "On Narcissism: An Introduction." *The Standard Edition of the Complete Psychological Works*, ed. James Strachey, vol. 14.

Gallop, Jane. 1997. *Feminist Accused of Sexual Harassment*. Durham, NC: Duke University Press.

Gorra, Michael. 1995. "The Autobiographical Turn." *Transition* 68.

Kraus, Chris. 1997. *I Love Dick*. New York: Semiotext(e).

Laplanche, J. and J.-B. Pontalis. 1973. *The Language of Psychoanalysis*, tr. Donald Nicholson-Smith. New York: Norton.

Tompkins, Jane. 1987. "Me and My Shadow." *New Literary History* 19: 169–78.

Veeser, H. Aram. 1996. *Confessions of the Critics*. New York: Routledge.

Whitebook, Joel. 1995. *Perversion and Utopia: A Study of Psychoanalysis and Critical Theory*. Cambridge, MA: MIT Press.

Index

Page rages in **bold** refer to chapters in the present volume.